SWASHBUCKLING

SWASHBUCKLING

A STEP-BY-STEP
GUIDE TO
THE ART OF
STAGE COMBAT
AND
THEATRICAL
SWORDPLAY

REVISED AND
UPDATED EDITION

by
RICHARD LANE

Certified Teacher and Fight Director/
Society of American Fight Directors (SAFD)
Executive Director/
The Academy of the Sword

LIMELIGHT EDITIONS
118 EAST 30 STREET NEW YORK NY 10016

FIRST LIMELIGHT EDITION, MARCH 1999, SECOND EDITION, MARCH 2003

PUBLISHED BY PROSCENIUM PUBLISHERS INC.
118 EAST 30 STREET NEW YORK, NY 10016.

LANE, RICHARD (RICHARD J.)
    SWASHBUCKLING: A STEP-BY-STEP GUIDE TO THE ART OF STAGE COMBAT
  AND THEATRICAL SWORDPLAY / BY RICHARD LANE.
        O.   CM.
    INCLUDES BIBLIOGRAPHICAL REFERENCES.
   ISBN 0-87910-091-5
    1. STAGE FIGHTING 2. STAGE FENCING. I. TITLE
  PN2071.F5L36 1998
  792'.028—dc21   98—7290
                                                                      CIP

MANUFACTURED IN THE UNITED STATES OF AMERICA
DESIGNED AND TYPESET BY THE WHOLE WORKS® NEW YORK CITY

DEDICATION

TO MY PARENTS, STANLEY AND CAROL LANE,
ON THEIR FIFTIETH WEDDING ANNIVERSARY:
TRULY THE MEASURE OF COMMITMENT
AND TRUST.

It is customary to say that a book is "long awaited, much needed, and a welcome addition." This book is beyond all such clichés. It is a necessity! It is more than a manual. Richard Lane's concepts are vital to the approach. The "why" and "when" of stage fighting are explained and make the "how" easier to understand and execute. No longer is it possible to mount a production, whether opera, theater, or film, where the combatants flail the air and on cue, fall down and expire. The public is too aware, too exposed to swashbucklers on the screen. However, I've yet to see one stage fight where I couldn't find some grave error to criticize. Now the bible is available, the commandments have been inscribed and brought down from the mountain. Read this, pay heed and you will avoid sin and suffering.

This is the book I would have written had I the discipline, time, energy, youth and literary ability.

Fortunately Richard Lane has all these qualities and I've overcome my envy, with its attending resentment at the fact he did it and I didn't, to the point that I raise my sword on high and salute you, Richard. Well done!

Oscar F. Kolombatovich
Fencing Master Emeritus

Former Fencing Master: Metropolitan Opera, New York,
and U.S. Military Academy, West Point.
Coach: U.S. Team World Championship.
Executive Secretary: Historical Fencing Society.

ACKNOWLEDGMENTS

TO SOME EXTRAORDINARY PEOPLE

Stage combat is a cooperative art, one in which two—and sometimes many more—people come together to make an audience think one thing has happened while, in reality, something else has taken place. Books are like that, too. If authors are worth reading, it's because their teachers, mentors, colleagues, students, friends, and family—including a host of unsung professionals in publishing and many other fields—all did their jobs first, and well.

Over my years of studying movement and stage combat, I've been privileged to work with and learn from a large number of such talented, creative, and knowledgeable people. How could I have guessed that by merely opening my mind to their ideas and pursuing my craft a book was being born? Whatever value you find in these pages is owed entirely to them. Whatever missteps or fumbles you see are entirely my own. In life we are all apprentices; if we're lucky, the cycle of learning never stops.

First and foremost, I am grateful to all the Fight Masters, Fight Directors, and Certified Teachers of the Society of American Fight Directors who have selflessly dedicated their time, patience, and expertise to an art form that is still largely unappreciated by many in the theatrical community. If it had not been for their great passion, mine would certainly have never been kindled.

I give my highest homage and humblest gratitude, too, to Maestro Oscar Kolombatovich who showed me the true romance and panache of historical swordplay and taught me, through his example, what it means to be a gentleman.

To Steve Vaughan, I give thanks for my introduction to the world of stage combat and athletic-style dueling, and extend that enthusiastic handshake, too, to all those who helped make the Academy of the Sword a reality: Fight Master J.R. Beardsley, Fight Director Dexter Fidler, Martino Pistone, Todd Gunter, Jonathan Scott, Maggie Taylor, Randall Miller, Jonathan Rider, Donna Ducarme, Alf Adams, Tina Hansen, Richard Buckingham-Clark, Nancy Thompson, Certified Teacher John Cashman, Aikido Sensei Nick Scoggin, and my board members and good friends Carolyn Reynolds and Miguel Najera. I wish also to thank Fight Masters Christopher Villa and David Woolley who paid us extended visits while we were growing, as well as Maestros David Boushey, Richard Raether, and Erik Fredricksen who conducted our adjudications and left their indelible mark on students and teacher alike. I am personally indebted, too, to J. Allen Suddeth, J.D. Martinez, David Leong, and Drew Fracher for their astute and generous instruction; and to Linda McCollum of the Department of Theatre Arts, University of Nevada, Las Vegas, for her historical expertise and tireless work on behalf of the SAFD. I hope you will all be proud of what you find in these pages, and forgiving of any mistakes.

Nearer to home, I am indebted to Steve Smuin and Lee Shult of the Odyssey School, Willene Gunn of the San Francisco Conservatory of Music, Bob and Lesley Currier of Marin Shakespeare Festival, and Robert Kelley of TheaterWorks for giving me so many opportunities to practice my craft and pursue my art. I'm grateful, too, to the multi-talented Kit Wilder, and my assistant Bob Borwick—a fine fighter and actor—and our other photo models, Christine Cannizzaro, Roberto Caraballo, Lawrence Homulos, and Deborah Marcus, for their participation in this project. I wish to thank also the publishing professionals who helped to bring it to fruition: Mel Zerman of Limelight Editions, our editors and book designers, Ettie Steg and Charles Peach; photographers, Frank Pryor, Chely Simon, and Larry Merkle; illustrators, Andrew Fox and Alex Daye; the Everett Collection in New York, and Archive Photos for their extensive selection of vintage and contemporary production illustrations; Matt Gales of Belgium and Andrew Fox for technical information; Alan Reichert for administration of the stage combat mailing list; and Dennis Graves, swordcutler, Hank Reinhardt of Museum Replicas, Larry Milligan of The Colonial Armory, American Fencers Supply, Arms & Armour, and Maestro Oscar F. Kolombatovich for stage combat weapons used in our illustrations.

Finally, I reserve my biggest hugs for my parents, (may they now know what I do for a living!); my black-belted brother, Jerald M. Lane, for his boundless faith and support of my decisions; my wife, Alison, for her encouraging words (and well-researched facts) when I needed them most; and my collaborator and student, Jay Wurts, for his literary contributions and persistence in turning my experience into words; and his wife, Peggy, for asking me that first, fatal question: "Have you thought about writing a book?"

R.L.
San Francisco, 1998

|CONTENTS

INTRODUCTION
ACTING WHILE IN ACTION

Good actors approach stage combat as they do any other professional challenge: with energy, self-discipline, and the desire to entertain and move the audience. (Photo by Chely Simon.)

The performing arts have never been more physical than today. Audiences demand realism—or at least the illusion of reality—in opera, theater, and film. Theatrical violence is most demanding on stage since there is no "take two." Sooner or later, you as a performer will face the challenge of your first stage fight; how you rise to that occasion will help determine the applause you earn.

How then does one make a fight safe and effective? How do we override the primal instinct and conditioned response system to portray conflict without fighting? How can we bring blood to boil, tears to the eyes, and a smile to the face of the audience while keeping it all safe? These are the questions the artist must ask continually, for there is no single procedure that will protect an actor from carelessness, ignorance, or "horsing around." Only through constant practice and questioning of techniques and procedures can stage combat be made safe for the artist. Only by understanding the entire procedure, both how and why it is safe, can the actor truly be *On Guard*.

Dale Anthony Girard
Actors On Guard: A Practical Guide for the Use of Rapier and Dagger for Stage and Screen

Going back to Victorian times, when the play demanded that the duel should be played, a number of well-known routines (known as "Standard Combats") were often used, the most appropriate being selected according to the requirements of the play, but not specially created as nowadays. These were referred to in the profession of that time as "The Square Eights," "The Round Eights," "The Glasgow Tens" (known in England as "The Long Elevens"), and even one called "The Drunk Combat." All these routines were made up from a series of cuts—not cuts as we know them today, but rather whacks at the opponent's blade. These could be repeated as often as required all over the stage.

William Hobbs
Fight Direction for Stage and Screen

Theater buffs may be surprised to learn that Standard Combats continued well into Hollywood's golden age, where stock moves known by such colorful names as "Ring the Bell," "Click-Clicks," and "Baronial Hall" were learned and practiced by itinerant swashbucklers everywhere. This may have expedited fight choreography, but it didn't do much for the drama.

R.L.

WELCOME TO THEATRICAL SWASHBUCKLING

Until the last few decades, actors and directors had little guidance for arranging safe (or even convincing) stage fights. Matinee idols and opera stars simply shuffled through a few stock moves, waved their swords, and delivered their lines. More athletic performers relied on the techniques of sport fencing to enliven their fights—making them more entertaining, to be sure, but more dangerous and undramatic as well. Unfortunately, even the best were about as faithful to historical fighting styles as Ben Hur driving a Buick. Well into this century, stage combat was viewed as a separate skill, like stunt work, that had little to do with acting and much more to do with keeping an audience amused until the *real* drama—the dialogue—could continue.

In modern theater, that nineteenth century taste for melodrama—grand gestures and grandiose productions—has given way to an appetite for truth. Even in stage combat, the theatrical gesture is out; the genuine gesture is in.

SWASHBUCKLING IS MORE THAN SWORDPLAY

Just as conflict is the essence of drama, so is combat the epitome of conflict. When two characters fight on stage, the conflict that has motivated them in the story escalates beyond words. What was before left to dialogue, stage direction, and voice inflection now becomes the province of pure motion. Audiences, too, become more focused during a fight, and more critical of what they see.

Many experts believe that Shakespeare's audiences, living as they did in the heyday of dueling, were connoisseurs of swordfights. However, even in our own era of graphic violence on film and TV, most of us have never seen—in person, up close and personal—an actual gunfight; let alone enough of them to become experts in their techniques. In fact, those who *are* experts in dealing with human violence—police officers, military combat veterans, and so on—often criticize Hollywood's action films as being too slick, their staged violence too pat and well rehearsed, and their hero's opponents too cooperative to mimic real life. As a result, performers and directors are left with the same challenge Shakespeare faced: how to stage violence that looks authentic and serves the story while keeping the actors safe.

A SWORD IS MORE THAN A PROP

One way actors can make historical stage combat more convincing is to "get inside" the fight, just as they get inside their characters. In Western culture, the sword has always been a symbol of rank, status, and privilege—a symbol of the indomitable human spirit. To the ancient Greeks, a sword given to a mortal by the gods (such as the sword Perseus used to slay the Gorgon) made that person a hero—someone fit for great, mythological tasks. To the Celts, the magic sword *Caladbolg*, called "Excalibur" in the

Arthurian legends, forged on the mythical Isle of Avalon, became the symbol of the entire British nation. Later, this special relationship between the weapon and its wielder was reflected in the names heroes gave their favorite swords, such as Orlando's "Durindana" (said to have been forged for Hector) and Rodrigo de Vivar's (El Cid's) companion broadswords, "Tizona" and "Colada." Even Elizabethan duelists (whose rapiers clashing against their small, round shields, called bucklers, sounding out a challenge to all who could hear, led to the term "swashbuckling") saw themselves not as rowdy thugs but as an elite whose swordplay set them apart from others. Since many of these stories have been preserved in dramatic form, modern actors have become, in a very real sense, the custodians of our Western warrior heritage.

THE MAGIC OF MODERN SWASHBUCKLING

Something happens when you pick up a sword: your smile becomes a little wider, your step a little jauntier. The hilt fits naturally into your hand—and that's not by accident. Most swords were designed to roughly double the reach of the human arm. Even two-handed broadswords and the Elizabethan's "outrageous rapier"—so-called because of its five-and-a-half foot length—were, in essence, little more than extensions of the "knife edge" flattened hand.

Now notice the weapon's "heft." Feel how its weight is distributed from tip to pommel, and look at the shape of the hilt and blade. These aren't dull museum statistics: they are the very soul of the sword. They reveal its designer's intentions, the capabilities of the fighter, and the social values of its era.

Take, for example, a staple used in many theatrical productions: the humble rapier. To most performers and directors, one sword is pretty much like another. In staging *Romeo and Juliet*, they'll often settle for foils from the nearest sporting goods store, since these are relatively inexpensive, easy to obtain, and bear a superficial resemblance to the stereotypical swashbuckler's sword. Because this particular piece of sporting gear also comes with a small cap (called a button) to blunt the tip, such people also think the actors wielding them will be safe. In truth, neither the actors nor the drama should be approached so cavalierly.

Now imagine that our performers examine a true rapier—any one of a dozen "rapier types" found in museums or catalogs of various stage-combat weapon suppliers. The first thing they notice is the wide range of weapons that fit the term rapier, all considerably different in shape, length, and heft. At one end of the spectrum is what appears to be a highly tapered broadsword, somewhat stout, with a heavy, no-nonsense hilt and perhaps a few bands of steel curving back from the crossguard to protect the hand. This earliest rapier was derived from the medieval broadsword and its heavyish, double-edged blade seems perfect for cracking light armor or exploiting chinks in that armor with its point. If our actors handle the

Although in his days the new-fangled "rapier" had become quite acclimatized in England, in Henry VIII's time, and indeed as late as the first years of Elizabeth's reign, it was only known to a few traveled courtiers as an outlandish weapon much used in Italy and Spain, and sometimes in France. The national weapon was the "sword," with a plain cross hilt, and perhaps a half-ring guard. It was intended mainly for the cut, and usually accompanied by the hand buckler or targate. Notwithstanding general restrictions, a great deal of obnoxious swaggering was common among the fencing gentry, who were as a rule looked upon with dislike and suspicion by the quieter portion of the community. The contemptuous name of "swashbuckler," applied to obtrusive devotees of the art of fence, graphically described these shady braves, and the clattering noise they created in their brawls, or even when merely swaggering down a narrow street..." They got their name," says Fuller,* "from swashing and making a noise on the buckler, and that of ruffian, which is the same as a swaggerer," because they tried to make the side swag or incline on which they were engaged.
Egerton Castle
Schools and Masters of Fence

*Worthies of England

"Rapier" was the name given to the Spanish weapon. A Frenchman called his arm, "espee," an Englishman, "sword." Both, when they talked of the Spaniard's sword, called it a rapier. In France, the word "rapier" soon became a contemptuous term, signifying a sword of disproportionate length—in fact, the weapon of a bully. In England, "Rapier," meaning the "Spanishe Sworde," would be applied to all swords used for thrusting in the Spanish style."

Egerton Castle
Schools and Masters of Fence

Although Webster's links the term "rapier" to the French *rapiere* (from *raspiere*, the action made by a rasper or poker), our word for the thin-bladed weapon may ultimately trace its roots to the Spanish *espada ropera*, or "sword (*espada*) worn with clothing (*ropera*)" as opposed to the broadsword, which was worn with armor—or from *raspar*, to scratch or graze—a deadly barb concealed within Mercutio's curse on Tybalt in *Romeo and Juliet*: "A plague o' both your houses! — Zounds, a dog, a rat, a mouse, a cat, to scratch a man to death! . . ."

R.L.

sword, they will find it surprisingly maneuverable, mostly because of the blade's modest size: about an arm-and-a-half in length. Still, it would be hard to imagine Shakespeare's lovestruck teenager, Romeo, wielding such a hefty weapon against Tybalt.

The main reason we don't see such rapiers even in well-staged, well-financed productions of Romeo and Juliet (*especially* in such productions) is that these rapiers went out of fashion a century or two before Romeo's famous duel. Their use would be anachronistic—like James Bond packing a flintlock. Even in their own day, these heavier rapiers were considered military weapons—as their design suggests—rather than accessories for dandies. However, if our players were renting swords for a production of Peter Shaffer's *Royal Hunt of the Sun*, a drama about Spanish conquistadors, such a rapier would fit very naturally and correctly in the gauntleted hand of Francisco Pizarro, conqueror of the Incas.

Suppose now that our performers glance up the historical timeline to the top branch of the rapier's family tree. There they would see a host of lightweight, beautiful weapons with long, slender blades and delicately carved hilts—deadly weapons disguised as works of art. Clearly, these are gentlemen's swords, worn as much to proclaim the nobility and fashion consciousness of their owners as for protection. But when protection was needed, these extremely sharp, handy blades—much quicker, longer, and more flexible than Pizarro's—were equally deadly. In fact, their very design suggests more a thrust-and-parry, fencing-oriented duel between agile, lightly clad athletes than a brutal, close-quarter melee among armored soldiers. Indeed, the decorative finishes of the later rapiers evoke images of refined manners and courtly passions—the essence of Romeo's world.

In short, what historians have always known and more directors and performers are now discovering is that the sword shapes the swordfight, indicates the fighters' time and place, and symbolizes their values, fears, and aspirations. Understanding these attributes and how to use them to reveal the essence of the character at the moment of truth is a crucial test of any performer.

THE BENEFITS OF THEATRICAL SWASHBUCKLING

As an actor trained in stage combat, you should be able to call upon the fighting style appropriate to any character in any era—a career-enhancing asset that lasts a lifetime. But knowing which weapons to choose and how to wield them—including the techniques of unarmed combat—is only half the challenge of swashbuckling. The other half is *acting* while in action, the reason you're on stage. Unless you can convince an audience that the story continues during the fight—that this most dramatic form of conflict can and does reveal still more about a character—you will have failed at your primary task.

Unless we care about the fighters, we won't care about the fight. (John Cashman, left, and Kit Wilder, in The Academy of the Sword's production, "Duels and Assassination.")

Fortunately, just as your skills as an actor enhance your ability to act in a fight, so will the techniques you learn as an actor-combatant increase your value in non-combat roles. These benefits include:

- *A better ability to concentrate.* Waving dangerous weapons at another person—and having the same done to you—has a way of focusing your mind. Like other activities involving risk and precision (such as flying a plane, skiing, rock climbing, and the martial arts) theatrical swashbuckling teaches you to *stay in the moment*, to concentrate intently—and eventually effortlessly—on what's happening here and now. After awhile, you'll discover this ability extends to other parts of acting: learning lines, giving and receiving nonverbal cues, prospecting a role for its most significant elements and then communicating them effectively on stage.

- *Improved coordination, strength, stamina, and appearance.* Athletes, runners, and body builders who have studied stage combat report that a typical session with rapier or broadsword (preceded by proper stretches and warmups), delivers the same physical and aerobic benefits as a workout with light weights or other body-toning equipment. As you shed weight, firm up, and build endurance for marathon performances, you'll also develop quicker reflexes and the keen motor coordination associated with trained dancers and martial artists. And where there is good physical conditioning, physical injury usually stays away.

- *Inner calm and confidence.* People who combine healthy physical activity with fulfilling work and a balanced life often report a sense of well-being—the state of "alert relaxation" that is the hallmark of happy, successful people everywhere—that helps them cope with the vagaries of life. For actors who face the stress of auditions, new roles, and rejection, this ability to channel stress in positive directions and exude self-confidence and optimism (knowing what to do when you "don't know what to do") can be crucial to launching and sustaining a successful career.

WHAT THEATRICAL SWASHBUCKLING ISN'T

Novice actors and directors sometimes confuse stage combat with other activities, sports, or disciplines. As it is taught by teachers certified by the Society of American Fight Directors (SAFD), stage combat is *not*:

- *Competitive fencing.* Like other modern sports, fencing is all about rules and competition, winning and losing. It bears no closer relationship to human combat—real or staged—than the superficial resemblance its foils, épées, and sabers have to historical weapons. Although modern fencing derives much of its form and terminology from the teachings of the early "masters of fence," only stage combat remains completely faithful to the letter and spirit of those sources—recreating both the inner world and outward reality of our sword-bearing ancestors. From this perspective, experienced fencers have no special advantage over others in learning theatrical swashbuckling. Indeed, expert fencers must often *unlearn* old habits before succeeding in this unique and collaborative art.

- *Stunt work.* Despite its physical demands, stage-combat training will not qualify you as an expert stunt performer. Although you'll learn the techniques of deadly (or at least deadly *looking*) combat using a variety of fearsome weapons, you won't be asked to jump from tall buildings, get blown up by pyrotechnics, or crash a car. All stage combat requires is self-discipline, reasonably good health (including freedom from any debilitating or recurring injuries, such as chronic back prob-

During the restoration of Charles II, after the reign of the Puritans, the demand for displays of skill with the sword revived, it formerly being the province of The Various Masters of Defense. "The Prize," was an English Tradition but now there was no Gild of Masters of Defense to organize the Prize, and no rules. However, there were plenty of disenfranchised soldiers and soon they had organized, calling themselves gladiators. "It is true that they styled themselves Fencing Masters, but this was a title awarded themselves by themselves." The first report of a Gladiator's Prize mentions that they fought with Sword and Buckler.

James Figg (The Atlas of the Sword) was as much impresario as gladiator, and staged, among other attractions, an all-woman fight. The ladies fought also with sword and dagger and sword and buckler.

After the death of James Figg in 1734, one of the most noted names of the Gladiator's Prize, his place was taken by a man who presented Bare Knuckle Fighting.

Origin of the Prize Fights.
The Fight Master
April, 1983

lems), and a willingness to learn and have fun in a safe environment. This brings us to the last major misconception some people have about stage combat. Most emphatically, theatrical swashbuckling does *not* involve. . .

- *Foolish risk-taking.* Although stage fights can take a comic turn and most qualified teachers give instruction in a friendly, low-key manner, theatrical swashbuckling is not about clowning around with sharp objects, taking unnecessary risks, or bullying other people. Although simulating historical swordplay is lots of fun, its enjoyment comes mainly from increased self-control, better communication with others, and the mastery of techniques that entertain while keeping performers safe. New moves are introduced step-by-step, and all techniques, when properly performed, have been designed to minimize the chances of even a nuisance injury. Each session begins with stretches and warmups aimed at preparing specific muscles and muscle groups for the demands ahead. Of course, injuries can occur in any athletic endeavor, so it is *your* responsibility to perform all techniques properly and observe all safety precautions.

CAN YOU REALLY LEARN STAGE COMBAT FROM A BOOK?

Without question, competence in stage combat comes only through personal instruction from a qualified teacher. Only an experienced instructor can tell you how well you are performing a given technique and help you separate unconscious bad habits from good muscle memory.

However, a book like this *can* go a long way toward preparing you for such instruction, then help you remember and perfect the techniques you've learned, even if they differ slightly from those presented here. This book can also do things many instructors, because of lack of time or resources, can't do, including:

- Showing you the beginning, intermediate, and end positions of desired movements in a permanent, visual form so that you can refer to them outside the practice studio. In this book, we also give you a wealth of cues and clues—both in photos and in the text—for performing techniques convincingly and avoiding common mistakes.
- Sharing stage lore and historical details that form a vivid backdrop for your training, increasing your ability to understand a particular role and allowing you to interpret your role through your swordplay.
- Providing specific tips, maxims, checklists, and do's and don'ts that enhance the dramatic value and historical accuracy of your perfomance, whether swordplay is involved or not.

Each "how-to" chapter opens with a list of performance goals: ways to measure your progress when you practice by yourself. Of course, as with any training program, the real value of this book lies in your thoughtful, faithful adherence to its techniques, safety precautions, and the sequences it prescribes.

In Part I, you'll get both the wide-angle and close-up views of theatrical swashbuckling, learning a bit of "hoplology" (the study of human violence), the history of the sword and its construction, the rules of safe sword-handling, the evolution of swordfighting techniques, and ways to bring these dramatic elements together—and give them life—in a performance.

In Part II, you'll begin your training as an actor-combatant. Following a chapter filled with special stretches and warm-ups, you'll learn the fundamentals of unarmed stage combat: how to deliver, and roll with, simulated punches, slaps, and kicks. After that, you'll practice swordfighting footwork as a prelude to attack and defense with a single rapier—the weapon used in many plays and Hollywood's best-loved swashbuckling films. You'll learn not only the basic parries, cuts, and thrusts used in theatrical swordplay, but how to use your hands and feet—even the hilt of the sword—as offensive and defensive weapons. By the end of Part II, you'll be able to perform an exciting martial-arts style solo rapier form simulating the desperate battle of one swordfighter against many—just as you would rehearse it for performance. You'll also learn how to adapt those basic skills to the unique demands of the medieval crosshilt, or broadsword: the scourge of Macbeth and Henry V, Lancelot and Ivanhoe.

In Part III, you'll get a glimpse of partnered work with a director, fight choreographer, and other production specialists; encouraging you perhaps to continue your training with rapier and dagger, smallsword, quarterstaff, and other exotic weapons. And, if your talent, desire, and skills are strong enough, you'll learn how to win acknowledgment as a Recognized or Recommended Actor/Combatant—earning professional credentials that show you have met the safety and performance standards of the Society of American Fight Directors.

Finally, in the appendices to this book, you'll find useful forms for organizing stage-combat productions; a glossary of stage-combat and historical-swordfighting terms; a roster of suppliers for stage-combat worthy swords and accessories from every era; a list of books and videos recommended for further study; and a directory of SAFD certified instructors, colleges, and other individuals and institutions offering formal stage combat training.

Most importantly, you'll finish this book with greater confidence in yourself as a performer—someone capable of meeting and mastering any challenge with a positive attitude, resourcefulness, and a wealth of solid technique. After all, that's what good acting—and swashbuckling in every age—has always been about!

PART I

COMBAT
AND
THEATER

1

"THEY FIGHT"

Actors are the most dangerous people to have to deal with. . . because we don't know how to handle ourselves. . . We come out charging, whirling all around, forgetting the prepared routines of swordplay.
Errol Flynn *My Wicked, Wicked Ways*

1-1. *"You killed my father: Prepare to die. . ." Mandy Patinkin as the brilliant Spanish swordsman Inigo Montoya, finally has the evil Count Rugen (Christopher Guest) at sword's point in "The Princess Bride." Fight Director: Bob Anderson. (The Everett Collection.)*

The prospect of stage combat intimidates many actors who aren't prepared mentally or physically to fight "in character." By the end of this chapter you'll be able to:

- Name the basic motivations for any fight
- Diagnose a fight's dramatic or comic potential
- Describe the simple four-step sequence that helps keep stage combat safe
- Identify and avoid the most common mistakes made in stage combat
- Add originality and style to even well-known stage combat roles

SAFD Fight Master Rod Colbin cofessed to once knocking off the pendulous nose of Cyrano de Bergerac in that play's opening duel, leaving the hapless star somewhat short of motivation for the rest of the play. Similarly, a production of Henry V went suddenly, terribly wrong when young King Harry made his grand entrance clad in a suit of authentic fifteenth century armor, only to fall flat on his face and struggle like an over-turned turtle until stagehands helped him up. Fortunately, with modern techniques and costumes, gaffs like these are rare, but they do raise important questions: Are the fighters prepared to fight? Is reality always better than illusion?

R.L.

Few things strike terror into the hearts of actors and directors faster than the two little words tucked away in virtually every script containing stage combat: *They fight.*

After pages and pages of clever, moving dialogue, the playwright (including Shakespeare) stops the action and leaves to others all decisions about what to do with the knives, spears, swords, and fists the characters have been brandishing at each other. This splash of cold water leaves many actors and directors all at sea—and scouring the Yellow Pages for fight arrangers who might somehow save the day. To experienced fight directors and actor-combatants, however, these are the two sweetest words in theater (second only to "check enclosed"): a chance to show most vividly the nature of their characters *in extremis.*

TO FIGHT OR NOT TO FIGHT

Directors and performers fear stage combat for a variety of reasons. Some think the action will interrupt, and not complement, the story. They've simply had no training in how to *act* during a fight. Others are afraid the actors will get hurt. That's only human nature and is, in fact, a healthy instinct. Still others think that even if the performers escape injury, they'll look foolish or unconvincing at the time they need to look most heroic and adept.

Fortunately, these are all things you can do something about—provided you start well before the curtain goes up.

Most playwrights put their combat sequences at the climax of a scene or at the end of an act, or even at the end of the entire production, when motivation has been well established and performance energy is high—although this placement is not always guaranteed. In Mozart's opera, *Don Giovanni*, the Commendatore must fall to Giovanni's sword within the first six minutes—before many patrons have settled into their seats. How actors in these circumstances create the illusion of violent passion (when all they're really feeling is opening night jitters!) is a good example of how *any* performer can do the same in all dramatic situations.

TO CARE ABOUT THE FIGHT, WE MUST CARE ABOUT THE FIGHTERS

The best stage fights, no matter when they occur, are fueled by life itself: those experiences shared by actors and audience. At the root of any combat are the intense feelings we've each experienced during conflict as children, teens, or adults. As the stakes in a dispute get higher and tempers flare, our natural "fight or flight" reaction kicks in. Our respiration, heart rate, and blood pressure all increase. Our muscles contract. Our eyes focus more sharply. Our fingers roll into fists. As we mature, our conflicts may become less violent, but the physiological reactions remain the same. These are the symptoms, the palpable signs, that performers can use to show that the violence about to happen is not only believable, but inevitable.

A far better plan is to have Romeo win because, over the course of the fight, he is shown (through the use of specific moves, techniques, vocalizations, timing, gestures, and expressions) to become the more fiercely committed fighter—his intense, focused, raw and deadly determination eventually overcoming Tybalt's arrogant overconfidence—a dramatic outcome any audience can understand. John Waller's "interpreters" at the Royal Armouries in Leeds, England, in their demonstrations of historical swordfights using stage combat techniques, cleverly resolve this same fight by having Romeo use the "slash and bash" methods of George Silver, an Elizabethan-era theorist while Tybalt employs the fancy "fence tricks" of his contemporary Italian masters. The result is a compelling fight wherein the less sophisticated fighter wins convincingly, though with much effort. In some of our productions, we've even staged Romeo's victory as a startling accident: he lands a lucky thrust to the obvious surprise of both fighters, showing vividly how Romeo may indeed be "fortune's fool."

The point is, each phase of a fight should depend directly on the action that precedes it—including the motivations provided by the script and the way those motivations change as the fight develops. Each phase, too, is a separate chance to explore the psyches of the characters and showcase the actors' talents, lending depth to what too many directors still view as a diverting but essentially *un*essential part of the story.

AGREEING TO DISAGREE: ACHIEVING THE ILLUSION OF CONFLICT

Strange as it sounds, fighting on stage is one of acting's most cooperative tasks. It has to be. Nobody loses an eye from singing off-key, but that (and worse) can happen if a collaborative fight turns competitive. Sadly, cooperation like this does not come naturally to some performers. They cut each other's throats (figuratively, of course) to win roles and awards, upstage each other shamelessly in performance, and schmooze producers and directors into giving them parts that throw other actors out of work. Hypercompetitive performers like these find, after being cast in a stage combat role, that they must somehow put such feelings aside and collaborate to achieve the illusion of conflict: agreeing—and clearly understanding—that it is the characters, and not the performers, who fight on stage.

Unfortunately, even when personal feelings are under control and mutual trust is genuine, a host of other factors can make even a well-planned fight unsafe. Stage combat produces adrenaline: one of the world's most dangerous drugs. Mere exuberance—the joy of action—has probably injured more people on stage than bad feelings. Yet *that* problem pales to insignificance behind two more dangerous enemies: carelessness and fatigue.

The key to overcoming these problems and keeping stage violence safe and convincing night after night lies in the four-step sequence you'll employ for each combat move: *eye contact–preparation–reaction–and action*. Here's how it works:

EYE CONTACT (Fig. 1-3a) Speech is only one form of communication and in a play, most of that is scripted. Actors in a fight may grunt and groan, but unplanned vocalizations—to cue a forgetful partner or get a derailed fight back on track—sometimes makes things worse and can kill the fight's credibility. In other words, you can't yell "Are you ready?" before launching a surprise attack, although you'd be surprised how many actors do.

Because of this, you must learn to communicate effectively with your eyes—a basic acting skill that becomes even more important in stage combat. By establishing eye contact with your parner and resuming it after the action, both of you can ensure you are "in the moment" and ready for the next move, all the while maintaining the illusion of conflict. In a real fight you'd keep a sharp eye on your opponent and the audience expects no less.

PREPARATION (Fig. 1-3b) Here, we don't mean rehearsal, but a purposeful motion (often made opposite to the planned attack) that signals your intention—much the way a boxer in a cartoon telegraphs a punch by making an exaggerated windup. In a rapier fight, for example, the attacker cutting to the defender's left shoulder would begin by drawing the sword *back* toward his own right shoulder. This preparation, or prep, before committing to a movement serves several vital functions.

First, it signals the defender that the choreographed action (in this case, a cut to the left shoulder) is about to be performed. This assures the defender that the routine is still on track, and serves as a reminder in case his or her attention has wandered: "Oh yeah, I'm supposed to parry 4 now to protect my left shoulder!"

1-3a. Eye-contact.

1-3b. Preparation.

1-3c. Reaction.

1-3d. Action!

Second, it lets the audience know that something is about to happen. This builds a little tension—however brief—before the release of action.

Third, because the prep is executed in the same rhythm as the subsequent action, it tells the defender how fast a particular attack will come.

Finally, good preps allow the fight to unfold in a lifelike, irregular way. Nothing looks worse than a mechanical "I attack, you parry; you attack, I parry" kind of fight that unwinds with clockwork regularity like the Anvil Chorus. A good prep, and the reaction that follows, gives the actors time to act.

1-4. Commitment to the character and to the fight make the scene believable and safe. Errol Flynn, right, and Basil Rathbone in swashbuckling action in "Robin Hood," 1938. Fight Director: Fred Cavens. (The Everett Collection.)

REACTION (Fig. 1-3c) Even more than the prep, the reaction has both practical and dramatic value. After the defender has seen the prep, he or she reacts—that is, begins to make the planned, choreographed response. This tells the attacker that it is safe to continue with the action that's been rehearsed—in this case, a cut to the defender's left shoulder. If the defender does *not* react, or reacts with the wrong response—say, by moving to parry on the wrong side of the body—the attacker knows that a mistake is in progress and aborts the planned move in the interest of safety and good theater.

Since acting is really *reacting*, the way the defender responds to the attacker's prep goes a long way toward selling the fight to the audience. After all, the defender who scrambles awkwardly, reacting in the nick of time to make a parry conveys an entirely different feeling to the audience than one who stands calmly, flipping the sword back and forth from the wrist, parrying blows effortlessly while stifling a yawn.

ACTION (Fig 1-3d) The last step in the cycle, the attacker's action—what the whole sequence has supposedly been about—is probably the least important of all. Of course, the action must be rendered properly, with the right technique, timing, and degree of energy; but it's the *defender's reaction* that makes the attack look dangerous. If the defender doesn't look worried, the audience won't be either, no matter how expertly the attack is delivered.

Ultimately, the quality and timing of this eye contact-prep-reaction-action cycle gives each fight its flavor. For example:

- To give the impression of two experts dueling, keep the cycle and its movements short, crisp, and simple. Remember K-I-S-S, "keep it simple, stupid"—the actors may not be as expert as the fighters they portray.
- To make a fight look one-sided, the stronger fighter's movements should be short and crisp while the weaker fighter's motions should take longer, be more exaggerated, and saved until the last possible moment.
- To give the impression of fatigue or extra brutality, both fighters should use ragged rhythms and exaggerated motions, although all preps and reactions should still be crystal clear.

Once a basic framework like this has been set for a given fight, the actors can then, and only then, concentrate on bringing other aspects of their characters to life through vocalizations, collateral gestures, and so on—factors we'll talk more about in the next chapter.

ARE REAL FIGHTS REALLY BETTER?

Novice actors and avant garde directors sometimes experiment with "full contact" or improvised stage fights, but this is almost always a mistake. The obvious reason to avoid such "organic" or unstaged combat is the chance of injury, which goes up enormously (our experience has shown that it is much more upsetting to be the actor who has inflicted an injury than to be the one who received it), but there are other reasons, too.

Although well-trained partners used to working together can perform a routine safely at blinding speed, most stage combat is performed at two-thirds to three-quarters the speed of an actual fight. Any faster and the audience can't follow the action. Any slower and the fight becomes unconvincing and (oddly enough) chances for mistakes increase. At the Academy of the Sword, we never perform a fight faster than we can do it "perfectly"—a rule that has proven its worth over many years and hundreds of performances.
R.L.

From a dramatic standpoint, unrehearsed fights usually end up looking amateurish, not real. Even dedicated actors aren't suicidal—or homicidal—so they end up pulling their punches and otherwise trying to avoid injury: a fine goal, but the results are often unconvincing to an audience. Just as bad, if the improvised fight is performed more than a few times, the actors inevitably settle into comfortable routines of their own, so even the spark of spontaneity (if it ever really existed) is eventually lost.

But the best reason to avoid "real" fights goes even deeper. Part of the covenant between actor and audience is that whatever happens on stage is make-believe—one reason the audience is willing to suspend its disbelief. If an action on stage isn't pretend, then the event—whatever it is—stops being art and becomes something else: an athletic contest, a gladiatorial match, psychotherapy for the director, or whatever—but it is no longer theater. Most people feel uneasy when they sense that another human being is in real danger. Just as each actor-combatant trusts the other to keep stage combat safe, so must the audience trust the performers to let them enjoy the show in peace.

That master of illusion, George Lucas, was once asked how he managed to make his exploding planets look so real, since no human has ever seen one. Lucas replied, "I don't have to know what they look like. I only have to know what the audience *thinks* they look like."

This is wonderful advice for anyone involved in stage combat. Realism is fine, but the illusion is often better. It's cheaper, safer, and more satisfying. Remember, great art doesn't just hold a mirror up to life, it improves on it when it can. R.L.

SMILING AT DANGER, LAUGHING AT DEATH

Great performances don't come from the script, but from the actors who bring it to life. Few people remember the name of Robin Hood's (Errol Flynn's) nemesis, the evil Sheriff of Nottingham (it was Sir Guy) or Levasseur (the villain in *Captain Blood*) or Esteban Pasquale (treacherous *commandante* from *The Mark of Zorro*) but no one forgets the actor who played them all to such perfection: British-born Basil Rathbone. What we saw in his inspired villainy wasn't just his devilish looks and sly manner, or even his exceptional swordplay, but his *commitment* to that villainy, to that style, to that fiendish way of thinking and fighting. Rathbone gave us antagonists whose total commitment to their own twisted ends made the travails of the heroes seem not only admirable and exciting, but necessary.

If you take nothing else from this chapter, it should be this: commit yourself fully to every character you play. Whether it's fighting or drinking, cavorting or wooing, a soliloquy or a mob scene, engage yourself completely in what that character is thinking and doing at that moment. It will make your conflicts more intense, your action more exciting, your victories more stirring and your defeats more moving. In today's era of naturalistic methods, we may not always consider Flynn and Rathbone to have been great actors, but they were always great performers. Not a motion, breath, or gesture escaped them that was not completely in sync with their characters—and that's what we still respond to, even generations later. As Maestro Kolombatovich affirms, "There are no secondary roles, only secondary talents." Roles involving combat—conflict on the knife-edge between life and death—affect audiences most deeply. If you wish to make your mark as an actor, you can find few better ways than by committing yourself fully to the action roles you play.

OF SIDEKICKS, SQUIRES, AND JESTERS

No less an expert than Shakespeare reminds us that just as drama depends on conflict, tragedy must be leavened by comedy if it is to rise to its greatest heights. Few of Shakespeare's tragedies lack comic relief, and experience shows it is far easier for good comics to play tragic parts than the reverse. As actor Edmund Gwynn (or W.C. Fields, or Molière—all have been credited with this line) reputedly said on his deathbed, "Dying is easy, comedy is hard!"

COMMEDIA DELL'ARTE Physical humor is as old as theater. The fine lines between tragedy, comedy, and farce were trampled on early and often by the ancient Greeks and Romans. In the sixteenth through eighteenth centuries, stock characters in the Italian "commedia dell'arte" were thrust into provocative situations solely for the audiences to experience the comedy and drama inherent in those situations. From this, modern actors have learned that a physical gag—a comic act done seriously or a serious act done comically— can be as effective as drama in releasing tension or resolving an audience's aroused emotions. While good drama compels an audience to identify with the actors, good comedy sets audience and actors apart and allows the audience to laugh at that "comic other." After all, what is comedy but a tragedy that happens to someone else?

THE COMIC COMBAT STYLE This mix of preconceived ideas and audience expectations plus the intimate link between laughter and tears—including that nervous laugh that flows from a dangerous situation—forms the basis of most comic combat. Since timing is the essence of comedy, the prep-reaction-action cycle here, makes its toughest demands on performers.

For example, in a real duel, a defender might be forced to jump back from a rapier cut aimed at the legs. In a stage fight, we would simulate this using various realistic techniques you'll learn about in Part II. In a comic fight, however, the defender must react in a way that, while remaining faithful to the logic of the weapon and the fight, stands drama on its ear. You *could* exaggerate your jump, wave your arms frantically and screech in terror, but that's exactly the kind of funny business most audiences don't find funny. A better choice might be for the defender, even one who is outclassed, to simply stand squarely and lift only one foot. The illusion of danger and the reality of the moment are maintained, but with a comic twist: the reaction is out of proportion to the action.

If you are ever called upon to perform a funny fight, you can usually make a move more humorous by:

1. *Delaying it.* A slight pause fools the audience and gives your partner more time to react—with more comic schtick, a double-take, or whatever. A longer pause builds suspense and can help even a lame gag seem hilarious.

2. *Giving it to the other performer.* From the tradition of Roman farce and the commedia dell'arte, we expect certain stock characters to do certain

The stage property most associated with Arlecchino, and the one which gave its name to physical or mock-comedy is the slapstick. The slapstick was a bat made of two limber pieces of wood bound at the handle. A blow delivered by one made a resounding slap, hence the name "slapstick." The blow was fairly harmless, as the energy of the blow was dissipated between two pieces of wood. . . . A variation of the bat was used as an instrument of corporal punishment in China, one side of the bat being weighted. The weighted side lent impetus to the blow, the resulting injury being a severe bruise. Whether the genesis of the slapstick can be found in this Chinese weapon I do not know, but it cannot be discounted.

Lloyd Caldwell
"Slapstick in the Commedia Dell'arte"
The Fight Master

funny things. When they don't, and a different performer does them, we find it even funnier.

3. *Starting the move, then stopping.* Like the long pause, a series of well-timed false starts builds comic tension while the audience waits for the other shoe to drop.

4. *Over- or under-performing preps.* Preps are cues for both the performers and the audience, and therein lie their comic potential. Greatly exaggerated preps, like slapstick, are easy to do and even easier to overdo. Sometimes, subtle gestures work best.

5. *Using non-combat props and ideas.* In most dramatic fights, the attacker tries to defeat the defender as soon as possible. The longer (and more plausibly) the defender frustrates this intention—sometimes using props like tables and chairs, or pseudo-weapons like candelabra, bottles, and dishes—the more he or she creates tension and excitement. In a comic fight, or brawl, using these non-weapons in an unexpected way can enliven the action and make it seem less threatening—but beware. Good actor-combatants spend lots of time training with swords but only a few know how to jump safely from balconies or swing from chandeliers—and most shouldn't try. If a director calls for such stunts, a specialist should be used, or the stunt written out of the fight.

1-5. Laurence Olivier (Oscar—Best Actor) scores a "touch" in the 1948 version of "Hamlet" (Oscar—Best Film) with Terence Morgan as Laertes. Fights by Denis Loraine. (The Everett Collection.)

WHEN ART IMITATES ART

After you've gained some stage-combat experience, you will begin to recognize certain moves used habitually in plays and films. These include not just the visual clichés (blades lopping off candles and opponents glaring combatively over locked hilts), but also moves drawn from historical practice and phrases borrowed (called "homage") from previous productions. Soon, the question occurs to any conscientious actor or director: "Is there really any *new* way to stage a fight?"

This question arises often when staging combat in plays like *Hamlet* and *Macbeth*, standard repertoire where the moods and outcomes of the fights are so well known; or in remakes of film classics like *Robin Hood*, where everyone knows that Robin and John Little must duel with quarterstaffs before the end of reel three. Do the actors and director staging these fights owe more to theatrical tradition, to peers and critics who demand innovation, or to the audiences who simply want to be entertained?

The answer is: you have a duty to all, but mainly to the author, to realize the highest potential of the story. If you do justice to the characters—and make clear their motivations for the conflict—audiences will be entertained and the critics (well, most critics) will be satisfied.

Take, for example, the concluding swordfight in *Hamlet*, which, after 400 years, has been staged in almost every conceivable way—from Lord Olivier's florid and athletic fencing exhibition (including that extraordinary leap) to Mel Gibson's gritty minimalism. No one approach is necessarily better than another, since all tend to reflect the values and esthetics of their day. What each Hamlet has had in common has been its director's desire to please and surprise the audience, and the actor's desire to leave his mark on the part. Since *Hamlet* is one of the Western world's most frequently produced plays, it is likely that someone using this book will be called upon to direct or perform its final, fatal fight. What would *you* do to bring new life and luster to this best-known of all stage combats?

One way to tackle such challenges is to forget about the precedents. Don't try to "out-Olivier" Olivier—it simply can't be done. Instead, go back to the primary material: the play itself—its characters, dramatic construct, and historical setting. What Shakespeare gives us in his stage direction and dialogue is that the melancholy Dane must "hit" Laertes—score a point in their friendly duel—and call for a judgment by the referee. He must then hit Laertes a second time, then Laertes must say, "Have at you now!" and wound Hamlet. . . then, in scuffling, they change rapiers. "Hamlet wounds Laertes. The Queen falls." After that, and more dialogue, Hamlet must "hurt the king."

Given everything else we know about the young prince, there is nothing in the play that would prevent us from showing Hamlet as the weaker swordsman. (He is usually shown as the stronger, partly because he's the star, and partly because directors and actors assume he must be in order to score those initial hits, but is that necessarily so?) We *do* know that Hora-

During *I Hate Hamlet* at Broadway's Walter Kerr Theatre, actor Evan Handler, playing Laertes, suddenly left the stage after the dueling scene with Hamlet played by Nicol Williamson. During the first act, Williamson began coaching his co-star, saying, "Put some life into it. Use your head. Give it more life!" The act continued until the final scene, in which the actors duel. In the first movement of the fight, when the swords are supposed to hit, this time they missed. Nicol later said said he thought that Handler was pulling something on him, and Evan felt that Nicol was pulling something on him. . . when it came to the part where Williamson is supposed to nick Handler from behind, he actually hit him with the sword. Evan walked straight through the door on the set and out. . .
Alex Witchel
The New York Times
Saturday, May 4, 1991

tio believes, "You will lose, my lord," and that Hamlet has "been in continual practice" and believes he will "win at the odds," (that is, achieve the
expected difference in the final score). Hamlet goes further to say, "I'll be
your foil, Laertes; in mine ignorance your skill shall, like a star in the darkest
night stick fiery off indeed." (Act V, Scene 2). If we staged the fight to show
Hamlet as merely a game sportsman whose early hits came at Laertes' suffer-
ance—perhaps to lure Hamlet in for the kill—or as the result of good luck,
wouldn't the audience's vicarious sense of danger for the hero actually *increase*
instead of diminish?

The point is, good theater is about creating, then fulfilling, audience
expectations in ever more inventive and entertaining ways. If an actor-combatant is a star or has special abilities not normally associated with stage
combat, don't hesitate to use them if it makes for a better and more entertaining fight. If an old chestnut seems tapped out in terms of creativity, go
back to the primary material—the play's historical period, dramatic construct, and characters—for the resources you'll need to stage a new and
compelling fight.

Theatrical swashbuckling gives us the almost unlimited means for doing
these things, and more, whenever the dialogue stops and the playwright
utters those two most terrifying and energizing words in Western drama:
They fight.

YOUR ROLE AS ACTOR-COMBATANT

A famed eighteenth century duelist arrived at the field of honor one misty morning only to send his hired carriage back to the city. His trusty second, sensing a bad omen, asked in alarm, "What's this? Have you so little confidence?" The duelist only yawned, "Never fear. I always return in my *opponent's* carriage."

Now *there's* a swashbuckler!

R.L.

2-1. *The fight, with the single rapier, according to Capo Ferro. (Re-rendered by Alex Daye.)*

Even the best-planned fight needs skilled performers to achieve its potential. In this chapter, you'll learn:

- More about the differences between real and theatrical combat
- How to use body and mind to achieve an effective illusion
- The anatomy of a good stage fight
- How swashbuckling differs from other forms of stagecraft
- How to minimize the chances of physical injury during training, rehearsal, and performance

In the real world, human combat tends to be violent, bloody, and short. Real fistfights are usually over after a few blows have landed and knife fights are even shorter. Genuine swordfights have long since passed from living memory, but we have no reason to think they departed from this pattern.

HISTORICAL COMBAT WASN'T PRETTY

Eyewitness accounts of historical swordfights suggest that many, if not most, were inconclusive. Few wounded combatants actually died on the spot; most succumbed later to loss of blood or infection. Generally, a duel ended when blood was drawn and honor was satisfied. Sometimes, one or both blades broke and the combatants finished the fight grappling in the mud—punching, kicking, and gouging each other's eyes. Fists, knees, elbows, and feet were used freely, as were other parts of the sword—knuckle bow, pommel, and quillons. Despite the traditions of chivalry, the Marquis of Queensbury rules, and the etiquette taught at fencing academies, real duels were sometimes vulgar brawls where art went out the window as soon as rage came through the door. Many successful swordfighters weren't the dashing swashbucklers of films and novels, but cold-blooded killers who were shunned by polite society.

War in the age of edged weapons wasn't much better. Isolated, one-to-one combat was rare and even for those who could afford armor, sometimes it wasn't much help. Battles were exhausting, chaotic melees where injury threatened from every side: pole arms, swords, daggers, axes, mace and flail threatened front and flank; arrows, javelins, sling stones, darts, and other missiles rained down from above. Even the battleground itself was sometimes seeded with barriers and booby traps. Caltrops (pointed "jacks" strewn across a field to cripple horses), sharpened stakes, pitfalls, boiling water, hot oil and even caustic chemicals, made fighting in the ranks a nightmare.

Most battles followed the same depressing pattern. After minimal maneuvering, both armies would collide and after a brief period of fighting toe-to-toe (where few were killed outright), one side would lose heart, break ranks, and run. This was when most of the casualties in ancient and medieval combat occurred, explaining the lop-sided results of most engagements. Thousands or tens of thousands were killed on the losing side at the cost of a relative handful to the winners. The victors chased the demoralized, disorganized victims from the field and pursued them as long as it was light, striking them down from behind.

Still, the chances of being killed in battle were far less for the average soldier than those of dying from disease in camp. Except for the nobility, their retainers, and a few well-paid mercenaries, warfare before and during the dawn of gunpowder was no picnic. Anyone with any sense avoided it like the plague, which itself took more lives than all the combat in antiquity and the Middle Ages put together.

In former days training was designed so that the trainee would be able to defend himself in everyday life with the weapon he carried, or so he could defend "his honour" in a duel.

By a duel we mean a fight between two opponents, carried out with lethal weapons, organized by arrangement and conducted in front of witnesses for both sides.

Today we would probably consider a duel to be murder sanctioned by law, but formerly its purpose was to prevent assassination, revenge, and a whole number of bloodthirsty repressive measures, particularly in the case of judicial duels.

This legal measure was meant to prove the guilt of the person defeated, but in practice the reverse was often the case. Hence at a fairly early stage this type of duel was forbidden, as for instance, by Theodoric the Great.

Charlemagne chose to recognize the judicial duel as an expression of God's will, but on the other hand the Fourth Lateran Council banned this form of duel in 1215, though in France, King Philip the Fair permitted it again in 1306, but with certain limitations. Other duels were alternately banned, tolerated, and once more, strictly forbidden.

Eduard Wagner
Cut and Thrust Weapons

Obviously, even the most graphic play or film, viewed in the safety and comfort of a theater, can't duplicate the horror and exhilaration of real combat. Fortunately, they don't have to.

WHEN ILLUSION IS THE REALITY

Just as an actor needn't be on stage during the whole play to win applause, a stage fight needn't draw blood (or turn stomachs) to be effective. What constitutes an effective fight?

1. *It lasts long enough to tell a story.* Good stage fights are self-contained mini-dramas that have a beginning, middle, and end. Skip or short-change any part, and the audience will notice. Sometimes, an artful fight can even reflect the larger themes of the play.

   For example, the fight between Tybalt and Mercutio in *Romeo and Juliet* usually begins in a light-hearted vein, then becomes serious, then ends in tragedy—as does the play. When staging this swordfight in our school, the Academy of the Sword, we sometimes mark the passage from Act I to Act II of the fight by having Mercutio kiss Tybalt between swords locked *corps a corps*, just as Romeo kissed Juliet in the marriage scene. Such touches are certainly not crucial to the combat, but they surprise the audience, feel intuitively right, and better integrate the fight with the rest of the story. We'll say more about telling a story with a fight at the end of this chapter.

2. *It completes all illusions.* You already know that the four-part sequence— eye contact, prep, reaction, action—is the basis for all stage-combat moves. Its quality dictates everything the fight can or will become. Yet even performers who follow it religiously sometimes ruin a fight if the audience sees them anticipate the next move, or if they stop acting after completing their part of the sequence.

   To make this clearer, let's go back to the fight between Tybalt and Mercutio. In one of our productions, it was necessary for Mercutio to disarm Tybalt—to make him drop his sword. There are lots of ways to do this in stage combat, but we chose to have Mercutio appear to bite Tybalt on the wrist—a counterpoint to the comedic kiss. We worked up a series of moves where this became a natural part of the fight, and the actors performed it flawlessly. The only problem was, the audiences at the first few performances didn't respond the way we expected them to. We discovered that Tybalt, after crying out and dropping his sword, did not complete the illusion. Instead, he did what most fighters would do in that situation, and what the choreography called for: he shoved Mercutio away to put some distance between himself and his armed opponent. The audiences read the disarm and the danger, but not the bite. We solved this problem by giving Tybalt time to stare momentarily—and in obvious disbelief—at the bite. After that, the audiences got the cue, and reacted appropriately.

> The true Way of sword fencing is the craft of defeating the enemy in a fight, and nothing other than this.
>
> Miyamoto Musashi
> *A Book of Five Rings*

It is far more common for a defender to spoil a move by anticipating the action, reacting to the prep not by beginning the defensive move, but by completing it. For example, a defender is already in a squat evading a sword swipe aimed at the head, or has assumed the end position for a particular parry, while their partner is still preparing. This obviously makes the entire exchange look fake.

Some actors go to the other extreme. They begin their next move before the current one has been completed. On attack, this means hurrying through cuts or thrusts, giving the audience the impression that the attacker never thought the blows would succeed. When on defense, this shows up as a partial parry: one that never quite reaches its proper end position before the defender goes on to the next move, reducing the sense of threat. The result on both sides is a sloppy routine that looks tentative, amateurish, and unconvincing, or worse: unsafe, which it is. This leads us to the last general rule for an effective fight:

3. *Good stage combat uses eyes and swords as pointers to guide the players and audience toward the action.* The actors know what's going to happen next in a fight—and why—but not the audience. To keep up with the action, the audience needs frequent cues about where to look next. The tools *always* available to give these cues are the actors' eyes and the tips of their swords—two things both observers and participants instinctively look at in a swordfight. To use these tools effectively, remember that:

- Combatants looking each other in the eye seem more focused and aggressive than those who look elsewhere.

- Attackers looking at a target area while they prep, show the audence, and their partner, their intention. If you're going to take a swipe at the defender's feet, for example, look at the feet—not into the defender's face. This makes the action safer and more believable.

- A defender watching the attacker's sword during the action phase of the four-part cycle shows the audience that the actor thinks the sword is a threat. This is only human nature. If you're about to be shot, you look at the gun; if you're about to be stabbed, you look at the knife. This also makes the reaction easier than if you had to perform it using peripheral vision.

- Sword tips guide the eye to wherever they are pointed. A naked blade is always communicating with the audience—so you'd better know what it's saying. A sword pointed down at the stage (Fig. 2-2a), or behind you toward the wings *reduces* the sense of threat. A sword held with the point straight up sends mixed signals (Fig. 2-2b)—it may or may not be threatening. A sword pointed at the opponent, however (Fig 2-2c), is *always* perceived as a threat—so if it is drawn and not engaged in some other purposeful activity such as a salute, let the audience know that the sword means business.

2-2a.

2-2b.

2-2c.

HOW GOOD ACTORS "ENDOW" THE SWORD

By now you've seen that "acting the fight" means more than remembering lines and choreography. It means actor-combatants must understand at all times the effect each move, sound, and gesture has upon the audience, as well as the safety of the fight.

One mental trick actors use to ensure that this effect is the right one is to endow the sword with dangerous—even mystical—properties whenever it's on stage. By "endow" we mean that you treat the sword like the deadly, enchanting weapon it is, and not like an umbrella or walking-stick (as Marlon Brando's surrendering Napoleon pointed out to Jean Simmons in *Desiree*, "...please don't hold it like an umbrella"). As with most techniques in theatrical swashbuckling, endowing has both practical and dramatic benefits.

First, it makes the sword an important "actor" in the play. By increasing the atmosphere of danger when one is present—even if it's still in the scabbard—you will help the audience sense that danger, too.

Second, it can lend historical accuracy to any scene. As you'll see in the next chapter, swords were expensive weapons and not just anybody owned one. Since the users' lives depended on them, they were kept clean, rust free, and sharp. Since swords were also a sign of nobility and high fashion, they drew respectful, admiring glances much the way expensive cars and designer clothes do today. Like police officers' pistols, they were drawn only when they were going to be used—not for idle threats or play. Consequently, good actors never abuse their swords on stage—resting them on their points, leaning on them, bending them, sitting on them, and so on—but they endow them with the properties of a real weapon.

Last but not least, endowing the sword makes stage combat safer. If you treat the sword like a gun—a deadly weapon that is always loaded and can inflict a serious wound in a split second—you'll go a long way toward avoiding that most avoidable of accidents: the careless injury.

SOME GENERAL RULES FOR FIGHTING ON STAGE

In the theater, we tend to use whatever works. Creativity, not slavish rule-following, is the order of the day—but there are exceptions. Here are some principles experienced fight directors have discovered to make any stage combat technique work—and look—better.

1. *In attack, move the sword first, then the body; in defense, do the opposite.*
   Real swordfights were about keeping one's balance while inflicting harm and avoiding being injured. Whoever fell was finished, so like all martial artists, good duelists worked hard to coordinate their hands and feet. The same principle applies to stage combat. Unplanned falls here may not be fatal, but they are painful and embarrassing.

Actors are so used to handling dull, blunt weapons that they don't think of them as being sharp or of inflicting injury so they don't portray that and the audience doesn't pick up on that. . . Everyone thinks of a knife as being a dangerous instrument. If you are facing someone with a three-inch knife you feel the real threat of being cut and you can imagine the injury that it can inflict, but the same people don't see a three-foot sword as being very dangerous. Drawing a sword in a crowded room three hundred years ago had about the same impact as pulling a machine pistol out from under your coat today. People understand what they are looking at and would have some fear of it. People of Shakespeare's time would have had that same fear of a naked sword.

Linda McCollum
"Dennis Graves, Premier Swordcutler"
The Fight Master

When attacking with a sword, lead with the blade, then let your body follow. This will help you avoid becoming over-extended. For example, to thrust at your partner's hip from a lunge, you would prepare by bringing the hilt of the sword back to your hip, (tip facing your partner) extending the blade toward the target, then stepping forward into the lunge. Because your sword is already extended, the lunge now becomes a simple repositioning of your feet, and not your torso, which can tilt you off balance.

When you defend—parry or evade—move your body first, then reposition your sword. This sequence makes sense because the instinctive reaction to a threat is to get out of the way, as one would from a punch, or remove one's hand from a hot stove. To evade the lunging thrust described above, step back with the targeted leg, *then* move your sword to parry the thrust. In these cases, the body movement is the primary defense; the parry is added insurance. Some experts advise moving and parrying at the same time, but making this look unplanned and spontaneous can be difficult.

In Part II, you'll learn specific techniques for coordinating swordplay with footwork. For now, just remember that balance and control are as essential to good stage fights as they were to actual duels.

2. *Rehearse the fight as often as needed to make it perfect.* Perfection here means that all participants, including extras in the fight, know the choreography—including the preps, reactions, and actions needed for every move—and can execute them safely *in costume*, and do not vary their styles or rhythms from performance to performance. You'd be surprised how many actors forget what they have learned once those period costumes go on—including how hard it is to see and hear from inside a helmet. Also, inspiration is fine, but if you have a new idea for your fight, don't spring it on your partner in the middle of a routine. Instead, mention it to the fight captain or director and show it to the audience *only* when everyone concerned is ready.

3. *Handle the sword naturally—as if you were born to it.* On stage, treat the sword like a real swordfighter did: as if it has always been part of your life. This doesn't mean you stop endowing the sword; only that you retain the same sense of confidence and flair during non-combat scenes as when you are fighting. Here are the ways to avoid the sword handling problems that often trouble beginners:

   • *Don't* let the sword develop a mind of its own. *Do* control a sheathed blade just as you would a drawn sword. We've all seen comedies where an actor wearing a sword moves through a crowd breaking dishes and inadvertently goosing people when he bows—the infamous "Groucho stab"(see Fig. 2-3). If this sort of business is required for your character, fine; but most of the time, these unplanned incidents turn drama into farce. British Fight Director Mike Loads advises that if you have to bow while wearing a sword, push the hilt

Another problem one encounters is the conviction of everyone in the production that his contribution is the only notable and important one and therefore not to be tampered with. A very dedicated costume designer brought forth a totally armored Montano, destined to be wounded on the arm by Cassio in "Othello." Hysterical, hands waving in anguish, voice shrill, he declared that there could be NO changes in his gorgeous costume. I used the diplomacy for which I am famous and the singer's arms were uncovered so that the action could take place.

Oscar F. Kolombatovich
Murder and Mayhem at the Met

back (keeping the blade vertical), or away from your hip (tucking the blade safely behind your thighs) before you bend over. If you have to sit down, remove the sheathed sword from its hanger— a true swordbelt should allow the scabbard to be lifted easily out of its frog. If that's not possible, approach the chair from the rear and ease gently onto the seat from the side opposite to your sword (see Fig. 2-4).

2-3. The Groucho stab.

2-4.

- *Don't* let the sword dictate your gestures. *Do* continue to act in a relaxed, natural manner. It's okay to rest your hand on a sheathed sword's pommel but don't let that arm look paralyzed, or get into the habit of nervously squeezing or fingering the handle unless that, too, is a conscious choice for your character. When you draw a sword on stage, be sure there is ample room to complete the motion. Unless it's part of the choreography, don't whip the sword out in an extravagant, horizontal arc, flailing the air around you. If the sheathed blade is uncomfortably long (or if you have short arms), step back slightly on your right foot as you draw, to gain the extra leverage you need.

To sheath a sword, find the tip with your free hand and guide it down to the throat of the scabbard (see Fig. 2-5a); or grip the throat of the scabbard with your free hand and hit your thumb near the throat with the blade tip, then guide the tip into the scabbard (see Fig. 2-5b).

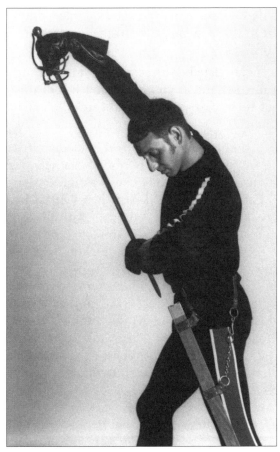

2-5a.

2-5b.

- *Don't* ignore other swords around you. *Do* take action if you see trouble coming. In some productions, the stage is filled with extras bearing swords, not all of them involved in combat or with their swords protected by scabbards. Typically (unlike the principal actor-combatants), these supernumeraries receive little or no training in sword handling. If you see problems brewing in dress rehearsal—extras behaving carelessly with their swords, for example—don't be shy about mentioning it to those involved, or to the director, stage manager, or fight captain.
- *Don't* over- or underplay fight-related death scenes. *Do* make dying as naturalistic as the rest of the fight. If your character has death lines, you should deliver them in a style that indicates the extent of your character's wounds.

The first thing to remember is that people seldom died immediately from mortal sword wounds. Grand opera got it right: a moribund character really would have time to sing that final aria. Serious chest wounds (that is, wounds that pierced the lungs but not the heart) killed their victims by literally drowning them in their own blood. If your fight calls for this kind of demise, don't be afraid to cough and wheeze. Serious wounds to other parts of the body, limbs, or the abdomen, meant bleeding to death in minutes, or dying from infection a few days or weeks later. Since you've got to die on cue, the best thing to do here is to simulate unconsciousness due to loss of blood. People who pass out from anoxia (a gradual reduction of oxygen to the brain) begin by getting light-headed and slurring their words. They can even act drunk or giddy. Eventually, they feel cold, lose muscular coordination, and must sit or lie down. When they finally lose consciousness, it's like a light bulb going out. Above all, have your character show the psychological shock of being wounded. Nobody expects to die, so your reaction should reflect, "This *can't* be happening to *me!*"

Staying faithful to the logic of the fight even after the fight is over makes the combat seem more real and can increase the power of the most improbable death speech.

ANATOMY OF A STAGE FIGHT

Just as this book progresses from sentences to paragraphs to chapters, so are choreographed fights built up from individual moves into phrases and longer sections. When you add that intangible ingredient called acting, a good fight becomes much more than the sum of its parts.

MOVES A move is the smallest unit of a fight that makes sense by itself. Just as a single word makes little sense until you use it in a sentence, a stage combat move must contain enough motion to show the intention and capability of the fighter—that is, *what* a fighter intends to do and *how well* he or she does it. Since the intention of most combatants is to win (or keep from losing), most moves should theoretically have the potential for doing just that: wounding the defender or foiling an attack. Sword cuts and thrusts, punches and kicks, etc., are all examples of attacking moves; just as parries and evasions are defensive moves. Even drawing the sword is a move, since it shows intention and advances the story of the fight. While a defensive move usually won't be enough to end the fight by itself, it should look as though it is sufficient to spoil a particular attack, and should therefore be made with the same conviction as the attack—more so, in fact, since the defender's reaction is what sells that attack to the audience.

PHRASES A phrase is a series of moves that tells one part of the overall fight story. Like a paragraph in a chapter or a scene in an act, it advances the story and leaves the combatants a little different at the end from the way they began. But a phrase does not tell the whole story—and phrases that follow may contradict what we thought was happening at an earlier point in the fight. At the very least, good phrases should show the momentum of the fight—who's winning and who's losing at any particular moment.

For convenience, most fight directors number consecutive phrases the way composers number bars of music. This allows actors to rehearse them in or out of sequence, concentrating at different times on different phrases that are giving them trouble. As useful as this is, we advocate giving phrases descriptive names as well—a way of identifying them by feeling and function as well as simple sequence.

For example, suppose a short swordfight consists of five phrases. In the first, the fighters probe each other for weaknesses. In the second, they seesaw back and forth, testing what they've learned. In the third, one fighter becomes recklessly aggressive. In the fourth, he makes a big mistake, which leads to his being disarmed and humiliated in phrase five. To help the actors keep the feeling and logic of these phrases in mind as well as their sequence, we might name them:

1. Probing
2. Testing for weaknesses
3. Pressing the attack
4. Making the big mistake
5. The ultimate indignity

Thus, the actors know from the outset that each phrase contains not just a specific set of moves, but a motivating force that changes the relationship between the characters and *tells a story* as the fight progresses.

SECTIONS A section is composed of several phrases—like the acts of a play or the chapters of a book. A section contains enough phrases to tell a self-contained part of the story of the fight. Most fights will have three sections, just as most plays have three acts: a beginning, middle, and end. In this scheme, the first section establishes the fighting styles and capabilities of the characters, as well as their initial degrees of commitment to the fight.

Motivation takes many forms. The will to fight requires the four basic motives we discussed in the previous chapter. They get characters into a fight but they do not always explain how the characters behave once the fight begins. Smaller motivations, called "targets of opportunity," explain those moment-to-moment needs and desires—often technical—that justify the moves within a phrase.

For example, if one character in a duel shows a preference for attacking along the high line—at the head, chest, or shoulders—the other might see some advantage to counter-attacking on the low line—at the hips, legs, or feet. This has nothing to do with *why* the characters fight; it only explains why one would select one form of attack or defense over another.

Just as every character should have a clear motivation for beginning a fight, every phrase should present targets of opportunity that drive it forward. Without them, fighters behave inconsistently and their styles become indistinguishable—lacking that stamp of individuality, spontaneity, and intention that turns the dramatic conflict into an exciting physical contest and test of wills.

R.L.

The middle section (or sections) develops the fight—just as the middle chapters of a book develop the plot. Middle sections reveal the momentum of the fight, shifting back and forth between the combatants, but end with only one having the advantage.

The final section resolves the combat. Either the stronger fighter overpowers the weaker, the better strategist outsmarts the poorer, or something unlikely happens to rescue the one who is obviously losing. Nothing bores an audience more than a really one-sided fight that ends as expected, which is why so many stage combats end as upsets. No matter how your fight ends, though, don't telegraph its conclusion. If the stronger fighter must win, have it occur in a dramatic fashion. If the weaker fighter wins, make the victory plausible, as we discussed in the last chapter. If the fight must end in a draw, make sure this serves the drama and does not leave the audience frustrated.

Finally, make sure the effects of the fight linger with the fighters in the scenes that follow. At the Academy, we call this the fight's "physical baggage" and the characters should tote it around with them, when appropriate, for the rest of the play. Part of this baggage is the wear and tear of combat. If your character is wounded in Scene 3, he or she should still be wounded in Scene 4 (unless the next scene takes place months or years in the future). And the signs of these wounds should include not just bandages and bruises, but the mannerisms that often accompany a traumatic experience: rubbing a sore arm, limping slightly, glancing about warily or using a different tone of voice—whatever is right for the character and the situation. Don't go overboard, but if the playwright hasn't built these subtler aspects into the script, add them to your interpretation.

One way to identify this baggage is to make a "biography" of the fight, just as you might write a brief biography of the character in preparing for the role. Itemize every punch, kick, stab, and slash you took or delivered (including *how* you took or delivered them), and imagine how that might change your character. Would that person become bitter? Sullen? Cocky? Reflective? Defensive? Nihilistic? The list seems endless, but in reality, only a few descriptions would logically apply to a given character. Adding that baggage to the inventory of gestures, inflections, and mannerisms available to your character adds depth to the performance and magnifies its impact on the audience.

Video stores are filled with swashbuckling movies that illustrate the structure of good fights. We offer the following "Top Ten" (in no particular order) as models of construction, style, and entertainment value:

1. Although their opponent in the opening duel is doomed from the start, both Jose Ferrer's and Girard Depardieu's *Cyrano de Bergerac* show how clever fight direction and strong acting can keep even a one-sided match exciting. Ferrer earned an Oscar for his performance as the long-nosed romantic. The opening poem/swordfight between Valvert (played by Cavens'

son Albert) and Ferrer is in the saber style of Hollywood's golden age. Cavens doubles for Ferrer when Cyrano fights eight people at once. William Hobbs uses a nice variety of weapons (including farm implements) for his battle scenes in the remake. (Fight Directors: Fred Cavens and William Hobbs, respectively.)

2. The final swordfight between Robin Hood (Errol Flynn) and Sir Guy (Basil Rathbone) in *The Adventures of Robin Hood* is the archetype for all good-versus-evil duels. Although their technique often looks stagey by modern standards, the ebb and flow of the combat and the swashbuckling energy shown by both Flynn and Rathbone, who fenced for pleasure nearly every day, is unsurpassed in this classic. There is a nice quarterstaff sequence between Flynn and Alan Hale (Little John) and a good staircase fight sequence—kids, don't try this at home! (Fight Director: Fred Cavens.)

3. Charleton Heston's "a outrance" joust (fight to the death) for the city of Calahorra in 1961's *El Cid*, is a good example of both a realistically staged medieval fight and a come-from-behind, underdog victory that leaves the victor caked in blood. Included are jousting with lances and contests with two-handed broadswords (Heston uses his saddle as a shield.) Canutt's sons, Joe and Tap, double for Heston and Christopher Rhodes. Earlier, Heston and Andrew Cruikshank engage in a rather lengthy and less inspired single-handed broadsword fight, supplied by Jean Heremans. (Fight Director: Yakima Canutt, perhaps the most active stager of tournaments since the Middle Ages.)

4. The tense gladiatorial match between Woody Strode and Kirk Douglas early in *Spartacus* shows one way to have the stronger fighter win a one-sided combat without disappointing the audience. Later, watch Spartacus bounce the chin of the gladiator instructor off a heavy iron pot before drowning him in the soup during the revolt—ouch! The film features numerous other examples of stunt-extras taking their lumps during the escape of the slaves. There is also the occasional soldier wearing a wrist watch and tennis shoes—see if you can spot them. Spartacus was directed by a young and untried Stanley Kubrik with Kirk Douglas as the Executive Producer—the credits do not list a stunt co-ordinator or fight director.

5. The fight between King Arthur (Graham Chapman) and the Black Knight (John Cleese) early in *Monty Python and the Holy Grail* though crudely photographed, is a masterpiece of comic combat. Notice how the Black Knight's brutal first fight, in progress when Arthur arrives, is absolutely essential to establishing the comic premise that follows. (Fight Director: John Waller.)

6. Although virtually every fight in *The Princess Bride* is a comedic and technical jewel, the initial duel on the Cliffs of Insanity between Cary Elwes and Mandy Patinkin is a marvel of construction, rhythm, and style—a real tribute to the Golden Age of Hollywood. (Fight Director: Bob Anderson.)

7. One of versatile actor Danny Kaye's best performances came in *The Court Jester*, where he plays a schizoid swashbuckler who must switch back and forth between two completely different fighting styles in the same routine—

must viewing for any serious comic actor. Rathbone and Kaye fence with rapiers even though the story is set in the Middle Ages. Faulkner doubled for Rathbone (who was an excellent fencer) in the "schizoid" scenes to allow Kaye more freedom for the comic bits which were somewhat dangerous and required split-second timing. (Fight Director: Ralph Faulkner.)

8. In the climactic duel in *Scaramouche,* Stewart Granger and Mel Ferrer successfully pull off the longest swordfight in film history, a full six and-a-half minutes—demolishing a theater in the process—though some viewers may feel cheated by the ending. A movie about little more than swordplay, it has other excellent scenes, including Granger's lesson and the initial and second fights. (Fight Director: Jean Heremans.)

9. Despite their annoyingly short takes, Tim Roth's two duels in *Rob Roy* are textbook examples of how to act the fight—rare examples too, of rapier versus broadsword. (Fight Director: William Hobbs.)

10. Michael York and friends (amongst them, Oliver Reed, and Richard Chamberlain) bring good-natured earthiness, convincing combat energy, and a solid historical feel to the swordfights in 1974's *The Three Musketeers,* the epitome of all modern rapier-and-dagger swashbucklers. (Fight Director: William Hobbs.)

PHYSICAL FITNESS AND SWASHBUCKLING

Of the dozens of fight-related injuries detailed by Laurence Olivier in his foreword to William Hobbs' venerable treatise, *Stage Combat,* more than half seem related to the famed actor's own lack of physical conditioning and questionable judgment—the type of injuries that can easily be prevented by a few common-sense precautions.

First, never practice or perform a fight when you are exhausted, sick, or on a medication that can impair your coordination, vision, or alertness. As young men, rakish performers like Errol Flynn and Richard Burton gloried in their ability to work hung over, dead tired, or both. In their later years not one of them failed to regret this needless abuse of their bodies.

Second, never begin a serious stage-combat practice session, rehearsal, or performance without a fifteen to twenty minute period of stretching and warming up. Most injuries occurring in the theater are *self inflicted* injuries— or accidents that happen when actors push themselves too hard or too far for their levels of conditioning and expertise. You'll find a complete set of stretching and warmup exercises aimed at injury-prevention at the beginning of Part II; and more information about the sword—and how to handle it—in the next chapter.

I live for a sigh,
I die for a kiss,
I lust for a laugh,
ha, ha!
I never walk
when I can leap,
I never flee
when I can fight

Danny Kaye
(as Sir Jockimo)
"The Court Jester"
1956

2-6. To show that you are out of control (when "the pellet with the poison's in the flagon with the dragon") you must first be in complete control. Danny Kaye and Basil Rathbone in "The Court Jester." Fight Director: Ralph Faulkner. (The Everett Collection.)

GETTING TO KNOW YOUR SWORD

A sword will never sing in your hand, unless it first sings in your heart.
Rod Casteel, Swordmaker

3-1.

...Italian theorists and practitioners of the sixteenth century had carried the art of personal combat with the sword a long way. The gymnastic play with broadsword and buckler, characteristic of the fifteenth and the earlier part of the sixteenth, had given way to a coherent system of fighting with the rapier. The cutting of the broadsword, accompanied by wrestling, tripping, striking in the face with the pommel, kneeing in the groin and blinding with tossed up earth, had all been seen to be less effective in the business of killing a man than a single thrust with a rapier blade through the face, chest, or belly.

Arthur Wise
The Art and History of Personal Combat

Swords come in all shapes and sizes—as diverse as any natural species. After you've finished this chapter, you'll understand:

- How swords and society developed together
- How a sword's design reflects its user's intentions, capabilities, and the values of its day
- Which types of swords are suitable for stage combat
- The "six commandments" of safe sword handling
- How to care for, store, and transport your swords safely

Throughout history, a good sword cost a year's wages, so many would-be swashbucklers stole, scavenged from battlefields, or waited to inherit the blades on which their lives depended. A well-made sword could last for generations, so its owners treated it like the valuable property it was. As an actor, you should understand and reflect in your performance this intimate relationship between sword and swordfighter.

A BRIEF HISTORY OF BLADES AND BATTLES

Before metallurgy was developed, stones (flint and obsidian prepared by pressure flaking), bones, antlers, and wood were fashioned into fighting extensions of the human hand: spears, arrows, and knives that could cut or pierce an animal or enemy. Since there were no stone tool factories, hunters made their own weapons, so the quality was uneven, to say the least.

The first metallic weapons were made of unalloyed copper—a very sharp, but very brittle material used mostly for daggers. Bronze Age (tin-bronze) weapons were an improvement, made better by hot forging, a breakthrough that forever linked technology to civilization. The smelting of ferrous (iron-based) metals in the last millennium B.C.E. finally made true swords practical, leading eventually to the use of carbon steel. Some biblical dramas involve these ancient, pre-steel weapons. A key plot point of at least one Hollywood sword-and-sandal epic, 1954's *The Egyptian*, featured the dramatic shattering of a Pharaoh's copper sword against a new, improved, Bronze-Age Hittite model.

Theorists love to argue about the relative merits and methods for using various weapons. Archaeologists contribute to this debate by unearthing and dating physical artifacts, while historians and anthropologists put those artifacts into cultural perspective. Little by little, we can reconstruct not only the kinds of weapons a society possessed, but a fairly clear idea of how they were used.

OFFENSIVE WEAPONS Without question, polearms (blades and other fixtures mounted on the ends of long poles and wielded by hand, not thrown) were the mainstay of human combat for most of history—well into the Iron Age. After all, spears had always been used for hunting and were undoubtedly our ancestors' most familiar weapons. That meant more people could use polearms in battle with confidence and without a lot of extra training. Missile weapons, like the javelin, sling and bow-and-arrow, were more difficult to master and were seldom decisive, so those were relegated to auxiliary uses, like skirmishing, until the advent of the longbow. Coupled with the fact that primitive swords were more expensive, harder to make, and easier to break than polearms, the age of spears was a long one. Indeed, the armies in the time of the founding of Western civilization—the ancient Greek *hoplites* (named for their distinctive shield, the *hoplon*), the pikemen of the Macedonian phalanx under Phillip and Alexander, and pre-Marian (early republic) Roman legions—all fought primarily with spears, the sword being a secondary sidearm until end of the first century B.C.E.

DEFENSIVE WEAPONS As with all arms races, improved offensive weapons gave rise to better defensive methods, which in turn promoted better weapons for attack and so on. Early body armor was made of leather or padded cloth, sometimes studded or reinforced with strips or scales made of metal or bone. Stiff, molded linen was also used in antiquity, mostly for breastplates. Helmets were made of molded leather or sections of metal joined by rivets, often with extra nose, cheek, and neck protection and reinforcement bands on the crest and forehead. Upper arms and thighs went bare; although some fighters wore shin guards (greaves) and wristlets for forearm protection. Gloves or gauntlets didn't appear until the Middle Ages, nor did plate armor, which required more extensive forging and thus didn't enter widespread use until the late medieval period. Chain mail, though time-consuming to produce, was used widely from antiquity onward—mostly in the form of long mail shirts (called *hauberks* in the Middle Ages), and coifs, which were worn under the helmet to protect the neck and upper chest.

Shields were first made of wicker or leather stretched on wooden frames, later of laminated wood trimmed with metal—the standard well into the Middle Ages. Finally, all-metal shields of the kite, target, and buckler type appeared and survived through the Renaissance.

Generally speaking, combatants preferred to dodge enemy blows or catch them with shields rather than block, or parry them with their offensive weapons (which might break), or give their trust solely to personal body armor. Interestingly, ancient Roman senators, like politicians today, complained about government contractors who sold "shoddy swords, and helmets that split after a single blow," to the army.

ARE LONG OR SHORT SWORDS BETTER? Because of their brittleness, copper and tin-bronze swords seldom exceeded eighteen to twenty-four inches—they were little more than glorified daggers. Even when carbon steel came into widespread use, making it possible for longer blades to be forged, certain cultures still preferred short swords. The most famous of these is the twenty-inch Roman "gladius," patterned after the Iberian short sword, adopted by Rome in the third century B.C.E. The Romans trained their soldiers to close with the enemy (after throwing a cloud of javelins to encumber opposing shields) then come up under the enemy's hedge of spears, thrusting with their short swords. Traditional armies, lacking room to wield their pikes or long swords effectively, had no defense for such tactics. Because of this and their iron discipline, Roman legionaries became the world's most effective soldiers. Only the collapse of Roman civilization and the onset of the Dark Ages—and the ascendancy of the northern European culture that followed it— allowed the longsword, or broadsword (and eventually the rapier) to assume a place of prominence in western arsenals.

I remember an occasion on a film location when a star (who must be nameless) complained about the weight of his expensive, specially made chain mail suit. On an extremely hot Spanish day, he staggered out of his caravan. . . carrying in his arms the chain mail leggings. "Just feel the weight of this. I'm not wearing it," he said to the director. . . a potentially explosive situation was quickly saved by the director saying that he himself would wear it whilst shooting— and for as long as he could stand it, so then could the actor, who returned to his caravan duly chastened. The crew then witnessed for some time the bizarre spectacle of a knight in full chain mail directing the shoot.

William Hobbs
Fight Direction for Stage and Screen

The Ten Principles of Knightly Conduct (from *Decalogue of Gautier*)

1. Unswerving belief in the Church and obedience to Her teachings.

2. Willingness to defend the Church.

3. Respect and pity for all weakness and steadfastness in defending them. [Sic.]

4. Love of country.

5. Refusal to retreat before an enemy.

6. Unceasing and merciless war against the infidel.

7. Strict obedience to the feudal overlord, so long as those duties did not conflict with duty to God.

8. Loyalty to truth and to the pledged word.

9. Generosity in giving.

10. Championship of the right and the good, in every place and at all times, against the forces of evil.

Arthur Wise
The Art and History of Personal Combat

By then, too, polearms like pikes and halberds had returned as mainstays of the infantry. In systems that glorified the individual—such as the feudal system and chivalry—the sword became the weapon of choice for personal combat, and was recognized as the mystical symbol of power on earth.

RISE AND FALL OF THE ARMORED KNIGHT Chivalry is a medieval term derived from the French *chevalier*, or mounted knight, ("cavalier" springs from this term also) and therein lies an important distinction for performers.

The cavalry, a body of mounted soldiers, was around long before the Age of Chivalry and lasted long after its demise. What distinguishes a mounted knight from a mounted soldier? How is a knight—say, a Lancelot in films like *First Knight* or the musical *Camelot*—different socially and psychologically from the dashing Napoleonic hussars depicted in *The Duelists*?

By about fifty pounds of armor, is one answer, but it's not the best, and tells only part of the story. The concept of knighthood, like so much in our culture, goes back to ancient Rome, where "eques," or middle-class citizens wealthy enough to own horses ("equus" in Latin), comprised the early cavalry. This connection between wealth, social status, and mounted troops laid the groundwork for the feudal system of knighthood.

In essence, knights were vassals wealthy enough to afford horses, armor, and retainers. They exchanged their services to an overlord in return for special favors. A favor often included a grant of land (which meant revenue from farms and peasants), a modest castle (where the knight could take refuge from those peasants), and the power to administer the king's justice: to police the countryside, collect taxes, and keep the peasants in line.

Chivalry and its ideals dominated the Middle Ages—in principle if not in fact. European knights committed some of history's worst atrocities during the Crusades, while the Arab and Turkish Saracens against whom they fought—already superior in art and science—developed their own brand of noble cavaliers, vying with Europeans in feats of arms. This tradition of presumed superiority among the European mounted elite survived the Middle Ages and persisted well into the nineteenth century, when men of merit, as well as hereditary aristocrats, assumed many knightly functions, even as knighthood faded as an institution.

Thus, an actor performing in a play depicting the time when "knighthood was in flower," should be constantly aware of the character's dual nature: the unique and unapologetic mixture of noble fantasy and thick-headed prejudice that formed such characters' lives.

GUNPOWDER AND ITS EFFECT ON THE BLADE Contrary to popular belief, gunpowder was first introduced to the West not by the Chinese (or Arabs or East Indians, as some claim), but by an English friar, Roger Bacon, in the year 1249. According to historian Sir Charles Oman, ". . .There would seem to be no doubt that the Chinese possessed incendiary compounds, as did the Byzantines, long before the tenth century of our era. But that they had explosive compounds is nowhere proven."

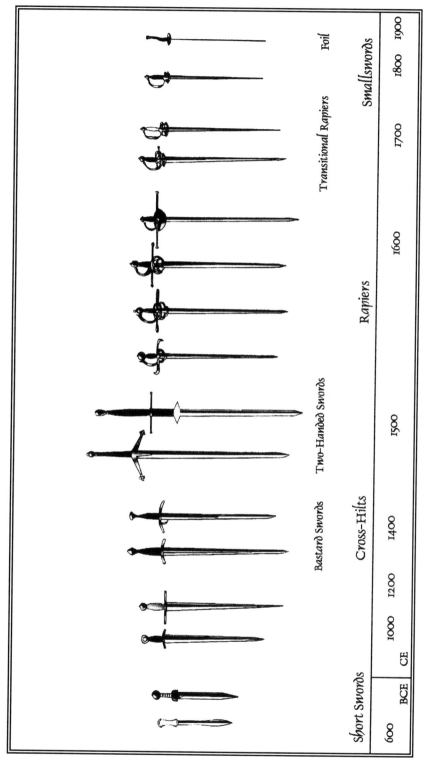

3-2. Sword length increased and decreased over the centuries, from the dagger-like Bronze Age weapons and the short swords of the Greeks and Romans to the long swords of Celtic Europe and the great two-handers of the high Middle Ages. During the Renaissance, the nimble rapier replaced the broadsword until its reign, too, was eclipsed by the courtly smallsword, forerunner of the modern fencers' foil. (Art by Andrew Fox.)

Second son of a lord, or perhaps of a lesser noble, he [the musketeer of Alexander Dumas] was probably given his choice of going into the clergy or seeking his fortune in war. The cavalry positions went to the first-born higher nobles, so a position in the King's musketeers was the next reasonable goal to achieve.

Richard Pallaziol
"A Musketeer History Lesson"
The Fight Master

According to Oman, the first visual record of firearms appears in the Millemete Manuscript of 1327. It shows an armored knight lighting the touchhole of a primitive bombard loaded with a massive bolt—a larger cousin of the crossbow arrow. Rather than revolutionizing warfare overnight, as atomic weapons did in the twentieth century, firearms wormed their way into Western military use gradually, year after year, until improvements in technology and tactics bore fruit. Instead of progressing from small to larger, as ships and warplanes have done, firearms began mainly as wall-smashing cannons. It required hundreds of years for early shoulder weapons to evolve into the smooth-bore matchlocks and flintlocks, used in quantity by European armies, let alone into the rifles, pistols, and rapid-fire, high-tech weapons we know today.

The real impact of firearms, though, was not the obsolescence of the armored knight—whose plate could already be pierced by longbow and crossbow—but the egalitarian effect it had on the soldiery. Within the span of a few hundred years, the monopoly that trained soldiers had held for millennia—competency with battle-winning edged weapons that took years to master—was broken. Suddenly, any peasant who could pull a trigger was a match for the most experienced knight, and a company of musketeers could slaughter a regiment of well-trained pikemen.

In this environment, battlefield armor, already in decline, disappeared very quickly. Instead, personal defense now depended on speed, mobility, and simply keeping one's head down. Oddly enough, rather than making swords extinct, firearms gave them a new lease on life. Blades became lighter, permitting people to move them more quickly, and since armor no longer posed so strict a barrier (and handguns were then rare and costly), more people carried swords as sidearms than ever before. The medieval broadsword became the slim, cut-and-thrust rapier—effective against armored and unarmored foes alike. As the centuries progressed and firearms improved and were mass produced, swords once again became the hallmark of gentlemen (accessories, like fashionable cloaks) while guns shouldered more and more of the deadly business of state-sanctioned killing.

SMALLER IS BETTER   The rapier held sway through the Renaissance and the Reformation: both as a military sidearm and for street defense. By Shakespeare's day, swept-hilt rapiers, in all their variations—from cup-hilts to shell-guards, from plain brushed steel to those etched and inlaid with ivory—were common throughout Europe (although the French were loathe to use a Spanish cup-hilt).

By mid-eighteenth century, lighter and shorter weapons were all the rage. Indeed, many of these swords looked more like elongated daggers, with cruciform hilts and vestigial knuckle bows and pas d'anes barely large enough to hold a finger. Their super-slim blades, used now entirely for thrusts instead of cuts, eventually became triangular in cross-section to increase their strength. The age of the rapier was over. The era of the smallsword—and the golden age of dueling—had begun.

3-3a. The broadsword had been, and remained, primarily a military weapon.

It is somewhat ironic that despite the really quite well-defined historical periods of operatic or theatrical works, one weapon overshadows the rest. The cup-hilt rapier seems to be the "all wrong" all-purpose theatrical weapon. . . . Interestingly enough, the French hardly used the cup-hilt . . . it was not in use anywhere until long after Athos, Porthos, Aramis, and D'Artagnan. Nevertheless, because the cup gives maximum protection to the hand, it remains the favorite of stage fighters . . . normally mounted with a triangular épée fencing blade. While the épée blade's lightness makes flashier and "prettier" movements, the purist would point out that it also leads to unauthentic and less dramatic swordplay.

Another stock theatrical sword is the swept-hilt rapier. A familiar swept-hilt is the Spanish Colada, the traditional rapier with a shorter, wider blade which many Spanish edged weapons manufacturers incorrectly attribute to the legendary Cid Campeador. . . . For some reason, it seems that every swordmaker in Spain. . . describes a late fifteenth century rapier as the "Tizona del Cid." When one asks how they can attribute that particular weapon design to a man who died in 1099 A.D., the answer invariably is: "Hombre, didn't you see *El Cid* with Charleton Heston?" The moral of this little story should probably be not to underestimate the power of Hollywood, history or no history.

Eiler Robert Cook, "Theatrical Weaponry" *The Fight Master*

3-3c. By the late eighteenth century, no gentleman was dressed without his smallsword.

3-3b. With the advent of the rapier, the sword became an article of fashion and a status symbol as well as a deadly sidearm.

DUELING—AND ITS DEMISE A duel is an organized fight between two opponents intent on bloodying, if not killing, each other. It differs from a street fight in that it lacks spontaneity; indeed, it must be scheduled, and witnesses summoned. For most of European history, it was sanctioned by the state. Judicial duels, or "Trials by Combat," arose early in the Middle Ages on the supposition that God would guide the blades of the innocent to the hearts of their false accusers. By the high Middle Ages, though, this unreliable form of justice was replaced by the duel of honor. It persisted with and without legal blessing well into the nineteenth century (during the reign of Louis XIV duelists faced execution, loss of property, defacement of their coats of arms, and the denial of a Christian burial. Yet even these draconian measures were no deterrent. In an era of poor communications, few judicial courts, and widespread illiteracy, such duels at least gave aggrieved parties a chance to settle their disputes without resorting to murder, vendettas, or clan warfare.

From the sixteenth century on, the growing demand for civilian sword training was met by various fencing academies run by "masters of fence." The description was derived from the "Art of Defense," although these academies covered all aspects of swordplay. Early schools took their missions quite seriously, and the manuals written by such masters as Marozzo, Agrippa, de Grassi, and Capo Ferro left as their legacy many of the moves we use in modern sport fencing and stage combat.

By the late seventeenth and eighteenth centuries, fencing had become part of a young gentleman's education, like athletics and instruction in courtly dances. Indeed, as more quarrels came to be settled with black powder instead of flashing steel, these friendly, competitive bouts took on the trappings of a sport—which, after the mid-1800s, is exactly what fencing became. With the last semblance of danger and chivalry thus removed from what was originally the deadliest of spectacles, swordfights to the death finally disappeared from Europe.

Modern penal codes define a duel as "any combat with deadly weapons, fought between two or more persons, by previous agreement or upon a previous quarrel." In California, the law is so strict about this that it even prohibits citizens from leaving the state with intent to duel in other places.
R.L.

IS FENCING REALLY SWORDPLAY? Swordmasters of old would have trouble recognizing in modern fencing much from their theories and manuals—or even the practical experience of duelists. Highly stylized, transistorized (electronic switches now keep track of points scored too fast for the human eye), and laden with rules and regulations based on the duel, modern fencing may be a fine way to hone one's reflexes and tone the body—but it offers only a shadow of historical swordplay. To experience and communicate what our sword-bearing ancestors thought, felt, and endured, we must turn to theatrical swashbuckling: in our opinion the last custodian of the original European martial arts.

LIVING HISTORY ON STAGE

By now you've seen that a character's relationship to the sword depends heavily on the era in which the drama is set. For example, a knight of the Crusades would most likely feel much more reverence for his blade (blessed by his village priest, or even the Pope) than a Spanish conquistador, who might regard his battle-scarred rapier as just another piece of military gear. Quite different from these experiences would be the dilemma of an eighteenth-century fop agonizing over which bejeweled courtsword to wear to the king's ceremonial ball.

Such attitudes, second-nature to the people who lived in those eras but elusive to many actors who portray them, make up the soul of a period performance—the bedrock upon which the other dialogue, gestures, and movements gain their authenticity. Whatever the attitude may be for your character, it should permeate not only the combat sequences, but all the other parts of your performance, whenever your character shares center stage with that most charismatic of co-stars: the European sword.

FINDING THE RIGHT SWORD FOR YOUR CHARACTER

Although we live in the age of computers and space travel, swords have never been easier to acquire. In the back of this book, you'll find a list of suppliers who make or sell quality, affordable swords, most designed especially for stage combat and historical accuracy. With such a selection, it's important to know, too, what kind of swords are *not* suitable for theatrical swashbuckling. You should avoid:

- Plastic or toy swords, and home-made swords regardless of the material from which they are fashioned. Even if these play swords look acceptable on stage, they won't stand up to combat.
- Fencing equipment. Foils, épées, and sabers are all wrong for the stage unless your play depicts a modern fencing match. Not only are the blades, hilts, and guards historically inaccurate, they are not designed for the abuse stage-combat swords often take on a daily basis.
- Asian swords. Unless you're playing a Mandarin warlord or a Samurai, Tai Chi swords and Japanese katanas, including the bamboo shinai used in kendo, all reflect the wrong culture for Western swashbuckling. Additionally, Japanese swords made in Toledo have no tang, making them very unstable for stage combat.

Other types of Western-style swords have their place, including decorative uses on stage, but it's usually not for fighting. These include:

- *Prop or decorative swords.* Also known as "wall hangers," these are usually made of inexpensive materials, (including fiberglass) or have untempered blades, such as stainless steel, too rigid for combat. Lavishly decorated and polished like mirrors, they may look great in non-combat,

"Somebody got the idea a long time ago that swords ring. Real swords don't ring," Dennis points out that the ring you get in a sword has less to do with the blade than with the fit of the blade in the hilt. The ring is caused by vibration. Too much vibration will cause the weapon to break. Cup hilt weapons can be made to ring like a church bell. Tightening the hilt to make it ring is a bad idea because the tang only understands torque, and too much torque will cause it to break.
Linda McCollum
"Dennis Graves, Premier Swordcutler"
The Fight Master

ceremonial scenes such as coronations, but if you bang them long enough against anything else, including other prop swords, they're liable to break.

- *Antiques.* Generally too expensive to use on stage, most look just like what they are: very old swords—not swords fabricated in the characters' own day. What's worse, even high-carbon steel loses its temper over time and you know what happens when people lose their tempers—they snap! Flexible swords, like flexible people, last longer.

- *Modern military swords and replicas.* Examples such as officers' swords from World War II may be found in surplus stores, cutlery catalogs, and other specialized outlets; but they, too, are unsuited for stage combat. Modern military swords are dress uniform accessories, not combat weapons; and blades of historical replicas, even if they look perfect for a part, are usually honed to semi-sharp chisel edges, not the wider, more durable edges needed for stage combat. "Real" swords like these can do lots of damage, too, to human flesh, so be careful where you swing them. Again, such weapons are fine for solo practice, to wear in historically appropriate non-combat roles, and for collectors—but they don't belong in theatrical swordfights.

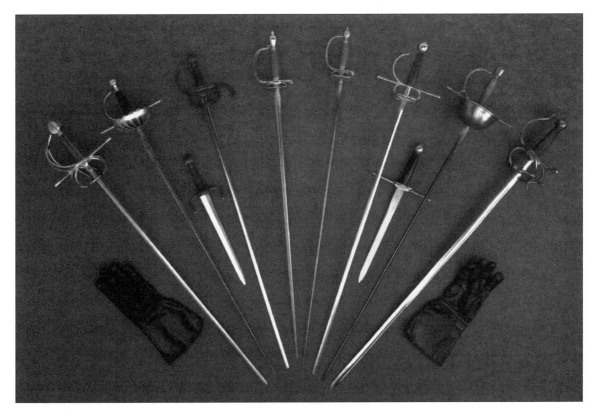

3-4. No matter what your character's historical era, there's a stage combat-worthy weapon that's up to the part. Swordmakers, from left to right: Lewis Shaw, American Fencer's Supply, Arms & Armor (including dagger), Oscar Kolombatovich, Oscar Kolombatovich, American Fencers Supply (including dagger), American Fencers Supply, American Fencers Supply.

- *Stage combat-worthy swords.* Obviously the best tool for the job, their blades are made of flexible, well tempered, high-carbon steel and possess slightly thicker edges (which should *never* be sharpened) that resist battle damage. Just as important, most are designed to be historically accurate—in styles appropriate for period productions—and are relatively inexpensive, at least when compared to less durable, museum-quality replicas. And if one component breaks, wears out, or becomes marred from constant use, it can easily be replaced at a fraction of the cost of a new weapon.

STAGE COMBAT SWORDS AREN'T TOYS

We should treat our theatrical combat swords with respect, just as real swordfighters treated the original articles. This is doubly true when you introduce such swords to novices. After all, swords are fascinating objects. When you bring one into a room, faces light up and everyone wants to touch it—pick it up, swing it, and admire it. People should not be permitted to handle swords, though, until they understand and agree to abide by what we call the "Six Commandments" of safe sword handling:

I. *A sword is always "loaded."* Knowledgeable people treat firearms as if they are always loaded. Because swords don't fire bullets, some people approach them casually, which leads to horseplay, complacency, and accidents. They forget that swords, too, can maim or kill in seconds—and the blade can't be "unloaded." It goes without saying, too, that despite the celluloid image of ale-guzzling swashbucklers, alcohol and steel don't mix. All swords should be stored securely, out of the reach of children or anyone else who may not handle them safely.

II. *Know where the sword's point is in the space around you.* In the old days, a lack of "point awareness" could mean injury or death in a fight. Today, it could mean a broken lamp, stitches, or worse. Swords are replaceable; eyes are not. Always know where the point of your sword (and others') is in the space around you. This is especially vital in battle scenes, where many pairs of fighters must share the same limited space.

III. *Speak first, then move the blade.* Never assume that people around you know what you are going to do with a sword. Communication builds trust, so if you are going to practice, tell the people around you. Never assume the en garde stance until you're sure that the area around *and behind* you is clear.

IV. *Carry the sword like a baby, with the blade close to your body.* Don't use the sword like a walking stick, ruler, pointer, or turn signal. When you transport an unsheathed sword, hold it point down close to your torso until you've reached a suitable practice area. Even a sword in a scabbard can cause lots of damage if you don't watch what you're doing.

The late Mr. Henry Wilkinson of London, a practical man of science, first proposed a formula for determining the center of percussion (for a sword) without the tedious process of experimenting with each and every blade. His system was based upon the properties of the pendulum...where the most effective cut can be delivered.

Richard F. Burton
The Book of the Sword

The center of percussion is that point on a blade where maximum force is delivered in a cut—usually the outer part of the middle third of the cutting edge. This can be determined experimentally (the blade reverberates unless it strikes with this spot) or with Mr. Wilkinson's calculation. In stage combat, where all cuts are illusory, this is of academic interest. Mr. Burton also describes why, based on Wilkinson's formulae, the curved blade is superior for cutting.

R.L.

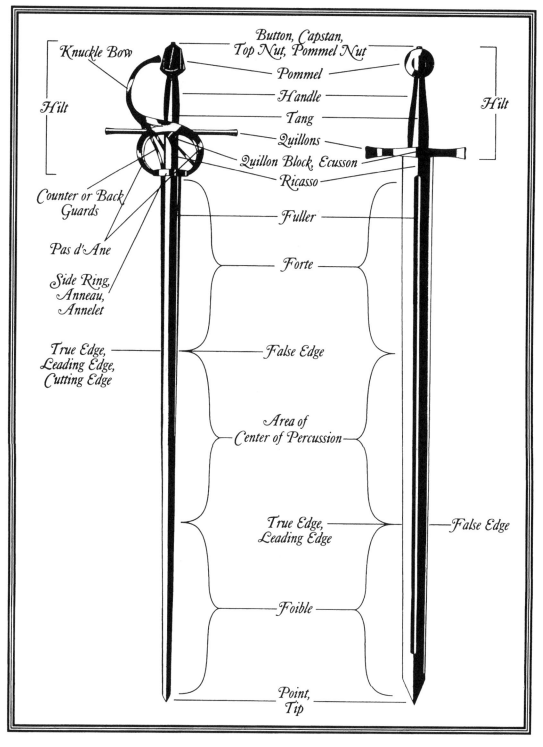

Knuckle Bow

Button, Capstan,
Top Nut, Pommel Nut

Hilt

Pommel

Handle

Hilt

Tang

Quillons

Quillon Block, Ecusson

Ricasso

Counter or Back
Guards

Fuller

Pas d'Ane

Forte

Side Ring,
Anneau,
Annelet

True Edge,
Leading Edge,
Cutting Edge

False Edge

Area of
Center of Percussion

True Edge,
Leading Edge

False Edge

Foible

Point,
Tip

3-5. The anatomy of a sword. (Art by Alex Daye.)

V. *Never touch a blade with your bare skin.* Skin oil contains acid and is corrosive. Since all stage combat-worthy weapons are made of high carbon (not stainless) steel, fingerprints can and do cause rust and will etch a blade. Even worse, battle-scarred blades often have sharp nicks and burrs that can slice unprotected hands like razors. Consequently, if you're going to handle a sword blade, put gloves on. Gauntlet style gloves made by period costumers are best, since they also protect the wrists and forearms; but any supple leather, full-fingered gloves will do. Leather saber gloves with padded palms and fingers are excellent. Avoid heavy work gloves (too thick or too loose to establish a good grip) and rubber kitchen gloves (too hot), as well as open-fingered golf, bowling, or weight-lifting gloves, which defeat the purpose of protecting the blade.

Finally, keep an eye on prop handlers, grips, fight captains, extras, and others who may handle your swords in the course of a production and make sure they, too, follow this commandment.

VI. *Check the condition of the sword before wielding it.* Blades, handles, pommels, quillons, and other sword "furniture" are usually assembled mechanically and can therefore come loose. The last thing your stage fight needs is a sword that spontaneously disassembles at the crucial moment, flinging the blade into the audience. Never use a sword with a loose handle or handle wrapping, wobbly quillon, or pommel that spins like a top. This will cause parries with the flat of the blade. Don't use a sword with sharp edges or a finely honed point. Reject a sword, too, if its blade is heavily rusted or has obvious cracks or welds. Although welds themselves can be stronger than the original steel, the high heat needed to make them can weaken the temper in the surrounding area. Sword-cutler Dennis Graves, writing in *The Fight Master* (Fall, 1992, "Welded Tangs: Safe or Unsafe?") says that welded tangs can be as reliable as one-piece tangs if they are annealed, or heat treated, so that the weld is not used simply to "glue" the tang or tang extension to the weapon. Bottom-line: if you don't know who did the welding, use a different sword.

TAKING CARE OF YOUR SWORD

Like any precision tool, your sword should be kept clean and dry when it's not in use. The precautions we've mentioned, plus a periodic coating of light, high-quality machine or gun oil, should keep its steel parts (including wire-wrapped handles) glossy and rust-free.

However, swords sometimes get wet when they're transported or used *al fresco*, and try as you will, you'll inevitably pick some fingerprints up along the way. Even worse, "flash" corrosion can strike any blade that's stored in a damp environment, so you should always keep cleaning materials handy. Swords being stored or shipped can be coated with vaseline but remove it before using the sword.

CLEANING THE BLADE Light rust can be removed by gently scouring the blade with dry, fine-grain emery cloth, steel wool, or Sandflex's Hand Block cleaning and polishing rust "eraser." After all traces of rust or rusty fingerprints are gone, use a soft cloth to coat the steel with light lubricating oil, such as Hoppe's gun oil or 3-in-1 oil; a good habit to get into after the sword has been used, whether it's rusty or not. Or, you can use a non-abrasive polishing compound like Metal-Glo or Renaissance Wax that cleans, protects, and shines all at once. We've heard mixed opinions on products like Rust-oleum (some knife makers say it traps moisture next to the blade), and WD-40 (which is better for cleaning than protecting) so query your supplier before you use it.

Some suppliers and swordmakers offer to polish your stage combat blade to a mirror finish, but we discourage it. Not only do such swords lose their historical, battle-worn look, but that costly mirror finish seldom survives more than a few stage fights. One advantage to a mirror polish is the absence of porosity, which helps preserve the blade. So decide for yourself which characteristic is more important to you.

Some new blades come coated with a plastic spray to protect them during shipping. This gives the steel a satin finish look, but it will soon begin to chip and peel. Consequently, we automatically sand and oil all new swords from forte to foible, including hilt furnishings if they're made of carbon steel. Some suppliers suggest using lacquer thinner or mineral spirits to remove the plastic coating. If you can stand the smell and take precautions to protect yourself and the wood and leather on the hilt, use it. Just be sure to follow all the instructions on the container.

Brass hilts and hilts with brass components can be cleaned and polished satisfactorily with household products like Brasso—just be sure the cleaning agent doesn't contact wood or other non-brass materials and be sure to remove all residue. Gold- or silver-plated hilts, and etched or inlaid metals often need special care, but they can all be cleaned and buffed reasonably well without damage by using a soft, clean, chamois-type cloth. If you have one of these valuable, eye-catching weapons, consult your supplier before using a cleaning agent.

REPAIRING A BATTLE-SCARRED BLADE Even the best stage combat blades eventually show wear and tear and become saw-toothed with nicks and burrs. Burrs are little barbs of metal that stick up from a nick or cut—anyplace that the steel has been gouged. These can slice unprotected flesh, rip garments, and pose a hazard to anyone handling or being touched by the blade. Therefore, you should inspect your sword regularly for such damage both visually and by lightly running a rag or *glove-protected* finger down the edge. When you discover a snag or sharp blemish, hone it away with a medium file or a lightly dampened whetstone (the same tool that makes blades sharp can also keep them safely dull); or take the sword to a machine shop where a competent craftsperson can use an electric grinder to smooth the blade without damaging or deforming it.

Oh, Keep up your bright swords, for the dew will rust them.
Othello
Act I, Scene 2

Usually the weapon was worn in a scabbard hanging from the left hip, so that it could be easily grasped by the right hand and be pulled quickly out. As they were worn on the hip, they were sometimes called hip weapons. The scabbard hung either straight from the belt, as in the case of the knight's sword, or from two long hanging straps (as in the case of broadswords or sabers), or on a broad sling. . . bandoliers hung across the right shoulder and down to the left hip to where the sword was hung.

Eduard Wagner
Cut and Thrust Weapons

I encourage all actor-combatants to wear scabbards whenever feasible in performance. They keep the swords at hand but out of the way, allowing you to concentrate on other business. They also lend authenticity to period costumes and give better definition to characters. A sword also sounds more threatening *rasping* from its steel-throated scabbard when the fight begins. One way to make a low-cost yet functional scabbard (particularly for épée-bladed rapiers, which tend to be hilt-heavy and fall

CARING FOR HANDLES AND SCABBARDS Wooden handles often come varnished and need no special care until the varnish starts to wear off. Bare wood or old wooden handles can be rejuvenated with linseed oil or household wood-care products like Pledge. Leather-wrapped handles, leather ricasso guards, and sword belts and scabbards should be treated when you first get them. Use liberal amounts of Lexol, one of the best leather conditioners and preservatives around, or neatsfoot oil or saddle soap; then treat them periodically to keep the leather clean, waterproof, and supple. Lexol also works wonders at restoring old, water-damaged, or dried out leather. Some experts recommend paste wax to give leather a warm, glossy sheen, but beware. Paste wax builds up and can leave gripping surfaces sticky or too slick. We prefer clean leather's natural look and feel.

STORING YOUR SWORD Like people, swords prefer to stay safe, dry, and unstressed:

- *Safe.* Keep all swords in a secure area out of the reach of children and others who may not understand or respect their destructive potential.

- *Dry.* Moisture is carbon steel's worst enemy and leather scabbards hold it close to the blade. Don't store a sword in its scabbard for more than a few weeks without giving it some air, inspecting it for rust, and cleaning/oiling the blade as necessary. Don't keep swords in tool sheds or other semi-open shelters, even if precipitation can't reach them directly.

- *Unstressed.* Never lean swords on their tips with the hilts against a wall. Not only are such swords likely to fall over, risking injury to pets and people, or damage to furniture and the swords themselves, but such continual and unnatural pressure can eventually deform some blades and their scabbards. Resting sword on their hilts isn't much better. The blades can still fall over and cause injuries unless they rest on specially made display stands. As a result, we recommend storing swords on their sides out of their scabbards. Wall racks or sword stands provide the best of all conditions, keeping your blades safe and dry, with their weight properly distributed off the tips.

TRANSPORTING YOUR SWORD Walking to practice, a rehearsal, or a performance down a busy street with a sword over your shoulder is an invitation for unwanted attention—from alarmed bystanders, snatch-and-run thieves, or even the police. At minimum, wrap your sword in a blanket, raincoat, or other bulky cover that will give it some protection. Better still, buy an oversized gym- or equipment-bag large enough to accommodate your longest sword. Sporting goods stores sell a surprisingly wide range of these for carrying everything from fencers' foils and skis to weights and golf clubs. If you transport a lot of swords, or travel by air or train to perform, consider getting the rigid airline-style container used by golfers to ship their clubs. Not only do these containers lock, securing the contents, but they have wheels, making transporting them to and from the terminal easier.

AVOIDING PROBLEMS WITH POLICE Unfortunately, not everyone shares our love of history, swashbuckling, and the theater. Although laws regarding the transportation, use, and display of edged weapons vary from place to place, and these suggestions are no substitute for the advice of your attorney, most state and local governments allow weapons to be transported for bona fide uses in a safe and lawful manner. Although you must follow all applicable ordinances, you'll probably avoid legal complications if you take the following common-sense precautions:

- When driving, keep all weapons securely wrapped or in a closed container in the trunk of your car or in another area of the vehicle that is not accessible from the passenger compartment.

- If stopped by peace officers and queried about your swords, tell them you are a performer and the swords are props and part of your theatrical costume. *Do not*, even in jest, say that you carry the swords for protection, which is almost always against the law. We usually take the added precaution of carrying some promotional flyers or playbills in our sword bags—proof that we do, indeed, use the swords for theatrical purposes.

- If you want to rehearse outdoors, and do not have a private, enclosed area such as a fenced yard in which to practice, find a low-traffic area well away from buildings or casual observers who might mistakenly think you are disturbing the peace. Be advised that many public parks and recreational areas have strict rules about the possession and display of even lethal *looking* weapons, so check all signs and park regulations before you pick your spot.

- If you are approached by a peace officer, ranger, or other official in one of these areas (or even a citizen who complains), treat the person courteously and leave the area promptly if so requested. If a peace officer or ranger wants to confiscate your sword, don't argue. You can always pursue the matter later through the proper channels.

- If you are approached by children, teenagers, or suspicious-looking persons who ask to handle your sword, decline politely. Tell them you'll get in trouble if you lose the sword, are forbidden by your insurance company (or theater management) to let anyone else handle the sword, or use some other plausible, non-confrontational excuse. If they persist, tell them in a friendly way that they can see plenty of swordplay at the local theatre, give them a copy of the flyer for your current production or of the stage combat teacher's brochure, then pack up and go someplace else. If you don't, you may never see your sword again.

In the next chapter, you'll learn more about handling your sword—and yourself—safely and effectively when your swashbuckling training begins.

out of standard rapier hangers) is to cut off the ends of an old ski pole. This is a trick I learned from swordmaker Rod Casteel, founder of *The Colonial Armory*. Remember, though, a scabbard made this way will be rigid even after the sword is drawn and may get in the way when you go to the ground or perform other fight choreography. In these cases, do what real duelists used to do: discard the scabbard before the fight.
R.L.

4

GETTING READY FOR SWORDPLAY

A young squire begged a famous knight to help him become a master swordsman in the shortest possible time. The knight agreed, provided the squire swear a solemn oath to do everything he was asked, which the squire promptly did.

"Very well," said the knight, "for the first three years, you will tend my camp. For the next three years, you will carry my sword from place to place. For a final three years, you will oil and sharpen my sword. After that, we will begin your knightly training."

Martial arts parable

4-1. A knight before combat, in the lists, with a coffin next to him. (From "Cut and Thrust Weapons" by Eduard Wagner.)

Before beginning your swashbuckling training, you'll learn:

- Two types of sword grips and the basic "on guard" stance
- How to control your breath, balance and energy while in action
- How targeting, distance, and timing help keep theatrical swordplay safe
- Four swashbuckling rituals—how they help shape you as a performer

Impatience has never been confined to medieval squires. Inspired by action films and the lure of fame and wealth, many actor-combatants want to run before they can walk—to fight before they know how to hold a sword. In this chapter, you'll complete your grounding in the basics. As all veterans know, what you practice *before* you lift a sword makes all the difference in how well you handle it after.

BEGIN AT THE BEGINNING

A good swordfighter is basically a well-tempered blade connected to a pair of springy legs through an agile mind. Since most real swordfights were won or lost in the opening moments, early masters spent a lot of time thinking about how such fights should begin. They attached great importance to sword grips and preparatory stances. In swashbuckling, we add body-breath control and various mental tricks for focusing energy when and where it's needed most.

RAPIER GRIPS A sword is an extension of the human hand. It should be held naturally, comfortably, and in a way that takes the maximum advantage of the supple human wrist and the characteristics of the blade.

Figures 4-2a and 4-2b show the two types of grips used commonly with a rapier—the classic swashbuckling weapon. Place your right hand comfortably (not too loosely, and not too tightly) around the handle, with your forefinger hooked through the pas d'ane. This gives you much greater control over the blade than is possible with all your fingers on the handle.

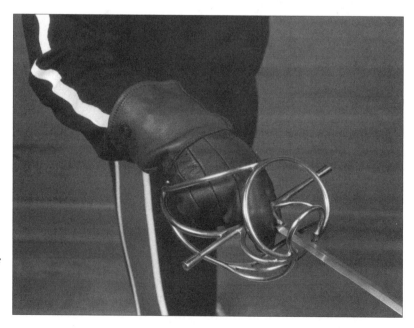

4-2a. Pronated en garde protects the outside line (right side of body).

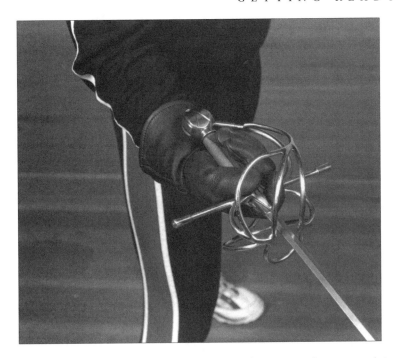

4-2b. Supinated grip exposes the back of the hand to cuts from the right. However, move this grip to the left side of the body, and the left side of the body (and knuckles) are protected from cuts coming from the left.

How tight is too tight? One legendary swordmaster advised his students to grip the sword as they might hold a small bird: "Too tight and you kill it; too loose and it flies away." A weak grip sacrifices control and invites an accident or a disarm. A vise-like grip, on the other hand, turns the sword into a club and is very tiring. Veterans can hold their weapons effortlessly for hours, while beginners holding a death-grip on their swords fade fast.

Because historically the rapier blade was most often flat like a dinner knife (unlike the triangular foil, épée, or "musketeer style" blade found on many theatrical weapons), the old masters chose grips that allowed flat blades to be thrust in between opponents' ribs, without being stopped by the bone. This meant holding the sword so that the flat of the blade was horizontal, with the palm of the hand facing up or down. A "pronated" grip means your knuckles are up, or facing the sky, and your palm is down, when you point your sword at your opponent. A "supinated" grip means your knuckles are down, or facing the ground, and your palm is up. We'll use these terms many times in this book to help you assume the proper sword position.

THE EN GARDE STANCE Most of us are familiar with the "on guard" (or "en garde," from the French) stance modern fencers use to begin a match. The right shoulder and sword arm are aimed at the opponent, making a very narrow profile. The free hand is cocked over the head for balance, and the feet are aligned for rapid movement along the line of attack. While this stance has its roots primarily in smallsword technique, it was not the way most people started swordfights during most of recorded history.

Back when swordfights were a matter of life and death, combat started from a variety of stances called "wards" designed to ward off attacks. Most of these preparatory positions were intended to help the fighters evade a sudden assault while giving them a good chance to draw first blood. As rapiers gave way to smallswords and dueling eventually became competitive fencing, the number of wards taught and used declined until a uniform en garde stance assured that both combatants would start off on an equal footing—the opposite of what wards were intended to do.

In theatrical swordplay, we emulate these earlier, more practical stances. The basic rapier en garde, in fact, tells you a lot about both the physical and psychological aspects of real swordfights. Figures 4-3a and 4-3b compare the classical fencing stance (a) to that used for the rapier (b).

In the stage-combat rapier stance, notice first that the trunk of the body faces the opponent, and is not turned in profile like the fencer's. This gives

4-3a. Lawrence Drefko Homulos in a classic foil en garde (sans mask). The left hand is not a target nor can it be used in defense.

4-3b. The author ready to swashbuckle. Notice how the left hand is forward and can be used to sweep the opponent's blade away, catch it, or otherwise engage an adversary.

the fighter better use of the left hand—to hold a dagger or buckler, defend or attack with a cape (wrapped around the arm like a shield or held loose to throw over an opponent like a net), grab the attacking blade (with or without the protection of a gauntlet), to block and deliver punches, even to hold a lantern for fighting at night. In fact, this active use of the free hand is one of the big distinctions between the historical swordfighting and competitive fencing styles. The fighter leads with the right leg (both legs are slightly bent in a springy "horse stance") just like the fencer's, but the feet are planted laterally farther apart, as if standing on the rails of a railroad track. This allows the fighter to move easily in any direction, not just forward and back.

Both modern fencer and stage fighter hold the head erect, establishing eye contact with their opponents. Overall, though, the stage fighter's posture gives us the impression of a body coiled like a spring, ready to leap in any direction.

PREPARING THE BODY FOR COMBAT As with any martial art, safe and successful stage combat requires that you use your body as a tool—to perform techniques properly, in balance, and with control over both the speed and range of motion. Most beginners think this means just controlling their arms and legs—literally going through the motions—but it is the torso, or trunk of the body, and its position relative to the feet, that gives the arms their power. When the feet and torso are poorly placed, the arms flail ineffectually and the body teeters off balance. As a result, much of your early swashbuckling training—and virtually all the stretches and warmups you'll learn at the beginning of Part II—are aimed at helping you control your center of gravity and coordinate the movements of your limbs with precision, grace and fluidity.

CENTERING THE BODY You've probably heard martial artists talk about centering the body and focusing their energy, or *chi*. What does this mean, exactly, and how do we use it for stage combat?

Physically, the body's center of gravity "CG"—the point of perfect balance around which the rest of the weight is evenly distributed—lies a few inches below the navel, just above the hips, halfway between the belly and the spine. To walk, we simply tilt our CG forward and "break" the resulting fall (or, more accurately, break the resulting series of mini-falls) by putting one foot before the other. Thus it is our displaced CG, not our legs, that moves us forward. As our CG becomes even further displaced, we find ourselves running to keep up. If we are bumped and our CG is displaced too rapidly or too far, we must scramble to stay balanced—or we fall down.

Unfortunately, CG management doesn't end here, on stage or in life. If you *raise* your CG by carrying a heavy object in your arms, on your back, or above your head, your body becomes less stable and is harder to balance. On the other hand, if you *lower* your CG, you become more stable—this is one technique from the martial arts we employ often in stage combat.

Foot position and body stiffness also affect how you keep your balance. A wider stance is more stable than one where your feet are close together;

Be still as a mountain, move like a great river
The Essence of T'ai Ch'i Ch'uan: The Literary Tradition

The *ch'i* (breath) should be excited, The *shen* (spirit) should be internally gathered.
Chang San-feng, *T'ai Ch'i Ch'uan Ching*

and a relaxed person, standing with feet apart and knees slightly bent, retains balance better than someone standing with heels together, rigidly at attention.

The point is, most martial arts moves, including those used for Western swordplay, begin and end with the body in balance, and we try to maintain a dynamic balance throughout the move.

FOCUSING YOUR ENERGY   Centering the body—that is, being aware of, lowering, and controlling your CG—is only half the story. The other half is projecting your performance energy from that center; a more difficult thing to do, but achievable through practice.

When we are *not* centered, physically or psychologically (as when we are learning to do something new and difficult, or are forced to do something we dislike or don't believe in) the body and brain are at odds. Movement is awkward, concentration is difficult, and we tend to make mistakes. When those barriers are removed—that is, when we gain mastery over a technique, see our objectives clearly, and are motivated to accomplish them, the body and mind tend to work in harmony. Thus previously difficult moves seem easy and their effects are greatly magnified. The mind feels clear and we can see possibilities that eluded us before.

Athletes experiencing this wonderful synchronization of physical and mental energy call it a state of *flow*—an apt description for the euphoria it produces. When you visualize this natural energy flowing out from your center, through your limbs and into the space around you, your body becomes much more balanced, manageable, and effective in its motions—a perfect tool for your intentions.

People experiencing this flow during a fight are said to possess the "combat high." In Nordic tradition, such warriors were called "berserkers" because they seemed to fight with boundless energy, win without struggling, and were indifferent to wounds that would disable lesser fighters. Part of this was undoubtedly due to a rush of adrenaline, but their companions were pumped with adrenaline, too—though it had vastly different effects on them. Trained and experienced warriors—those who viewed their calling as an art—were able to channel that energy through their physical and mental centers, boosting their performances and producing the combat moves needed to win. Untrained fighters were overcome by the rush of adrenaline and became paralyzed by it, employed it ineffectively, or used that extra energy to run away. As an actor-combatant, your ability to focus that natural energy in positive ways can make the difference between an adequate performance and a great one.

AND DON'T FORGET TO BREATHE   Breath means life—and that's more than just a metaphor. A good actor-combatant literally "breathes life" into a fight by coordinating inhalations and exhalations with the rhythms of the routine and the movements of the body. Indeed, good breath control helps you center and attain the poise, focus, and performance energy you need.

Most people are surprised to learn that they've been breathing wrong all their lives. Believe it or not, this most natural of all human acts is corrupted by the habits we acquire as we go through life: poor posture, breathing too fast when upset, holding one's breath when lifting something heavy, and so on. Part of your swashbuckling training is to unlearn these bad breathing habits.

First, you must realize that good posture induces good breathing—and good breathing means better control of all bodily motions. (In Part II, you'll learn specific techniques for better breathing, both in action and at rest.) For now, it's enough to know that in stage combat, bad breathing leads to bad technique because your body isn't using its resources to the best advantage.

The vast majority of novice swashbucklers habitually hold their breath while performing stage combat moves—say, sword cuts or parries. Not breathing, they think (if they think about it at all), lets them concentrate more on learning or performing a given move. To a certain degree, that's true—eliminating complications and distractions makes it easier to learn any new action. However, swordfights aren't stationary contests, like chess or checkers. They require movement—lots of it—and movement requires breathing. If you isolate one part of the body and consciously put it out of action—that's one less resource you have for your performance. When that resource happens to be breath, with its intake of life-giving oxygen and elimination of poisonous CO_2, not breathing can be crippling indeed.

In short, poor breath-control can lead to short-windedness or its opposite, hyperventilation (taking in too much oxygen, which results in dizziness), both of which diminish control and reduce performance. In stage combat, we generally follow these guidelines for better breath control:

- Begin each stretching and warmup session by assuming the "breath stance."

- Take a moment to center yourself when you come on guard, even in practice. This includes assuming the upright breathing posture that is part of this basic stance.

- Inhale on preparations. Collecting a breath tells your body and partner that something significant is about to follow—and helps communicate that gathering of energy to the audience.

- Exhale as you perform the action or the reaction. Breathing out— even forcibly expelling air, sometimes with a shout—when you perform a combat move is a basic martial arts technique. Called "ki-ai," (pronounced "key-eye") it helps you focus your energy, both mental and physical, on the object of the action. In real combat, this increases the power of your blow. In a stage fight, it increases your performance energy, shows more aggressive intent, and makes your technique crisper and more convincing. Fencers shout "Eh-la!" for much the same reason.

MORE SECRETS TO SAFE SWORDPLAY

Among the last general rules we'll offer before your swashbuckling training begins are three keys to a safe and effective performance: managing targets, distance, and timing.

TARGETING In theatrical swordplay, a "target" is a reference point related to, but physically removed from, a particular part of the body. An example will make this important distinction clear.

In a real sword fight, the target of a cut might be the defender's shoulder—for our purposes, from the point of the shoulder to just above the elbow: a large muscle area that, if slashed, could cause the arm to be useless. To inflict such damage, you would have to be close enough to contact the opponent in the desired area with the foible of your blade and deliver

4-4. Imagine throwing a drop of water from the tip of your sword past the defender's targeted area.

the cut hard enough to rend clothing, skin, and muscle. That takes a pretty good whack—real swordfights weren't for the squeamish.

In stage combat, we want to project to the audience all this aggressive intent, but without the gory side-effects. To do that, we must simulate danger-ous *looking* swordcuts but assure ourselves and our partners that the cut will never actually land. How can this be done?

One of the best ways is to simply *displace* the target slightly from the ref-erenced part of the body. That is, instead of aiming for the shoulder itself, aim a few inches to the side and past the shoulder area. (To your right, if it's your partner's left shoulder; to your left if it's your partner's right). When your blade arrives at this position, extend your sword arm as in fly-casting, aligning the sword with your outstretched arm, using the energy that flows from your properly positioned feet, hips, and torso (see Fig. 4-4). This gives a good the-atrical illusion of striking something solid—like steel or flesh and bone—when in reality, the attacker has stopped the blade in mid-air. Of course, it's up to your partner to complete the illusion. If the choreographed reaction is a parry, your partner's blade will catch yours at this precise location, giving the illu-sion that it was the defender's sword, not your targeting, that stopped the cut.

That's why we say a target in stage combat is a reference point related to, but removed from, a particular part of the body. Of course, there are excep-tions to every rule. Low thrusts made to "cross parries" with rapier and dag-ger, and certain techniques for simulating wounds require targets that cannot be displaced—but those are advanced techniques performed only under the supervision of a qualified fight director. In Part II, you'll learn more about targets and the ways to deliver convincing attacks against them.

DISTANCE Distance is nothing more than the space between the fighters. Like targeting, it is a key to both creating a realistic illusion and keeping the rou-tine safe.

In early swashbuckling films, actor-combatants often fought "in distance." This meant that both partners were close enough to actually strike one another with their swords unless precautions were taken. One of those pre-cautions was to aim their attacks well "off target"—much further, even, from the bodily reference point we just discussed. Sometimes, this "off target" target was so far away it was hard for the audience to tell what the attacker intended or where the blow would have landed. This technique gave fights in early movies the appearance of what the critic Rudy Behliner referred to as "knife sharpening" ("Swordplay on the Screen," *Films in Review,* 1965)—blades being scraped together overhead to no particular purpose (see Fig. 4-5a). One reason this technique was so popular was that it allowed both actors to appear in the same narrow frame, glare combatively at each other, and exchange dialogue while the fight continued—a concession to small lenses and big egos.

Today, many fights (particularly those performed in live theater) are staged "on target, out-of-distance." This means that the actors aim directly at

The "time, distance, and proportion" of the early Anglo-Italian masters of the six-teenth century are still the first notions to be grasped. They are now called "time," "mea-sure," and "guard."

Egerton Castle
Schools and Masters of Fence

Benvolio: Why, what is Tybalt?

Mercutio: More than prince of cats, I can tell you. O, he is the courageous captain of compliments. He fights as you sing prick-song, keeps time, distance, and proportion; he rests his minim rest, one, two, and the third in your bosom; the very butcher of a silk button, a duelist, a duelist. . .

Shakespeare
Romeo and Juliet

It was Rocco, an Italian fencing master of Shakespeare's time, who said he could, "hit any English man with a thrust, just upon any button in his doublet."
R.L.

the bodily reference points instead of somewhere way out in space, increasing realism. They compensate for the increased risk of on-target fighting by making sure their distance is so great that blows can never land. How big is this safety margin? How great *can* it be and still present the illusion of danger?

At the Academy of the Sword, we define minimum safe distance as the longest arm/weapon combination of the attacking partner (arm held out to full extension), plus the width of the defender's fist. (Remember, both partners will attack and defend, so if one partner's reach is considerably greater, make sure you use that distance.) Before partners begin learning a new routine, they physically measure this distance, then check it periodically during rehearsal if they think they are—literally—cutting things too close. As you'll see in Part II, both partners are responsible for maintaining safe distance— managing cooperatively their shared space as they execute the choreography.

The physical danger of an on-target fight performed in distance is obvious, but many performers overlook its dramatic problems as well. Actors

4-5a. "Knife sharpening" in "Under the Red Robe" (1937) with Conrad Veidt (Gil) and Raymond Massey (Richelieu). (Archive Photos.)

who feel threatened in a stage fight usually pull their punches or unconsciously displace their targets even more. This gives what is in reality a very dangerous fight a tepid, half-hearted appearance that audiences can detect.

TIMING Timing here means just what it has meant to swordfighters throughout history: responding to a partner's move with a specific move of your own. In our case, though, well-timed moves don't surprise anyone except the audience. The four-step sequence of eye contact, prep, reaction, and action is the basic ingredient of timing, but timing is affected by targeting and distance, too. For example, the partner whose character is "on defense" at that moment *always* controls the timing of the fight, making it the attacker's job to adjust to the defender's moves, extending preps and delaying the action until the defender's reaction shows it is safe to continue. Most fight directors insist that you practice your timing with your partner until it is so close that your reactions look to the audience as if they are just in the nick of time.

All of these techniques, of course, depend on good communication between the partners; first in rehearsing and adapting the choreography, then in performance.

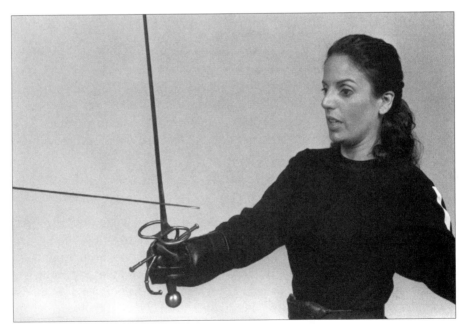

4-5b. Reacting to the off-target attack is what will make this move look dangerous.

SWASHBUCKLING RITUALS—FREEING YOUR SPIRIT TO ACT

A ritual is any meaningful act regularly repeated. The key words here are: meaningful and repeated. The more we practice specific actions, the more we build "muscle memory." The more a specific action is combined with a particular thought, or feeling, the easier it is to evoke that idea or feeling when the motion is performed.

Real sword fighters performed various rituals prior to practice, and when possible before their fights, to instill proper attitudes. In theatrical swashbuckling, we borrow some of these rituals to add not just realism, but "spiritual energy" to our performances. For us, as for them, rituals help us learn—and earn—our places on center stage and the applause we hope to win.

RITUAL #1:   WEAR YOUR GLOVES WHEN YOU PRACTICE

You already know two practical reasons for wearing gloves when you handle a sword; to protect the sword from rusty fingerprints and yourself from nicks and burrs. To these you can add a third. A sword simply feels different when it is wielded by gloved hands. If you rehearse without gloves and then perform with them, or vice versa, be prepared for a mild surprise when your big fight scene begins.

There are important psychological reasons to wear gloves as well. Gloves show your respect for the sword as a weapon and a work of art (or at least of high craftsmanship), and as a symbol of Western culture. It also shows courtesy to the sword as a significant "co-star" in your period drama—a consideration that should extend to your human partners as well. Wear gloves whenever you conduct a serious sword workout, rehearsal, or performance.

RITUAL #2:   SALUTE IN, AND SALUTE OUT, WHEN YOU PRACTICE

Modern soldiers salute each other as a sign of recognition and respect. Roman gladiators raised their weapons to salute the Emperor and cried out, "We who are about to die, salute you." Medieval knights lifted their visors, a precursor to the modern hand salute, and clasped right hands to show they bore no weapons. The Elizabethan and the later duelists acknowledged each other with courtly bows and flourishes—most learned from their fencing masters, who believed attitude was as important as technique in a fight. We continue this long tradition in swashbuckling training and, when possible and appropriate to the drama and the characters, in performance as well.

A sword salute, similar to the rapier salute shown in Figures 4-6a through 4-6h (which we use at the Academy of the Sword), links us to our sword-bearing ancestors, acknowledges the gift of instruction we receive from our teacher, and honors our partners—the actor-combatants we work with in performance. It also bestows some practical benefits as well. Mentally, ritual

A very interesting and, by the sound of it, a very old prayer before attack is recalled by Mikhail Sholokhov in his novel, *And Quiet Flows the Don*. . .

"Supreme Ruler, Holy Mother of God and of Our Lord Jesus Christ! Bless, Lord, this slave of God now entering battle, and my comrades who are with me. Also bless this my steed. Wrap us in cloud! With thy heavenly stony hail, protect us! Holy Dimitri Soslutsky, defend me, the slave of God, and my comrades on all four sides; permit no evil men to shoot, nor with spear to pierce, nor with sword to cut down, nor with butt-end of axe to thrash or stun, nor with axe to hew down, nor with sabre to smite or pierce, nor with knife to cut. . . Go arrow shafts, back to the forest, and feathers back to thy mother-bird, and glue back to the fish. Defend me, the slave of God, with a golden buckler, from steel and from bullet, cannon-fire and ball, spear and knife. And may my body be stronger than armor. Amen."

Eduard Wagner
*Cut and Thrust
Weapons*

salutes help us clear our minds of whatever we were doing before we began to practice or perform, bring us closer to the interior world of the sword fighters we portray, and help us focus on the reality—the discipline, joy, and demands—of swashbuckling in the here and now.

Physically, salutes duplicate many of the motions we'll use in stage combat, alerting our bodies to the challenges ahead. And we mustn't forget to smile or scowl as we make those final bows—to trigger that swashbuckler's *attitude* from which our energy flows.

RITUAL #3: PRACTICE YOUR FOOTWORK WHETHER YOU NEED TO OR NOT

Stuck at the airport waiting for a flight? Have a few minutes before an appointment or a date? Is your back stiff from working at a desk and you need to get the kinks out? No problem—even if you don't have a sword, you can put yourself through your paces by assuming the en garde stance and practicing your footwork: the foundation, literally, for every move in swashbuckling. Without a sword, you can simulate a rapier grip by extending the first two fingers of your right hand in pronation. Why go to all this trouble—especially if you've already achieved some competence in swordplay?

As always, the benefits are both physical and mental. Physically, practicing footwork builds calf, thigh, back and abdominal strength, promotes agility, increases body-breath awareness, and, when you're good enough at them, allows you to move freely and energetically during a routine without worrying if your feet will let you down or trip you up. Mentally, adhering to the discipline of footwork drills quells the restless spirit of the impatient squire in all of us—our desire to run before we can walk, or reach beyond our grasp. With appropriate humility, we affirm with every step the necessity of constant practice and admit, even if it's only to ourselves, that, no matter how good we become, we can never achieve true perfection.

RITUAL #4: PRACTICE YOUR SWORD FORMS RELIGIOUSLY

In Part II you'll learn a variety of sword forms, or solo exercises like a martial arts "kata," that allow you to practice the moves you've studied in a series of realistic, sword fighting movements—some of which enact one role in a partnered stage-combat routine. Even more than footwork drills, these challenging and exciting routines give you rehearsal experience, help you hold a sword more comfortably, develop eye-hand coordination, and build strength and stamina. They also promote the kind of body-breath awareness essential to channeling both your energy and the kinetic force of your blade to the proper point in space, in exactly the right way, at exactly the right time. And oh yes—sword forms are *fun,* too! Short of a paid performance, the mastery of these forms is the crowning achievement of your swashbuckling training. Learn them thoroughly, perform them well, and enjoy them—not forgetting to smile that swashbuckler's smile.

[Of gloves on student swashbucklers] They are historically correct (actually they wore gauntlets made of one material or another) and necessary for safety purposes. If they can't afford even imitation suede or something similar, they shouldn't be taking the class. Would a ballet master allow a student to take class without ballet shoes on his feet? What's more, would a student dare to take class from a ballet master without proper footwear?
David S. Leong
"Teaching Stage Combat, Helpful Hints"
The Fight Master

72

1. No swearing or using the Holy Name of God.
2. Do not use indecent language or sing dirty songs.
3. Do not tease anyone, as it is annoying and vulgar.
4. Do not make fun of anyone's fencing.
5. Do not draw your sword in the Salle d'Armes.
6. Do not fence without gloves.
7. Do not fence while wearing your sword.
8. Do not disturb people while they are fencing.
9. Do not drag the button of your foil on the floor.
10. Do not fence if you have been drinking.
11. No drinking or smoking in the Salle.
12. Be polite to visitors and offer to lend them foils, with the fencing master's approval.
13. Foils broken by visitors will be charged to the lender.
14. Foils broken by students will be charged to him who is holding the rest of the foil.
15. If one knocks the foil out of his opponent's hand, he should retrieve it promptly and return it politely.
16. If, unfortunately, there is a hit on the face, he who makes that hit should admit it forthrightly.
17. If they wish, students may exercise at the Salle d'Armes whenever it is open, except for Sundays and holidays.
18. Students should take fencing lessons regularly and not wait until they are obliged to fight duels.
19. The student must pay for all foils broken while exercising with the Fencing Master of Provost d'Armes.
20. It is to the honor of the student to pay for his lessons fully, the agreed upon price and on time.

Pierre Jacques Francois Girard
Traire des Armes
Regle que l'on doit Observer dans les Academies d'Armes
Paris, 1737

4-6a. First Position.

4-6b. To Your Heart.

4-6c. To Your Partner.

4-6d. To Your Lips.

4-6e. *To Heaven.*

4-6f. *To Your Heart.*

4-6g. *Swipe Open.*

4-6h. *Bow (but keep your eyes up. After all, your character respects, but doesn't trust, the other duelist).*

PART II

STAGE FIGHTING TECHNIQUE AND BASIC SWORDPLAY

5

STRETCHING AND WARMING UP

He made a somersault, fully armed except for his bascinet. He leapt onto a horse without placing foot in stirrup, fully armed. With a strong man mounted on a war horse, he leapt from the ground onto his shoulders by gripping his sleeve in one hand, without any other hold. Then, placing one hand on the saddle pommel of a war horse and the other near the horse's ears, seizing the mane, he leapt from the ground through his arms and over the horse. Next, between two high walls an arm's length apart, he would climb to the top and down again, simply using the strength of his legs and arms—fully armed. Again, wearing a mail hauberk, he climbed up the underside of a long ladder, without using his feet, just using his hands on the rungs.

Le Livre des Fais du Mareschal Bouciquaut 1368-1421 ("The Book of Deeds of Marshal Boucicaut")

5-1. (Art by Alex Daye.)

Being in good physical condition is a prerequisite to performing a good stage fight. In this key chapter, you'll learn:

- The physical and mental benefits of warming up before you fight
- When and how to exercise to get maximum benefits and avoid common injuries
- Twenty popular stretches used by experienced performers
- The eight Chairman Mao warm-ups used to prepare for stage combat

Historically, many swordfighters probably warmed up for a morning's joust by curling a few ales and gnawing on the bones of the previous night's feast. Like many of us in modern times with physically active jobs—such as police officers and soldiers—some swashbucklers in all eras probably let their official fitness standards slide, counting on their youth and contemporary courtly or rustic dances to keep them fit.

Today, many actors exercise just to look good in glossies and auditions rather than to develop the strength, agility, and endurance they'll need for performance. For an out-of-shape actor-combatant, even the briefest stage fight (often coming at the end of a long play) can add what feels like hours to a performance; and pulled muscles, strains, and sprains do nothing to enhance a career.

Physical conditioning—the gradual development of appropriate muscles and muscle groups, as well as endurance building—goes hand-in-hand with progress in swashbuckling. One important physical goal for all actors is to gain more control over their movements and not be governed by instincts. Stretches and warmups—performed consistently and properly before training sessions, practices, rehearsals, and performances—go a long way toward keeping you healthy, fit, and photogenic.

Warmups offer psychological benefits, too. Mentally, they help us make the transition from whatever we were doing before the practice or rehearsal—studying, banking, waiting tables, signing autographs—to our new roles as actor-combatants. They help us de-program old responses and activate new reactions. Actors familiar with Stanislavski's method know that a vessel full of one thing cannot hold another. Warmups help you empty your head of old thoughts, and your body of conventional muscle memories, so that the mind and movements of your character can more easily take over.

STRETCHING AND WARMUP OBJECTIVES

At the Academy of the Sword, we use both standard and non-traditional stretches and warmups to prepare for the demands of stage combat. We chose them specifically to:

- Engage opposing muscle groups because stage combat is, more than anything, an exercise in balance and recovery.
- Isolate and strengthen the specific muscles and muscle groups we use in swordplay.
- Warm us up—not wear us out!

WHAT TO WEAR, WHERE TO GO, WHEN TO START

The exercises in this chapter take about thirty minutes and should be performed unarmed (without gloves, gauntlets or sword) wearing light workout clothes or sweats. Tennis, fencing, or wrestling shoes are perfect

. . . I saw young Harry—with his beaver on, His cuisses on his thighs, gallantly arm'd,— Rise from the ground like feathered Mercury, And vaulted with such ease into his seat, As if an angel dropp'd down from the clouds, To turn and wind a fiery Pegasus, And witch the world with noble horsemanship.

Sir Richard Vernon
Henry IV, Part I,
Act IV, Scene 1
Shakespeare

for both exercise and swordplay. If possible, choose a floor that has some give to it, such as a sprung dance floor. Hardwood floors and very short-pile carpets (or carpet pads) are acceptable indoors. Avoid thick pile or shag carpets, and *never* exercise where loose throw rugs can trip you up.

Outdoors, short grass is preferable to cement, concrete, or asphalt, but the worst possible surfaces are loose dirt or gravel which invite slips, sprains, and abrasions.

Although you'll perform both stretches and warmups before each training session and rehearsal, there's nothing wrong with performing the exercises for their own sake, as part of a personal fitness program. If you do them at least three times a week, you'll improve your physical strength, muscle tone, aerobic capacity, and enhance your overall appearance and health—as well as drop those few extra pounds no swashbuckler needs. To avoid boredom, change locations from time to time. If you usually exercise indoors, go outside on a sunny day. If you're normally outdoors, use rainy days to exercise to music or in front of a favorite swashbuckling video. If you keep the experience pleasant, it will become a pleasurable habit. If you turn it into a chore, you'll find plenty of reasons to do something else.

STRETCHES

Many trainers and martial artists recommend a light warmup *before* stretching as a way to minimize even the unlikely chances of pulling a muscle while stretching. By light warmup they mean a few minutes' walk around the room—forward, backward, sidestepping, on toes, on heels, on the knife-edge of the foot (the outside of the foot tucked under), or a short jog around the house, yard, or neighborhood. This can be especially helpful to swashbucklers over forty, those who lead a sedentary lifestyle, people recovering from illness or injury, and *everyone* in extremely cold weather. As always, the motto for any physical fitness program is: Be smart, know your body, take it slow, and let it grow.

When you're ready to begin the stretches, always perform them in sequence. Take as much time as you need for your body to give you feedback about its readiness to continue. The initial "cracks and crackles," stiffness, and tingles are the way the body communicates. An "easy" stretch is one that's held for twenty to thirty seconds. A "developmental" stretch is held for a little longer—but not so long it becomes "drastic," or injurious. Unless you're an experienced athlete or body builder, no stretch presented here need be held longer than half a minute to receive the required benefits.

Completing all stretches is more important than doing them quickly or perfecting any particular one. Your capacity to increase your range of motion will grow gradually over time, so don't rush. Unless the instructions tell you otherwise, begin and end each exercise in the relaxed, neutral position described in "Neck and Upper Back Stretches" on page 81.

"A stretch is not a warmup!!!"

The best warmup is exactly what it says. . . a warmup. It should be designed to increase your body temperature, increasing the flexibility and range of motion of your joints and muscles. The most effective way to warm your body up is to move it, warming it from the inside out. Any rhythmic, repetitive, low intensity move will do it for you. If you tailor your warmup to the expected activity, it will benefit you even more. Walk before you run. Spin before you race. A low intensity version of the expected workout or activity will prepare the right muscles more fully, but even a general rhythmic warmup will suit the purpose, which is to prevent injury. A good warmup will prepare your body for more strenuous work to follow. At the completion of your workout take a few minutes to work on flexibility, taking advantage of the internal heat generated by your activity. Your muscles and ligaments are ready for a well-designed static stretch.

Lisa Cross
Personal Trainer,
Fitness Instructor,
Exercise Leader
Certified by AFAA,
ACE and ACSM

5-2a.

5-2b.

UPRIGHT BREATHING POSTURE Begin by exercising the principal muscles of the back, those that most often cause muscle spasms and lower back pain. Stand with feet together, knees slightly bent (see Fig. 5-2a). Place your hands on your lower back. The dorsal erectors are among the weakest muscles in the human body, although, along with the abdominals, they're the ones that help us to stand erect (see Fig. 5-2b). Breathe deeply, sending your breath to your hands and feel your lower back expand laterally. Inhale through your nose and exhale through your mouth. Repeat three times.

To see how the power of our limbs really does radiate from the center of the torso, and how one side of the body affects the movement of the other, wave one hand over your head while leaving the other hand in place. Notice how the dorsal erector on the opposite side of your body responds to the movement of your arm. You needn't do this test each time you assume the upright breathing posture; once should be enough to convince you that proper extension, balance, and recovery depend on *all* parts of the body working harmoniously together.

5-3a.

5-3b.

NECK AND UPPER BACK STRETCHES   These exercise the triangular muscles that support the head from the back, and the thick muscles that support it from the side. These muscles are important to the rotation, flexion, and extension of the head. From the "upright breathing posture," open your stance by "walking" each foot sideways, toe-heel-toe, away from the other until your feet are about a shoulder's width apart. Bend your knees slightly so that they extend out in the direction of your toes. Take your right hand and reach over the top of your head to the left side of your face while extending your left arm out to the side, left hand in the "flexed" (fingers up) position. Use your right hand to "pull" your head down (eyes looking forward) until your right ear is touching your right shoulder (see Fig. 5-3a). After a short pause, turn your head down (nose to your armpit, see Fig. 5-3b) then look forward again. With your head still cocked to the right, rotate your extended left hand at the wrist eight times in each direction; then "push through" (extend your flexed hand out as far as it will go) and "wash the wall"—make a circular motion with the flexed, flattened hand eight times in both

Today's experts in the body/mind field of metaphysics, while differing on a wide variety of subjects, at least agree on the idea that man's motor function is intimately linked with his mental and emotional growth.

Mark Olsen
"The Metaphysics of Stage Combat"
The Fight Master

5-4a.

5-4b.

directions. When you're finished, use your right hand to "push" your head upright again. Neck muscles are relatively weak, and this little push really helps avoid strain after stretching. Repeat the entire sequence, using your left hand to "pull" your head down to your left shoulder and your right arm to perform wrist rotations and wash the wall.

"BANDAGE" NECK MUSCLE (TRAPEZIA) STRETCHES   These muscles help move, extend, and rotate the head. Place both hands behind your head and use them to help your head roll down to your chest (see Fig. 5-4a). Take a few deep breaths in this position. Now roll down further, trying to put your nose in your belly button (see Fig. 5-4b). Take another good breath after you've reached your lowest position. Place your hands on your face to help your head roll back to an upright position. Now let your head extend up and back(don't drop your neck behind), then stretch gently from side to side a few times (see Fig. 5-5). Let your jaw go slack and breath deeply and naturally. Place your hands on the back of your head and help it return to an upright, neutral position.

HEAD ROTATION   Despite its name, this exercise stretches those muscles used to maintain the body's posture. You must never rotate and tilt your head so far that you compress the vertebrae, which can cause a painful injury. From a neutral position, look purposefully over your right shoulder, pause as if you see something, then return to neutral (see Fig. 5-6). Repeat three times; then do the same to the left. Try to exhale with each stretch. Return to neutral. Now drop your chin forward and look at the floor. Letting your eyes lead, roll your head to the right and up. Let your head "follow" your eyes as your eyes track across the ceiling above your head and down the left wall until you are looking at the floor again. Don't allow your head to fall back as you track across the ceiling but rather keep your neck extended. Repeat four times in each direction.

5-5.

5-6.

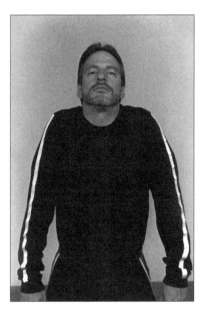

5-7.

SHOULDER SHRUG This exercise stretches the "delts," "lats," and "pecs" (deltoids, latissimus dorsi, pectorals) the muscles that support the collarbone and facilitate arm movement—and feels great first thing in the morning or at the end of a stressful day. Lift your shoulders almost to your ears, relaxing everything else, then drop them (don't force them down, just stop holding them up—see Fig 5-7). Repeat three times. Now move your shoulders forward as if you were trying to touch them to each other, then do the same while moving them back. Repeat three times. Now combine the movements by rolling your shoulders up, forward, down, and back in both directions three times each; then relax.

5-8a.

5-8b.

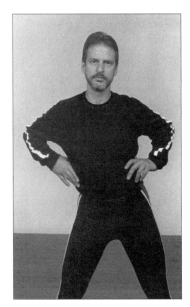

5-8c.

CHEST ISOLATION Dancers will recognize this exercise: it stretches the same muscles as the upright breathing posture but with a wider range of motion. With hands on your waist (upper fingers just touching the bottom of your rib cage), push your chest forward (Fig. 5-8a), then to the rear (Fig. 5-8b), then back to neutral. Repeat three times. Now push the bottom of your rib cage to your right (see Fig. 5-8c), then to your left, and return to neutral. Repeat three times. Now roll your chest through all four positions going to the right (forward, right, back, left) four times; then repeat to the left (forward, left, back, right) four times and return to neutral.

5-9a.

5-9b.

5-9c.

WAIST ROTATION This exercise employs the "abs" (abdominals) and "obliques" to compress and rotate the torso—important muscles for doing sit ups. Extend your back up and to the rear, pushing your belly button out (like stretching after a big meal—see Fig. 5-9a), then bend forward, keeping your head erect, eyes looking to the front, and push your tailbone back as far as it will go, taking your weight mostly onto your heels. Feel the stretch in your hamstrings (the large muscle behind the thigh—see Fig. 5-9b). Repeat four times, breathing deeply and naturally as you reverse directions. Now, from a neutral position with your hands on your hips, displace your hips to the right, keeping your head aligned with your center (see Fig. 5-9c). Return to neutral and displace your hips to the left, again keeping your head aligned with your center. Repeat four times. Finally, from a neutral position, arms held loosely out to the side, rotate your hips through a large circle (forward, right, back, left) four times in each direction, rocking on the toes, sides, and heels of your feet as you do so. We call this part of the exercise the "drunken sailor." If you imagine that you are trying to wipe the inside of a barrel with a towel tied around your waist—without using your hands— you'll get the right motion.

5-10a.

5-10b.

5-10c.

PELVIC ISOLATION   This exercises the muscles used to keep balance and rotate the hips. Tilt your pelvis forward by tucking your tailbone under (see Fig. 5-10a). Tilt it back by pushing your tailbone back (see Fig. 5-10b). Repeat four times. Now tilt your pelvis to the right (see Fig. 5-10c), then to the left. Repeat four times. Finally, roll your pelvis through all four positions—forward, side, back, other side—four times in both directions. Some people tense up in this exercise, so make sure the rest of your body stays loose—no lip-biting or breath-holding allowed, so you might as well smile.

5-11.

5-12.

KNEE ROTATION   This exercise stretches the muscles that are among the weakest (the sartorius hip flexors) and strongest in the body, (quads, or quadriceps, a bundle of four muscles on the front of the thigh)—so be careful and don't overdo it. Caution; if you have a history of knee problems, do not do this exercise. If you feel any pain whatsoever, stop the exercise. Try again only after the muscles have rested and then with a much smaller range of motion. Place your feet together, heels and big toes touching, and bend your knees slightly. Put your hands on the outsides of your knees, *not* on your kneecaps, and rotate your knees slowly in a small circle, keeping your heels flat on the ground (see Fig. 5-11). Repeat eight times in both directions.

SIDE BENDS   This exercise stretches the same muscles used in shoulder shrugs and waist rotations. They all attack those "love handles" that come with age and fine living.

Stand in a neutral position and imagine that you have a weight in each hand. Let the weight in your right hand gradually pull you down and over, letting your head go with it (see Fig. 5-12). Now let the weight in your left hand pull you back over to that side. Try to reach down and to the side as far as you can. Touching the outside of your foot is fine, but keep the opposite shoulder high. Remember, we are stretching the muscles on the side of the body, not the arms. Repeat twice in each direction then return to neutral, mentally dropping the weights.

Your muscles are protected by a mechanism called the *stretch reflex.* Anytime you stretch the muscle fibers too far (either by bouncing or overstretching), a nerve responds by sending a signal to the muscles to contract; this keeps the muscles from being injured. Therefore, when you stretch too far, you tighten the very muscles you are trying to stretch! (You get a similar muscle reaction when you accidentally touch something hot; before you can think about it, your body quickly jerks back from the heat.) Holding a stretch as far as you can or bouncing up and down strains the muscles and activates the stretch reflex. These harmful methods cause pain, as well as physical damage due to the microscopic tearing of muscle fibers. This tearing leads to the formation of scar tissue in the muscles, with a gradual loss of elasticity.

Bob Anderson
Stretching

5-13a.

5-13b.

SCRATCH THE WALL This exercise takes shoulder shrugs a little farther. Standing upright in a neutral position, extend your arms and fingers down toward the floor. Imagine reaching down with long claws or having bolts of lightning or streams of water shoot out of your fingers. With straight arms, begin raising your hands to the sides (see Fig. 5-13a) imagining that your claws, lightning bolts or streams of water are hitting the floor, then the walls, and finally the ceiling overhead. This tactile visualization is very important in getting the muscle extensions you need—simple arm-raising just won't do it. Now with both arms above your head, and knees slightly bent (see Fig. 5-13b) stretch one arm and then the other as if you were climbing a rope. Make sure you're extending enough to feel the stretch in your torso and "obliques," (the muscles on the sides of your stomach). After you've stretched both arms a few times in this manner, go directly into the next exercise. Do not go back to a neutral position.

SIMON SAYS This exercise helps you "come down" from the scratch-the-walls extensions and gain more control over each joint in your arms. Isolation exercises are important for sword control. With both arms still straight above you (see Fig. 5-14a), drop your right hand at the wrist. Don't push your hand over, just relax the wrist muscle and let it drop forward on its own. Sometimes it helps if you visualize the energy you had been shooting at the wall through your fingertips, now emanating from your wrist (see Fig. 5-14b). Now drop your left hand the same way. Now drop your right arm at the elbow (see Fig. 5-14c). Now drop your left arm at the elbow. Drop your right arm at the shoulder (see Fig. 5-14d). Drop your left arm at the shoulder. Drop your right shoulder. Drop your left shoulder. Roll down, vertebra by vertebra, leading with your head, arms dangling, until you are hanging over at the waist, knees straight (see Fig. 5-14e). Do not return to neutral, but go immediately on to the next exercise.

5-14a.

5-14b.

5-14c.

5-14d.

5-14e.

HAMSTRING STRETCH   This exercise—familiar to most athletes—moves your focus back to the lower half of your body, beginning with hip and knee joints. From the relaxed hanging position, "walk" your hands over to your right foot. Try to keep your right leg straight, but not locked. Now walk both hands over to your left foot. Relax and breathe into your lower back. Walk your hands back to your right foot, hold your right ankle, and with your back and leg straight, try to extend, reaching with your nose down toward your toes (see Fig. 5-15a). Relax and walk your hands back to the left, holding your left ankle and extending, reaching with your nose toward your toes. Walk your hands back to the right and grab the outside of your right ankle (over the top) with your left hand and extend your right hand up toward the ceiling (see Fig. 5-15b). Continue to breathe easily into your lower back. Lower your right arm and walk your hands back to your left foot. Grab that foot with your right hand and extend your left hand up behind you toward the ceiling; again, breathing easily into your lower back. Drop your left hand, walk both hands to the center, and roll up vertebra by vertebra to a standing position, head coming up last.

5-15a.

5-15b.

TRIANGLE STANCE This exercise stretches the hamstring again, plus the calf muscle and the "glutes" (gluteus maximus, medius, and minimus), the muscles of the buttocks. From the neutral stance, turn your body so that the toes of your right foot point to the right. Keeping your right leg straight, bend over and try to extend so that your nose reaches towards your toes. Massage any tight muscles in your leg (see Fig. 5-16a). Bend your right leg slightly and roll up, vertebra by vertebra. With your torso erect, step out with your right leg into a slightly deeper (demi- or half-) lunge. Make sure your right knee does not extend farther than your toes. Now swing your left arm eight times in backward circles, as if doing the backstroke in a swimming pool, eight times (see Fig. 5-16b). Now swing your left arm in forward circles eight times, as if doing the Australian Crawl (overhand) stroke. You should do these circles briskly enough to feel the energy flow from your arms through your fingertips.

Now step out into an even deeper lunge to the right (let your weight sink down and make sure your left heel stays on the ground), squaring your hips and shoulders in that direction (see Fig. 5-16c), and lean forward, putting your left hand on the ground by your foot while reaching forward with your right (see Fig. 5-16d). This is the "passata sotto"—the "all or nothing"—lunge that either killed the opponent or, because it left attackers vulnerable, allowed them to be killed instead. (The passata sotto was usually executed as a low line evasion with a stop thrust). This is a very effective stretch for the side of the body.

Now switch hands, bracing yourself with the right hand and extending the left (see Fig. 5-16e). Remain there a moment, then balance yourself on your feet alone, staying in your deep lunge (it helps to raise your torso slightly) and extend both hands in front of you (see Fig. 5-16f). Now pull your left hand back as if you are drawing a bow and arrow and open it out behind you, turning your torso to the front, arms open wide in the "hero" pose (see Fig. 5-16g). Recover by bringing your left arm forward while shifting your weight towards your right leg. This will allow you to bring your left foot forward and place it by your right foot. Rise slowly from the resulting crouch, vertebra by vertebra. When upright, reverse direction and repeat the entire sequence going to the left. Remember, you will step out on the left leg, rotate the right arm first, and reach out with the left arm first in the passata sotto lunge, opening out, eventually, into the hero pose to the right.

5-16a.

5-16b.

5.16c.

5-16d.

5-16e.

5-16f.

5-16g.

5-17a.

5-17b.

DROP STANCE Although your thigh muscles are no more prone to injury than any others, you often feel strain there first because of their rich supply of nerves. This stretch will challenge the hamstrings and glutes at the same time as the quads. Step out to the right in a wide horse stance, still facing forward, until your feet are a double shoulder's width apart. Shift your weight to the right and lower yourself until your buttocks are over your heel (see Fig. 5-17a). Be sure that right heel stays flat—it will have a tendency to come off the ground as you go lower—and keep your left foot flat as well. If you feel like you'll lose your balance, steady yourself with your hands. Now shift your weight to the left, keeping your CG low, and drop as low as you can while keeping your left heel down. Shift back to the right, but this time let the toes of your left foot rise and point to the ceiling (see Fig. 5-17b). Repeat the same move to the left, letting the toes of your right foot rise. Shift back to the center, staying low, and go immediately into the next exercise. Do not return to a neutral standing position.

5-18a.

5-18b.

5-18c.

SPIDER STANCE Both the "drop stance" and "spider stance" use the flexors of the thigh (the flexors of the thigh allow you to squeeze your legs together: the adductor longus and brevis pectineus)—useful muscles in swordfighting footwork. Still in the open squat from your previous stretch, place your palms flat on the ground in front of you, roughly in line with your toes (see Fig. 5-18a). Keeping your head down, straighten your legs, raising your tailbone as high as you can. Lower your tailbone and return to your open squat. Now press your elbows to the ground (see Fig. 5-18b). Raise your tailbone again by straightening your legs. Lower yourself again, but this time try to press your belly button to the ground between your feet. You won't be able to do it—but the idea will help you stretch (see Fig. 5-18c). Don't hold your breath, but breathe easily and naturally. Now "walk" your feet together, toe-heel-toe-heel, staying low. Staying in a squat, get your feet as close together as you can without raising your heels. Brace yourself with your hands behind you, and gently lower your tailbone to the ground. Remain seated and go directly into the next exercise.

5-19a.

5-19b.

5-19-c.

When you grow up athletic and know how good you feel, you want to share this information. You know it has not only great physical but psychological benefits. When you feel so good and you hear people around you saying they feel tired, don't feel healthy, and don't have energy, and you see them overweight—you feel you should do something about it.

. . .Everyone should do something every day. It will create a healthier nation, a healthier environment, and people will be more productive. . . . We have to help one another. That's what makes everything work.

Arnold Schwarzenegger
USA Weekend
April 2-4, 1993

THE OCEAN WAVE This exercise uses all the muscle groups, including the abdominals. Sit on your buttocks, back straight and legs in front of you, knees bent, with the soles of your feet together (see Fig. 5-19a). Now "fall" forward, vertebra by vertebra like an ocean wave breaking on the shore, beginning with your pelvis, then belly button, stomach, chest, collarbone, neck, chin, nose, forehead, and finally your arms extending past your feet (see Fig. 5-19b). Now roll back up, leading with the small of your back, vertebra by vertebra, continuing past the vertical. When you start to fall backwards, let your hands slide up to your knees and stop (see Fig. 5-19c). Now start forward again in the same manner, then let the wave fall back, beginning with your hips. Repeat this ebb and flow three times. Return to an upright sitting posture and go immediately on to the next exercise.

ANKLE ROTATIONS These movements exercise the muscles used to rotate the feet and maintain balance while your weight shifts. Still seated with the soles of your feet together, pick your right ankle up with your right hand and place your left hand on your right toes (see Fig. 5-20). Rotate the foot from the ankle eight times in one direction, then eight times in the other. Gently lower the foot and repeat with your left foot and ankle. Stay seated and go on to the next exercise.

5-20.

We have come to accept the notion that armor worn in the fifteenth and sixteenth centuries was so cumbersome that a knight dislodged from his horse could not move or that he had to be lifted onto his horse by a crane. Complete field armor before the seventeenth century averaged between 55 and 60 pounds which is no heavier than a fully equipped field pack worn in today's army. The big difference being that this weight was distributed over the entire body and not suspended from the shoulders like modern military equipment. A fully trained man (and we know that they received training) was hardly inconvenienced except for his ventilation. Modern experiments in fifteenth and sixteenth century armor show that an untrained man wearing a properly fitted harness can get on and off a horse, lie on the ground, get up again, bend over, stoop and move his arms and legs freely. For tournaments, extra defenses were added to the field or fighting armor, even though special armor for jousting that was totally unlike anything worn in battle was also made. This increased weight (jousting armor weighed between 80 and 85 pounds on the average) promised security in the saddle. Tournament armor sacrificed mobility in exchange for greater safety. A knight armed for the joust could not mount to the saddle and portions of his armor had to be fitted on after he was mounted.

Linda McCollum
Weight Consciousness
The Fight Master

BACK TO STANDING From an upright seated position, bring your knees up together and hug them to your chest, trying to make yourself as small and compact as possible (see Fig. 5-21a). Breathe deeply and easily letting the breath go into the small of your back. Brace yourself with your hands on the floor behind you and return to a squatting position, weight resting on your feet (see Fig. 5-21b). Shift your weight slightly forward and begin raising your tailbone, bent over with head down, heels on the floor, straightening your legs as you stand. Once standing bend your knees slightly and roll your body upwards, vertebra by vertebra, until you've returned to the full upright, neutral standing position.

SHAKE IT ALL OUT You've just given your body a pretty good mini-workout and it's bound to react a little. Keep those muscles from tightening by standing on one foot and shaking your arms and your raised leg vigorously for a few seconds (see Fig. 5-21c). Shift to the other foot and repeat.

5-21a.   5-21b.   5-21c.

THE CHAIRMAN MAO WARMUPS

Developed in China and used for years by many SAFD-certified teachers, the Chairman Mao warmups consist of eight, four-count exercises repeated eight times in opposition—that is, to both sides of the body's centerline with right hand and left foot working simultaneously, and vice versa. Consequently, each exercise has a left-side and a right-side component to help develop bilateral coordination, improve circulation, and enhance overall fitness—ideal for stage combat. The eight-exercise series begins and ends with an aerobic-style marching- and running-in-place exercise to help you get into, then out of, the warmup mode—mentally and physically.

Some of the exercises will seem complex at first, but the four-count process breaks them down into sequences anyone can manage. Go slowly until you've mastered each exercise, then gradually increase your speed. As with stretches, it's more important to complete the movements thoroughly through their full range of motions than to perform them quickly. Just as important, the Chairman Maos contain many of the same motions we'll use for both armed and unarmed stage combat; so the time you spend learning and using them will pay dividends in performance.

THIRTY-TWO-STEPS MARCHING IN PLACE This cross-lateralization of arm and leg movements gets both hemispheres of the brain in gear—valuable for rapier and dagger work. Start by raising your left knee (at least waist high) and right elbow (at least shoulder high) and march in place at a brisk, even pace for a count of thirty-two steps. Keep your arms swinging freely in opposition to your legs (see Fig. 5-22).

5-22.

1. CHIN-UPS These are "phantom" chin-ups. You won't need a bar but you will have to imagine the effort needed to pull up on one to receive the maximum isotonic benefits for your biceps and triceps, as well as for the hand flexors and extensors used for sword-gripping. Done correctly, you'll "feel the burn" in your arms as the flexors and extensors resist each other, and in your legs as the deep horse stance stimulates the adductors and abductors (muscles on the inside and outside of hips and thighs). Begin in the same, relaxed neutral position you used for your stretches.

- Count One: Step left into a deep horse stance. Raise your arms over your head and make fists, knuckles forward, as if you are grasping a chin-up bar (see Fig. 5-23a). Vigorously pull your parallel fists down to your chest (see Fig. 5-23b).
- Count Two: Repeat the chin-up motion.
- Count Three: Open your hands and push your arms sideways to full extension—as if you are trying to push the walls of a very tight corridor apart (see Fig. 5-23c).
- Count Four: Drop your arms to your sides and bring your left foot back to the neutral position. This completes one repetition of the exercise.

Step out on your right foot and repeat counts one through four. This constitutes the second repetition of the exercise.

Repeat this left-right cycle for a total of eight repetitions (four to each side) and return to the neutral stance.

5-23a.

5-23b.

5-23c.

2. PUNCHES These martial arts-style punches exercise the pectoral and latissimus muscles as well as the deltoids, biceps and triceps (upper chest and arm muscles) used in sword thrusts and lunges.

- Count One: Leaving your right foot in place, turn your body to the left and step out into a moderate (demi-) lunge—similar to the position you assumed in the triangle stance stretches. Keep your back straight with both feet on the floor. As you do this, draw your left elbow to your side, forearm parallel to the ground with fist in supination—the martial-arts readiness position—while you punch straight out with your right arm, rolling your fist to pronation as your arm extends (see Fig. 5-24a).
- Count Two: Draw your right arm back to the martial-arts readiness position (rolling your pronated fist to supination) while punching out with your left arm, rolling your fist to pronation as your arm extends (see Fig. 5-24b). Be sure to get full extensions in your punches.
- Count Three: Draw your left arm back while simultaneously punching again with your right.
- Count Four: As you bring your right arm back, step back to the neutral position, facing front (see Fig. 5-24c). This completes the first repetition of the exercise.

Step out into a demi-lunge to the right and repeat counts one through four on that side, beginning with a left-hand punch. This completes the second repetition of the exercise.

Repeat this left-right cycle for a total of eight repetitions and return to the neutral position.

5-24a.

5-24b.

5-24c.

3. BUTTERFLIES These exercises in displacement and recovery use the pecs and lats as well as the quads and muscles surrounding the knee.

- Count One: Leaving your right foot in place, step out diagonally forward on your left foot into a demi-lunge, keeping your back straight and both heels on the ground. Extend your arms to the side like the wings of a butterfly, (see Fig. 5-25a) then cross them, left over right, in front of your waist (see Fig. 5-25b).
- Count Two: Repeat the arm-crossing motion, but this time right over left.
- Count Three: Drawing your arms apart, let them continue up in a circular motion over your head, as you draw your body back to the neutral position (see Fig. 5-25c). Keeping your back straight, enter a squatting position as your arms come down (see Fig. 5-25d). At this point, try to keep your heels on the ground. Feet should be parallel, toes pointed to the front.
- Count Four: Return to the neutral standing position. This completes the first repetition of the exercise.

5-25a.

5-25b.

5-25c.

5-25d.

Step out into a demi-lunge on the right foot and repeat the four counts using the right side of the body. This time, cross right arm over left first, then right arm over left. This completes the second repetition of the exercise.

Repeat this left-right cycle for a total of eight repetitions and return to the neutral position.

4. KICKS These chorus-line high kicks from theatrical-looking reverse lunges (with arms held high) have show-biz written all over them. They exercise the glutes and hamstrings as well as many other coordinating muscle groups.

- Count One: Sink down on your right leg and step back deeply (reverse lunge) on the left foot while raising both arms straight overhead (see Fig. 5-26a). Your right knee will be bent in the demi-lunge position. Be sure to keep your left heel on the floor.
- Count Two: Bring your left leg forward and up into a chorus-line kick, simultaneously dropping both arms to your sides (see Fig. 5-26b).
- Count Three: Return to the count-one position: reverse lunge (left foot back) with arms held high.
- Count Four: Return to the neutral position. This completes the first repetition of the exercise.

Step back on the right foot into a reverse demi-lunge and repeat counts one through four on the right side (that is, kicking with the right foot). This completes the second repetition of the exercise.

Repeat the left-right cycle for a total of eight repetitions and return to the neutral position.

5-26a.

5-26b.

5. WINDMILLS These are other good balance and recovery exercises using the lats and external oblique muscles.

- Count One: Step to the left into the dancer's second position, legs turned out from the hips, feet a little more than shoulder's width apart, knees straight. Raise your arms to the side, parallel to the ground, shoulder high (see Fig. 5-27a).
- Count Two: Touch your left foot with your right hand while your left arm extends toward the ceiling. (Imagine that your arms are rigidly connected through your shoulders, like a scarecrow—see Fig. 27-b.)
- Count Three: Still bending over your left foot, touch your left foot with your left hand (see Fig. 5-27c) while the right arm extends toward the ceiling.
- Count Four: Return to neutral (see Fig. 5-27d). This completes the first repetition of the exercise.

Step out to the right into the dancer's second position and repeat counts one through four on the right side, beginning with the left hand touching the right foot. This completes the second repetition of the exercise.

Repeat the left-right cycle for a total of eight repetitions and return to the neutral position.

5-27a.

5-27b.

5-27c.

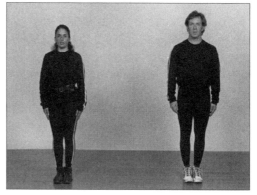

5-27d.

6. **SWANS** These graceful exercises, using the latissimus and external oblique muscles, have a surprise element: a martial-arts style "ki up," or energy-release vocalization, that gives practice in breath control and energy focus.

- Count One: Step to the left as you did for windmills, raising your curved right arm over your head (fingertips pointing to the left) while curving your left arm down along and just in front of your torso, fingertips pointing right. Your torso should tilt slightly to the left and you should feel the stretch of the raised arm and the right side of your body (see Fig. 5-28a). In the proper position, your left hand "cups" the body's center of gravity, the area just below the navel, which, according to Asian martial artists, is the energy center as well. The arms form a graceful S-shaped, yin-yang pattern. From this position, try to extend the raised arm slightly up and to the left, and the other arm down and to the right, feeling the stretch.
- Count Two: Try to extend the arms more, feeling the stretch.
- Count Three: Try to extend more, feeling the stretch.
- Count Four: Return to neutral, bringing your left foot back in contact with your right. As you do so, extend both arms in front of you at waist level, forearms up, hands in supination, and "grab" some air, crisply pulling it toward your energy center—ending with fists in the martial arts readiness position used in punches (see Fig. 5-28b). As your elbows come into position at your sides, exhale sharply through your mouth, thereby vocalizing a martial arts shout from deep in your abdomen—your energy center. This should sound like a deep, breathy "Hah!", not a nasal or throaty cry. This completes the first repetition of the exercise.

Step out to the right and repeat counts one through four on the right side, left arm up, right arm down. This completes the second repetition of the exercise.

Repeat the left-right cycle for a total of eight repetitions and return to the neutral position.

5-28a.

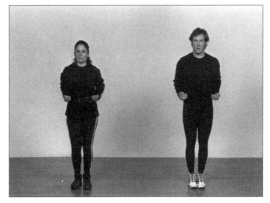

5-28b.

7. JUMPING JACKS These standard aerobic and coordination exercises are performed with four counts, not the usual two.

• Count One: Raise both arms to shoulder height, hands extended, palms down, while both feet jump to the dancer's second position (see Fig. 5-29a).

• Count Two: Continue to raise both arms, clapping the palms together as they meet overhead, while bringing both feet together quickly (see Fig. 5-29b).

• Count Three: Lower both arms to shoulder height, palms down, while both feet jump to the second position.

• Count Four: Drop arms to sides and bring feet together. This completes the first repetition of the exercise.

Repeat counts one through four another seven times for a total of eight repetitions and return to neutral.

5-29a.

5-29b.

8. TOE TOUCHES The familiar two-count toe touches are transformed by reverse lunges and arm lifts into a four-count finale that exercise the deltoids, gluteals, hamstrings, and abdominals.

• Count One: Raise both arms overhead (see Fig. 5-30a).

• Count Two: Bending at the waist, lower both arms and touch your toes (see Fig. 5-30b). This feels and looks better if your hands follow a graceful semi-circular pattern when you raise and lower your arms. Don't move them stiffly in front of your body like a robot.

• Count Three: As you rise from the toe-touch, step back on your left foot (keeping your weight on your right foot) into a reverse demi-lunge while raising both arms overhead again—a nice musical theater position (see Fig. 5-30c).

• Count Four: Return to neutral, feet together. This completes the first repetition of the exercise.

Repeat counts one through four, this time stepping back on the right foot into the demi-lunge. This completes the second repetition of the exercise.

Repeat the left-right cycle for a total of eight repetitions and return to neutral.

5-30a.

5-30b.

5-30c.

THIRTY-TWO STEPS RUNNING IN PLACE This is nothing more than a faster version of "thirty-two steps marching in place." It requires faster cross-lateralization, helps you "shake it out" after the eight Chairman Maos, leaving you relaxed, warmed up, and full of energy for a good stage-combat session. Begin by raising the left foot and right arm, and remember to raise the knee waist high and swing your arms in opposition to your legs with each step (see Fig. 5-31).

5-31.

A FINAL WORD ON EXERCISE

As with most other things in life and in acting, you'll bring to the physical side of stage combat all the strengths and weaknesses that characterize you as a person and a performer. Among typical actor-combatants, these strengths include talent, ambition, and the desire to excel. Among the weaknesses: over-competitiveness, procrastination—and sometimes a bit of laziness.

If these traits sound like yours, keep a couple of things in mind. First, exercise—stretching, warming up, training, rehearsal, and performing—is not a contest, even against yourself. Everyone wants to improve and achievement-oriented people want to improve quickly; but haste is the enemy of mastery. Let your body be your partner: learn from it as it learns from the exercises and you won't delay your success because of needless injuries.

On the other hand, exercise for some people is like eating broccoli: they just can't bring themselves to like it, no matter how good it's supposed to be. In truth, warming up is an integral part of the swashbuckling menu, not an optional side dish. People who try to learn stage combat without cultivating their bodies or improving their physical condition become, at best, mediocre and injury-prone performers. Breathing deeply, moving fully, and sweating, contribute to the joy of life. Don't cheat yourself of a minute of it!

It is necessary to appear animated with a brave Boldness, for nothing requires a Man to exert himself more than Sword in Hand; and it is as difficult to attain such an Air of Intrepidity without much Exercise, as it is to become perfectly expert.

M. L'abbat
The Art of Fencing or the Use of the Smallsword

6

STAGING UNARMED COMBAT

Many people only classify the ubiquitous fist fight as unarmed combat. I, however, also lump the multifarious gymnastics involved in chase scenes, vaudeville pratfalls, commedia dell'arte lazzi, food fights, reacting to gunshot wounds, and any other precision body work as unarmed combat. Hence, for me, the subject is vast and could fill many books.

J. Allen Suddeth, SAFD Fight Master (author of *Fight Directing for the Theatre*)
Handbill, Choreographer's Workshop Celebration Barn Theatre, 1993

6-1. *"Extremities" at Northern Kentucky University (1985)
with Lisa Rene and George Bellah.
Director: SAFD Fight Master David Leong.*

Fistfights and other forms of unarmed mayhem are as old as drama. By the end of this chapter, you'll know:

- Why unarmed stage combat can actually be *more* dangerous than fights with weapons
- The fundamentals of knaps, punches, kicks, chokes, hair pulls, rolls and falls
- Nine ways for performers to make unarmed fights safer and more effective
- Nine guidelines for performers or non-specialists staging unarmed fights—including the all-important duties of a fight captain

Chances are, your first stage fight will be unarmed. This is simply a matter of statistics: more plays involve this kind of physical conflict than any other type. To fight with swords, you'll probably have to appear in a period play; but people have been battering each other with fists and feet in every era—and that's reflected in our dramas.

THE SIMILARITIES BETWEEN ARMED AND UNARMED FIGHTS

Fortunately, the principles you've learned so far about swordplay apply equally well to unarmed combat.

First, slaps and punches, kicks, chokes, hair-pulls, and most throws, falls, and rolls, (see Figs. 6-2a through 6-2e) use the same four-step process of eye-contact, preparation, reaction, and action that applies to sword fights. Second, both armed and unarmed combat require you to "act in action." The drama doesn't stop when two characters come to blows; it's magnified. If you step out of character to fight, it's like switching channels on the audience. Much of what you'll learn in this chapter, in fact, involves completing the illusion: continuing to react as the victim of violence after the aggressor's action is complete.

6-2a.

6-2b.

6-2c.

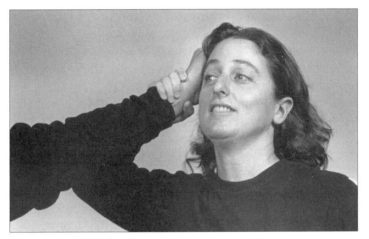

6-2d.

6-2e.

THE DIFFERENCES BETWEEN ARMED AND UNARMED FIGHTS

Beginners assume unarmed combat is safer than fights with swords, but as with so many initial assumptions in stage combat, that notion can get you hurt. Because unarmed combat takes place at much closer quarters, the margin for error is smaller: there is simply less time and distance available to recover from a mistake. Also, because unarmed combat often requires one or both of the characters to fall down during a fight, there are more chances for injury, including more serious injuries to backs and necks. While there are ways to do falls and rolls safely, there is simply no way to fake them, so the proper instruction in their techniques by a qualified teacher is essential.

The biggest cause of accidents, however, is complacency. "How badly can I get hurt just using my hands?" is a question too often answered by band-aids, plaster casts, and crutches.

Timing also becomes more important. For example, sound effects take care of themselves in a swordfight: A successful parry produces the sound of ringing steel. In a stage punch, the only skin-on-skin contact allowed comes in the form of a "knap"—the sound of a punch, kick, or slap. If this sound effect is performed too soon or delayed even a fraction of a second, it produces laughs instead of gasps.

Nonverbal communication, too, is of prime importance. Without adequate eye contact, a closely timed, in-distance stage punch can easily become the real thing: "Is that woozy, distant look in my partner's eye good acting or has he simply forgotten what comes next?"

Finally, unarmed fights are harder to sell to audiences than swordfights. After all, most of us have grown up punching and kicking each other in playgrounds, and we have all watched hours of expertly crafted violence on TV. This makes audiences more critical of what they see in live theater—and more pleased when an unarmed fight meets or exceeds their expectations.

One important rule shared by armed and unarmed stage combatants is that no blow is ever aimed directly at, or passes directly in front of, a vulnerable part of the body: neck, face, spine, solar plexus, or groin. The parts of the body *near* these areas, (breastbone, shoulder blade, stomach and thigh) are protected by bone or thick muscle and are targeted instead, while the "victim" reacts as if hit in the more vulnerable spot. Performed correctly, audiences seldom notice the difference in targeting and the action is infinitely safer.

Be sure you have adequate space, sufficient lighting, a soft surface to fall on, soft-soled tennis shoes or bare feet, non-restrictive clothing, and *no jewelry or sharp objects* of any kind on your person before you begin. If you wear glasses and cannot work without them, get a band to keep them on your head. If contact lenses will be used during a performance, wear them for practice to see if you have trouble with them.

J.D. Martinez
Combat Mime

Still, when studying a performing art, you can only learn so much from the printed page. If you're an actor, your job is to take this handful of key ideas with you into partnered work with a qualified fight arranger. If you're a stage director or anyone else with the task of choreographing a convincing stage fight—from a simple slap to a barroom brawl—this chapter will help you learn what may reasonably be expected from your actors, and how their performance can be shaped and made safer.

A SAMPLER OF UNARMED TECHNIQUES

You already know that *intent* makes the biggest difference between real and stage combat. The former is competitive; the latter cooperative—a collaboration to achieve an illusion. The biggest *similarity* between real and staged violence is found in the range of techniques available to the performer. Moves that would violate most rules in college wrestling and boxing, for example, are the very ones used most in unarmed stage combat. The techniques you'll survey below are employed not only in fully staged fights, but to physically punctuate intensely dramatic moments in non-combat scenes: the "drawing room" slap in the face, for example, or the collapse of a falling-down drunk.

The most frequently used techniques include punches, slaps, kicks, chokes, hair-pulls, various falls and rolls, and of course, the knap (the simulation of the sound of a blow). We'll look at each, including some of their derivatives. Again, while this book can introduce you to the basics and help you practice by yourself, it is no substitute for competent personal instruction.

Don't try these techniques with a partner until you can receive the supervision of a qualified teacher.

KNAPS Like the Buddhists' "sound of one hand clapping," a knap produces the sound of a blow that hasn't really connected. It's made by one or both partners slapping their hands together in a surreptitious way, deceiving the audience into thinking that the blow—perhaps a roundhouse punch—has actually landed. The hallmarks of a good knap of any type are concealment and timing. Here are the knaps we use most often in stage combat:

- *The Aggressor Knap.* This knap is the most reliable one. Here, attackers supply the sound effects by striking their own bodies or hands. This is the easiest knap to perform and get right, since one person—the aggressor— controls the sound effect and its timing.

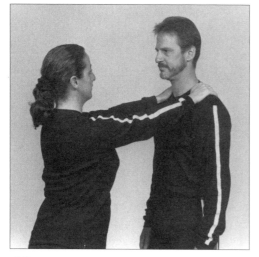

6-3a.

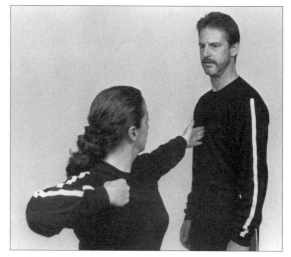

6-3b.

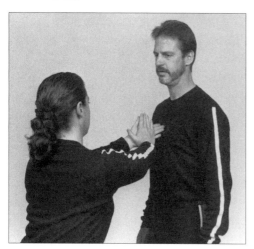

6-3c.

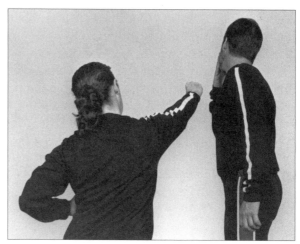

6-3d.

To get the feel of this technique, pretend to put both hands on the shoulders of an imaginary partner who is facing you (see Fig. 6-3a). On stage, your partner's back would be toward the audience. Begin by establishing eye contact. This ensures that both you and your partner are "sharing the moment" and that the ensuing action won't come as a surprise. Prepare by drawing your right fist back (see Fig. 6-3b). Begin your punch by moving your right fist toward your left hand and *not* toward your imaginary partner's face. As the fist goes forward, turn your left hand over while quickly opening your fist, letting the palm of your right hand brush against the palm of your left. This produces a satisfying skin-on-skin *slap* (see Fig. 6-3c). Before your right hand passes beyond the victim's right shoulder, roll it quickly again into a fist—then extend it as far as you can— really stretching yourself up and out from your right foot to your upper left side—completing the illusion of a bell-ringing punch (see Fig. 6-3d).

The aggressor knap can produce a good illusion of a powerful punch, perfectly timed, with the technique concealed from the audience by your partner's back.

- *The Victim Knap.* Also known as the slip-hand technique, this effect is provided by the partner "being struck." This is the next most reliable method, since one partner still controls the effect. The problem is that timing can be off—sometimes hilariously so.

To get the feel of this technique, pretend you are the victim. Stand in a relaxed, neutral position with your back facing the imaginary audience. Hold your right hand near your stomach, palm down, with your left hand, palm up, below it (see Fig. 6-4a). Let your upper arms and elbows hang naturally. Now imagine that your partner, the aggressor, after establishing eye contact with you, preps back for a roundhouse stage punch traveling from your lower left side to your upper right. As the aggressor's hand passes just below your chin, raise your left hand quickly against your right, and produce an audible clap (see Fig. 6-4b). Now—this is important—*continue* your own left hand's upward motion until it reaches the left side of your jaw, which you then cradle as you toss your head back to the right with the blow, giving the illusion of intense pain (see Fig. 6-4c).

An energetic punch requires a louder noise and a bigger response than a wimpy slap, so don't be afraid to lean or even stagger to the right as the aggressor's right hand passes you. As in all stage combat, *the defender's reaction sells the illusion to the audience.*

 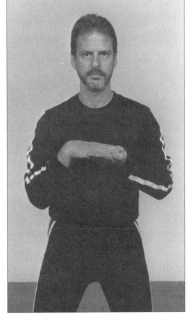 

6-4a.   *6-4b.*   *6-4c.*

- *The Shared Knap.* The knap in which the aggressor's action hand contacts the victim's concealed and passive hand is the most difficult to do really well. Chances for errors in timing abound and, because physical contact is actually made during the blow, minor injuries—from small cuts to jammed or broken fingers—are possible and must be avoided. To get a sense of this technique, adopt the victim's posture: back to the audience in a relaxed easy stance with arms dropped loosely at your sides. Now imagine that an aggressor, about to slap you, stands in front of you. He or she puts both hands on your shoulders and looks you in the eye—establishing distance, eye contact, and giving the audience a convincing sense of hostile intent.

  Now the aggressor preps for a back-hand face slap (to pass from your lower right to your upper left) by extending their right hand out to the left and, perhaps, leaning a bit in that direction. You react by looking at the hand—and the direction the threat is coming from. Here, in the shared knap, you *also* position your left hand, fingers up, palm facing to the left, a thumb's length away, in front of your chest. A quick way to find this position is to stick the tip of your outstretched thumb against the bottom of your sternum, or breastbone (see Fig. 6-5). Now imagine that the aggressor, seeing your reaction (ie: your hand in position), completes the action by passing the active hand from your lower right side to your upper left, contacting your palm with a satisfying *slap* as it passes. You toss your head quickly to the left and, using the impetus of the blow to help raise your right hand, cradle your jaw or cheek as if in pain.

  Naturally, neither hand involved in a shared knap should have jewelry, which can cut or bruise the skin. Some directors and actors extend this prohibition to anyone engaged in stage combat, whether knaps are used or not—a good way to eliminate any chance of this sort of injury.

- *Third-Party (Bystander) Knaps.* Another method is the bystander knap, where the sound is produced by another actor, extra on stage, or technician in the booth. Usually, this non-combatant is watching the fight intently, like the audience, and can use a slip-hand knap without being seen. This method has the greatest chance for an error in timing and should be used only when there are compelling reasons to avoid the other three, such as when the one-handed Captain Hook slaps a tied-up Peter Pan.

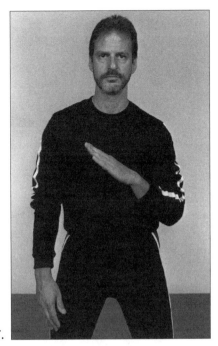

6-5.

Diane Keaton: "Allen, is that you?"

Woody Allen: "Yes."

Tony Roberts: "How'd it go, fella?"

Allen: "I got into a fight—"

Roberts: "What— you got into a fight?"

Allen: "Yes."

Roberts: "Who?"

Allen: "Some guys were getting rough with Julia, I hadda teach them a lesson."

Roberts: "Are you alright?"

Allen: "Yeah, I'm fine. I snapped my chin down on some guy's fist and hit another one in the knee with my nose."

Play It Again, Sam 1972

SLAPS AND PUNCHES   Three techniques are commonly used in unarmed stage fights: the roundhouse or John Wayne punch, the open-hand slap, and the back-hand slap.

- *The John Wayne Punch.* This crowd-pleaser looks just the way it sounds— and if you've never seen the Duke deliver it on-screen, go out and rent any John Wayne video today. The prep is an exaggerated draw-back, using the whole body like a coiled spring, that clearly telegraphs violent intent. To simulate delivering a John Wayne punch, place your hands on your imaginary partner's shoulders and establish eye contact and distance. Prep by stepping out to the side (not back) on your right foot into an easy right side drop stance and pull your right fist back to your cheek as if drawing a bow and arrow as you step. Let your left hand drift down to the bottom of your imaginary partner's sternum. This exaggerated prep lets the audience see the aggressor's "wind up" better, increasing the sense of threat.

When your imaginary partner has reacted by looking at your right fist, you are free to continue the action: passing your right hand quickly from your lower right to your upper left. *Do not* step forward with your punch, but leave your right foot out to the right. If the routine calls for an aggressor knap, your target is your own left hand. In this case, you should practice the quick unrolling of your fist prior to contact with your left hand, then re-forming it as it reappears in the audience's view.

The end-position for this punch is a nice, heroic, fully extended pose: your right arm stretching up and to the left from your extended right foot.

6-6a.

6-6b.

6-6c.

- *The Open-Hand Slap.* This basic slap is similar to the John Wayne punch but is delivered with an open hand. The preliminary position (hands on shoulders, eye contact) is the same. The first difference is that you step diagonally back on your right foot and extend your arm with your right palm open (see Fig. 6-6a). Instead of targeting the slap to pass under the chin of your imaginary partner (as in the John Wayne), the slap will pass upward next to your partner's left cheek (see Fig. 6-6b) and finish directly over the center of the head (see Fig. 6-6c). A slip-hand knap is effective for an open-hand slap since it is easy to execute and the victim of the slap controls the sound and the reaction.

- *The Back-Hand Slap.* A more aggressive variant of the above is the back-hand slap. It shows more hostility and aggressive intent since it leads with the knuckles. To get a feel for it, assume the ready position, hands on imaginary partner's shoulders, making eye contact, prep by dropping both hands and stepping diagonally back to the left and drawing your right hand back and down across your body to a point just past your left hip (see Fig. 6-7a). When your imaginary partner looks at your right hand, begin the action by drawing your flattened hand forward, knuckles first, toward the target: in a shared knap, your partner's open left palm on their chest (see Fig. 6-7b).

If a shared knap is planned, your target is the palm of your partner's left hand, strategically placed over the sternum. In this case, though, be sure you strike your partner's palm with the *fingers* of your right hand and not your knuckles, which can leave a bruise even at moderate speeds.

The end position is a fully open, theatrical stance as shown in Fig. 6-7c, lording it over your cowering partner, whose right hand now cradles a bruised and battered jaw.

6-7a.

6-7c.

6-7b.

OTHER TYPES OF SLAPS AND PUNCHES Stomach punches can be simulated by bringing the aggressor's fist to within an inch or so of the victim's stomach. This target area, above the navel and below the solar plexus, is well-protected by muscle or fat. The aggressor takes a small step back on his or her right foot and raises the right arm over the right shoulder, showing the audience the fist that is preparing to strike. The aggressor then brings the right elbow straight down to the right hip and, because the aggressor is only striking him- or herself, this technique can be executed with a lot of force. An illusion of extra power (and even better control) can be gained if the action arm is held still relative to the aggressor's body and the torso itself is pivoted to provide most of the illusion of the punching motion. With practice, the aggressor can place the knuckles at the point of attack (the victim's stomach) without leaving a gap between fist and stomach and never sending any force into the victim's body.

Stomach punches like these can be performed at any angle to the audience, though the upstage fist is best used, when viewed from the side. When viewed from the victim's back, a stomach punch can be especially effective as a set up for a John Wayne punch.

A two-handed punch looks devastating and can be effective despite one limitation: the *victim* must perform the knap. A two-handed uppercut to a bent-over victim should be targeted with the blow passing upstage and to the side, well clear of the victim's face.

An elbow to the stomach can be simulated by giving an exaggerated prep (raising the aggressor's action arm shoulder high) then bringing it crisply into the aggressor's own side, like the stomach punch above. This is seldom enough to provide a knap, though the victim's response—doubling over and exhaling or groaning loudly—often sells it without one.

A karate chop, like a punch, always targets the sternum from the front, or shoulder blades from the back, and never the neck, head, or spine. To perform one, prep by pulling the action hand back in Bruce Lee style—fingers together and pointed up, thumb to the side, and palm flattened into a deadly looking "knife edge"—then complete the action by *slapping* (not chopping) the removed target, and quickly withdrawing the hand into the same karate-style pose. The victim, whose back is to the audience, will react as if the vulnerable head, neck, or kidneys have actually been hit.

Multiple punches can be performed in any sequence; just make sure both partners complete one set of moves and re-establish eye contact before going on to the next.

KICKS Any purposive contact between an aggressor's foot and a victim's body is a kick. Always kick with the top or side of the foot, and never the toe (toes can break, get dislocated, or leave painful bruises on the victim). The energy of a powerful kick can be simulated by vigorously raising the thigh while leaving the lower part of the leg relaxed—then extending the foot gently toward the target area, contacting it with barely a tap then withdrawing it briskly. As with other unarmed blows, never target a vulnerable part of the body for a kick, but choose a nearby area that is naturally protected by bone or muscle.

- *Kicks to the groin.* These kicks read best when viewed from the side. Begin by putting your hands on the imaginary victim's shoulders, establishing distance and eye contact, then step back on your upstage leg. This is the prep for the kick. The victim should be in a relaxed, accessible, open-legged stance with the downstage leg forward and feet wide apart. The more the thighs are square to the body and parallel with the ground, the more accessible the stage combat target is, and consequently safer. When your partner has reacted to the prep by looking at your foot, bring your knee up smartly, then extend your lower leg so that the top of your instep, the soft part of your foot between the metatarsal arch and toes, lightly contacts the inside of the victim's downstage thigh (see Fig. 6-8a). The victim then responds appropriately, doubling over.

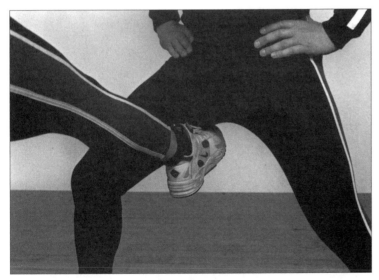

6-8a.

6-8b.

• *Kicks to the stomach.* Stomach kicks can be delivered to standing victims or, more easily, to victims already on their hands and knees. High kicks are discouraged because of the difficult stretch and the resulting loss of control. Don't try them unless you've had martial arts or dance training.

To kick victims when they're down on all fours, target the right side of the waist or the love handles, the band of muscle and fat just below the ribs and above the hips—see Fig. 6-8b. Step in next to the victim with the left foot. Don't get so close that you can't extend the right one. First raise the right knee smartly (see Fig. 6-9a), then extend the leg until the soft part of the right foot taps the target as in Fig. 6-9b, then pull the foot back energetically. The victim should respond by groaning and rolling to the left.

6-9a.

6-9b.

CHOKES Choking and strangling can be simulated convincingly without going near the throat. You can see this technique demonstrated often in films and on TV where a closeup of the struggling actors shows the aggressor's thumbs clearly on the victim's clavicle, or collar bone, and not near the windpipe at all. You'll also see the defender's hands on top of the attacker's—a clear sign that the victim, not the aggressor, is controlling all that thrashing.

- *Forward choke.* Face-to-face, the aggressor places both thumbs on the victim's clavicles with the fingers on the shoulders close to the neck (see Fig. 6-10a). The victim then covers the aggressor's hands (see Fig. 6-10b), or grabs the wrists, extending the chin forward and down, acting as if being strangled, even dropping onto the ground if that's necessary.
- *Choke from behind.* The aggressor approaches the victim from behind and extends an arm past the neck. The victim then places one hand on the inside of the elbow and the other hand over the outside of the elbow and pulls the elbow to his own neck. The aggressor then grabs his or her own wrist and *pushes*, rather than pulls, to keep any pressure from building up. The victim is now free to struggle and suffer in comfort.

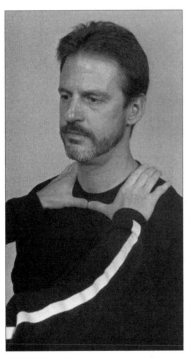

6-10a.

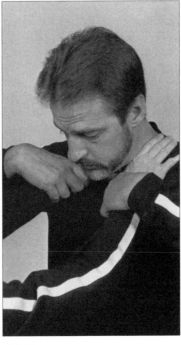

6-10b.

In his book, *The Sixteenth Century Italian Duel*, Dr. Frederick R. Bryson recounts the story of a sixteenth-century bully named Sergesto who spread the rumor that he had once defeated his old fencing master, the legendary swordsman, Pirro. At first Pirro took the boasts in stride, but later found it necessary to refute them, whereupon the younger man promptly challenged him to a duel on the field at Benevento.

The fight was well attended and had barely begun when Pirro saw that Sergesto's skill had improved little since his days at the master's school. Still, Sergesto was a strong fighter and Pirro knew he would have to employ all his experience to avoid having to kill the younger man.

The fight raged back and forth until Pirro finally managed to back Sergesto against the crowd where Pirro's son stood as a spectator.

"What's this?" Pirro roared with indignation as he glanced over Sergesto's shoulder. "Don't dishonor me, my son, by striking out with your dagger!"

When his opponent whirled to meet this new threat, Pirro spanked the back of Sergesto's knees with his blade, causing them to buckle. From there the old master had no trouble disarming his opponent and he ended the exhibition with a chokehold on his ungrateful pupil's throat.

R.L.

HAIR PULLS Hair pulls follow the same general procedure as chokes: The aggressor initiates the action but the victim controls it. To prepare for the hair pull, the aggressor displays an open hand (see Fig. 6-11a) which is thrust just beyond, and not onto, the victim's head (see Fig. 6-11b). The victim reacts by grabbing the aggressor's wrist, which cues the aggressor to make a fist. The victim then pulls the fist onto the hair and holds it in place (see Fig. 6-11c) while exhibiting a pained reaction—moving the head up and down, from side to side, or giving the appearance of being pulled backward and forward. Of course, the aggressor is just along for the ride, and has plenty of opportunity to look masterful.

The same technique can be used to simulate face scratching. The aggressor puts the heel of the hand on the victim's forehead or cheek and the victim immediately grabs it. The aggressor, keeping the fingers relaxed, now applies light pressure to remove the hand while the victim controls how close it is allowed to come to the face and the direction it is allowed to travel in. When the "scratching" is over, the victim throws the hand away (making it look as if the aggressor has finished and is pulling back) and clutches the "wound," completing the illusion.

THROWS, FALLS, AND ROLLS Like any complex tasks, throws and falls (and subsequent rolls) can be made easier by breaking them down into incremental parts—each of which has its own technique for increasing realism and safety. Before trying the basic sit-fall and several other related falls, it's important for you to grasp the three principles of going to the ground safely in a fight:

1. Use all the support you can get. A supported fall is one in which the aggressor helps the victim go to ground. Since virtually all fights are performed at very close quarters, this can be done more often than you'd think, making the fight safer and easier for beginning or older actor-combatants, without sacrificing the illusion of violence.

2. Distribute your weight evenly during a fall or roll. Concentrating your weight in one place is an invitation to pulled muscles, torn ligaments, and back injuries—even sprains and broken bones. Most of these injuries are caused by improper technique: actors responding with instincts rather than trained reactions. In reality, trained actor-combatants don't fall at all, they simply re-distribute their weight gradually while moving from a standing to a prone position.

3. Stay relaxed. Tension causes stressed muscles and ligaments to tear—it can even break bones. Muscles and joints that are relaxed have more give, and, like the limbs of a tree that bend with the breeze, resist damage. Remember to exhale when lowering yourself to the ground.

6-11a.

6-11b.

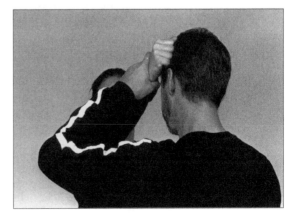

611c.

The use of breakable props in stage fights has been brought to near perfection by the motion picture industry but is rarely seen in the legitimate theatre. The most probable reason for this is the fact that breakable props create many problems on the stage and play-wrights realize this—hence few scenes are written for the use of breakable props. However, the prob-lems are not insur-mountable, and for stage violence, the best breakable props are the breakaway chair or small table. A scene in which a breaking bottle is used must be blocked far enough away from audience mem-bers so that the debris can be cleared off the floor between acts or scenes. Breaking a glass bottle over a person's head can be a brutal movement, but the audience's detachment will not be broken if the struck actor makes it clear by his reactions that the character being portrayed, and not the actor, was hurt.

Dr. John Callahan "Some Methods of Weaponless Stage Combat," Part V *The Fight Master*

- *The Sit-Fall.* As the name implies, this is a gradual way to lie down backwards, though it makes a very convincing backward fall to an audience. Don't try this technique on a hard surface until you've per-fected it on a tumbling or martial arts mat, soft grass, or other padded surface. Begin by facing away from the direction of the fall. Imagine that the aggressor has shoved your chest and you've got to fall back-ward. Simulate the reaction to a push to the chest by throwing your shoulders and arms forward and dropping your head forward. Step back as far as you comfortably can onto your stronger foot (see Fig. 6-12a). The leg you favor, or prefer, is the one that supports you best when you're off balance. Usually, it corresponds to the hand you use most often: right handed people tend to be "right legged." Let your head continue to drop forward and lower yourself onto your back-stretched heel, balancing yourself with your torso and extended arms (see Fig. 6-12b). *Don't* try to break your fall with your arms—it's a sure way to sprain a finger or wrist, or bruise an elbow.

  The trick here is to step back as far as possible, get low quickly by bending forward, then continue lowering yourself until your buttocks make contact with your backstretched heel. Continue the backward and downward motion by sliding off your heel onto the floor and unrol-ling, vertebra by vertebra, until you're completely flat (see Fig. 6-12c). Don't let your head or knuckles bang down; keep your chin tucked in and lower your head gently after your shoulders are on the floor.

  If you do the sit-fall properly, your arms, elbows and hands need never touch the floor. Performed at high speed by a competent actor-combatant, the sit-fall looks completely spontaneous and unrehearsed, when in fact, nothing has been left to chance.

- *Supported Sit-Fall.* If you can do the sit-fall comfortably alone, you'll find the supported sit-fall a cinch. The difference here is that your partner provides resistance, counterbalancing your weight for all or a portion of the fall. This is usually done by having the aggressor hold one or both of your arms; or, perhaps, by maintaining a simulated chokehold and straddling you while your hands grip your partner's arms, letting his or her back and legs take some of your weight as you lower yourself to the floor.

- *Forward Fall.* This might seem easier to do than the sit-fall because you're facing forward, but in reality it's more dangerous. Stand fac-ing in the direction you want to fall. Imagine that the aggressor has shoved you from the back. Throw your chest forward and down while taking a large step forward and slightly to the side with your stronger leg, bending deeply at the front knee, and continue to sink down as you travel forward. The movement is much like the passata sotto lunge. If stepping onto the right leg, take part of your weight with the heel of your left hand on the ground, then take some of that

6-12a.

6-12b.

6-12c.

weight on the right hand outstretched in front of you. With both hands now on the ground, turn your supporting leg out and ease your pelvis down, then your chest.

Like the sit-fall, the forward fall can look startlingly real when performed by a skilled actor. Marsha Mason takes a harrowing forward fall on a Manhattan street using exactly this technique after thugs steal her groceries in the Oscar-winning film, *The Goodbye Girl*. You can notice the protective gloves and leggings she wears in this scene.

GENERAL RULES FOR ACTOR-COMBATANTS

Like the play itself, the best-directed stage fight is no better—entertaining or compelling—than its actors. Good technique also keeps a routine safe; so proper training and diligent practice are essential. Here are some final pointers about unarmed combat to keep in mind when you start, or return to, partnered work with an instructor:

1. Once you've learned the basics, you'll be able to contribute new ideas to a fight—to follow where your character leads. But remember, the time to offer these ideas is in rehearsal, not in performance. *Never improvise a fight on stage!*
2. Stay focused in the moment. Complete each move, technique, or phrase before moving on to the next one. Always complete the illusion.
3. Don't forget to knap!
4. If you trust yourself to perform a technique or remember a sequence you'll be better able to trust your partner.
5. Keep your center of gravity low—let the energy flow back and forth from one partner to the other throughout the fight.
6. Don't forget to make eye contact between moves and before you prep.
7. Dress appropriately for rehearsals: no jewelry, hair clips, wrist watches, hard or sharp objects in your pockets. Wear protective gear if you need it—from special equipment like belly and knee pads to elastic wrist and ankle guards—both under your workout clothes and under your costume. If you need corrective lenses, wear contacts instead of glasses.
8. Be willing to take artistic risks and invest yourself fully in the move, the moment, and the part.
9. Don't forget to act and re-act!

THINGS FOR DIRECTORS TO KEEP IN MIND

Many productions can't afford a professional fight director or choreographer, so that responsibility often falls to the stage director, local fencing coach, or most experienced actor-combatant. This tendency—or temptation—is even more pronounced in productions that feature unarmed combat but no swordplay. If this responsibility falls to you, here are some things to remember:

1. Keep unarmed fights simple and straightforward—don't get carried away or put yourself or your actors in a situation where they'll have to perform beyond their competence. A few moves performed well are much better than a long routine that over-taxes the actors.

2. Stay ahead of the fight—envision the possibilities that could *follow* a move or sequence. Encourage your actors to share their feelings and ideas at any point, especially if you are involved as a performer and absorbed in your own character. After all, the fight is a mini-story within a story, and your actor-combatants are the story-tellers. Let the world of the play, including its time and place, guide the selection of techniques and let the emotions and traits of the characters help shape the fight.

3. Use the space and the environment to good advantage. If the stage offers multiple levels, platforms, obstacles, and props that could be used in the fight and to help tell the story, define the characters, or make the fight more exciting, don't be afraid to exploit them.

4. Make sure the actor-combatants have adequate dress rehearsals on stage (not just in the gym) so that they feel comfortable during the fight.

5. Watch for problems in logistics that might complicate or ruin a fight, such as awkward costumes or accessories; leather soles on a slick raked wooden floor; breakaway props that must be repaired or replaced after each performance and consequently may not be there the next time, and the possibility of weapons breaking.

6. Give training sessions in basic stage-fighting skills before introducing choreography.

7. Help actor-combatants "act the fight" during slow-motion run throughs. Don't hesitate to sacrifice action for acting if a performer is having trouble doing both.

8. Rehearse the routine for two hours daily in order to hone skills and sharpen the fight.

9. Unless you're prepared to do these things yourself, appoint a fight captain from the cast or crew to: a/ oversee the care and security of any fight-related props and weapons, both before and between performances, b/ monitor the actor-combatants in slow-motion run-throughs before scene rehearsals, c/ make sure an adequate first-aid kit (including an ice pack) is on hand for all rehearsals and performances.

In the next chapter, we'll extend your growing ability to coordinate body and brain into the realm of footwork—the foundation of all swordplay.

In unarmed combat, as with weapon work, success depends upon team-work and having complete confidence in your "opponent"—which as always can only be achieved by dedicated rehearsal. Moves must be worked out with exactly the same attention paid to detail, precision, distance, rhythm and timing. When working without weapons, it should also not be thought that there is less potential danger. In fact, in my experience, there can be more possible hazard in unarmed combat, because the actors assume there to be less danger, sometimes producing a cavalier attitude and this can lead to problems.

William Hobbs
Fight Direction for Stage and Screen

7

SWORDFIGHTING FOOTWORK

A certain eighteenth century English lord was said to be so clumsy that he couldn't walk down the hall of his ancestral castle without bumping into both walls. Justifiably concerned about his prospects in a duel, he hired a noted fencing master to be his private tutor.

The lord practiced diligently but eventually grew bored with his teacher's "preoccupation" with fundamentals—passes, advances, retreats, and lunges—and dismissed the swordmaster, with thanks.

"Of course, I shall commend your services to all my friends," the lord said pleasantly on parting.

"Don't trouble yourself on my account," the fencing master muttered, climbing into his carriage. "In fact, I would take it as a particular favor if your lordship would never tell anyone from whom he learned his footwork."

Anonymous

7-1. An example of the Coup De Jarnac as performed in the 1700's. (Art by Rowlandson.)

Good footwork is the foundation of good swordplay. In this chapter, you'll learn:

- How footwork changed over time to reflect new weapons and sword-fighting styles
- How good footwork helps keep stage combat safe
- Basic footwork for all swordfighting periods: passes, double passes, fleches advances, retreats, lunges, and recoveries
- How to assemble basic movements into a variety of challenging footwork drills

Good footwork is fundamental to the martial arts, and theatrical swashbuckling is no exception. Your feet carry you forward in attack and to safety in defense. In a real swordfight, your first slip might be your last, so perfecting hand-foot coordination was much more than a question of style. Today in performance, good footwork helps you and your partner keep the proper distance from each other. It can make a stage fight thrilling and safe, or it can put you, your partner, and the show at risk.

In this chapter, we'll discuss footwork for what it is: the foundation of all your future success in swashbuckling.

PUTTING SWORDPLAY ON A SOUND FOOTING

Like ballet dancers who spend long hours at the barre, you should practice basic swordfighting footwork until it becomes second nature. Your footwork in a specific stage fight will be mostly choreographed, and your ability to perform it virtually without thinking will free you to concentrate on sword handling and acting—what the audience came to see.

FOOTWORK AND PERFORMANCE You already know the safe distance for a partnered routine: the longest sword/arm combination held out at maximum extension, plus the width of your partner's fist held in front of the chest. The basic task of partnered swordplay is to manage this safe distance throughout the fight, moving nearer or farther away only as the choreography dictates. Since the defender (the partner "on defense" at a particular moment) controls the action and pace of the routine, attackers should think of themselves as being pulled around by a giant magnet attached to the defender's belt buckle. When the defender retreats, the attacker advances. When the defender moves forward, the attacker moves back—anything that's required to maintain a safe distance. This is different from traditional movements of "leader and follower" in ballroom dancing, in which the man leads at all times, but it's essential to safe stage combat.

You can also think of this managed space as a volume of air that (with only a few planned exceptions—such as closure for a punch or kick) stays fairly constant during a fight. The task of the performers is to move that fixed volume of air around the stage, keeping it inviolate, like their own box of safety (as explained in Chapter 8). Formal coordination between the footsteps of the defender and the footsteps of the attacker is required; and this is where swordfighting footwork comes in.

In real duels, basic footwork was used most often to *change* the distance between combatants: to narrow the gap in attack and increase it in defense. In stage combat, those identical moves are used more often to keep that distance constant: when one partner passes forward, the other passes back; one advances, the other retreats, and so on. As a result, you should strive during solo footwork drills (and in later sword practice) to visualize this

They in their rapier-fight stand upon so manie intricate tricks, that in all the course of a man's life it shall be hard to learne them, and if they misse in doing the least of them in their fight, they are in danger of death.

This is the manner of the Spanish fight: they stand as brave as they can with their bodies straight upright, narrow spaced, with their feet continually moving, as if they were in a dance, holding forth their arms and rapiers verie straight against the faces or bodies of their enemies: and this is the only way to accomplish that kind of fight. . . running and standing in Rapier fights, the runner hath the advantage.

George Silver
Paradoxes of Defence
1599

shared space so that preserving it will be second nature by the time you begin partnered work with an instructor.

FOOTWORK AND PHYSICAL CONDITION Many novices find footwork drills to be the most tiring of all swashbuckling training. Certainly, dancers and athletes used to spending long hours on their feet have an advantage here, but swordfighting footwork is sufficiently different from most kinds of sports and performing arts that even these veterans might find themselves challenged. Unless you have a medical reason to avoid them, give these fundamental skill- and stamina-building exercises a chance to work. Soreness in leg muscles can be reduced by adequate stretching and will go away in time. Your aerobic capacity will improve, too, if you drill on a regular basis.

BASIC SWORDFIGHTING FOOTWORK

Unless the instructions below tell you otherwise, begin and end each movement with the en garde stance (see Fig. 7-2) you learned earlier in this book. For now, leave your sword alone and simulate holding a rapier as described in Part I.

7-2.

Muhammad Ali's "float like a butterfly" was all about dynamic footwork to confuse, misdirect and thwart any attack made at him while still having the power to direct an attack at his adversary.

Payson H. Burt
Of Paces

PASS FORWARD In the long reign of edged weapons, the power of thrusts and cuts was amplified by the use of the legs. In this respect, a pass forward is simply a step, but it's not like walking. The lateral distance between the feet is strictly maintained (see Fig. 7-3a) and the stationary foot merely pivots and does not "push off," as it would to create the momentum to walk. To perform it, step forward naturally, but keep your CG low (maintaining that springy horse stance) with your hips aligned in the direction of the movement. Don't let your hips face to the right when passing the left foot forward, or face to the left when passing on the right (see Fig. 7-3b). When the pass is completed, both feet should be flat on the ground with the body in perfect balance, ready to move in any direction.

If you make your pass from the basic en garde position (right foot forward), your new foot position will be its mirror image—with your left foot now in front. Notice that your left hand is now just about parallel to your sword hand. This is perfectly acceptable for a left-footed en garde, where the free hand may be used for grappling or defending against an attack, and can be either empty or holding a dagger, cloak, shield, or other defensive weapon.

7-3a.

7-3b.

PASS TO THE REAR Now, from your left-footed en garde stance (see Fig. 7-4a), simply perform the pass in reverse: step back *exactly* the way you came, keeping your center low, hips straight, and pivot on the ball of your stationary right foot. You have just performed a backward pass, or pass to the rear (see Fig. 7-4b). From your new position (the standard en garde with the right foot forward) pass to the rear again, pivoting this time on your left foot. You should now be in the same position from which you started this move: the left-footed en garde.

Practice these moves, pass forward and pass to the rear, a few times before going on to the next section.

7-4a.

7-4b.

DOUBLE PASSES Now that passes from each foot, both forward and to the rear, feel comfortable, try combining them. This is a good way to cover ground quickly in a swordfight. A double pass is essentially two passes in the same direction, except that the first step is more like a "grape vine" step: as you move into the second step, your hips are already in the final position (see Figs. 7-5a through 7-5c). Your feet will end up in exactly the same relative position as when you started.

Remember, even though you're passing twice, keep your legs bent and springy (in that wide-track stance), your center low, and your hips facing forward. Your head shouldn't bob up and down, but it should move smoothly—a glass of water or a book balanced on your head should stay in place during the entire motion.

7-5a.

7-5b.

7-5c.

FLECHE A fleche (pronounced "flesh," French for arrow) is an energetic, rapid double pass with the first step (either forward or back) being extended slightly while the second is used to stop and stabilize your body in the original en garde position. In real fights as well as stage combat, the first "leaping pass" is useful to jump over small obstacles (such as slain bodies), intimidate an opponent by an aggressive assault, or, if made to the rear, to escape a surprise attack.

To fleche forward from the basic en garde stance, throw your left foot forward vigorously, raising the toes (see Fig. 7-6b). As it comes down, pass the right leg forward to regain the basic en garde stance (see Fig. 7-6c). Although your head will rise a bit when you take that first big step, try to keep your center low throughout.

7-6a.

7-6b.

7-6c.

Now try a fleche to the rear. Extend your right leg back and push off vigorously from your left (see Fig. 7-7b). As your right foot comes down, pass back on the left foot to stop your momentum and resume the basic en garde stance (see Fig. 7-7c). Again, try to stay low, with hips, arms, and eyes all focused to the front.

After you've practiced these awhile, you'll notice that fleches have their own unique cadence, quite different from double passes. If the rhythm of a double pass is two even beats (that is, your feet produce two evenly spaced sounds as they land, one after another), the rhythm of a fleche is a short pause followed by two quick beats—the leap followed immediately by both feet assuming the original en garde stance.

Practice single passes, double passes, and fleches in both directions awhile before going on to the next movement.

7-7c.

7-7b.

7-7a.

ADVANCES The advance was a latecomer to the swordfighting scene. It was quicker than the pass because it did not require moving the rear foot such a long distance, and so it became an instant favorite in thrust-oriented rapier duels. Along with the lunge, it was the preferred way to attack with smallswords. Its modern legacy is the rapid heel-to-heel attack used by competitive fencers.

To perform an advance from the basic right foot forward en garde stance, step forward on the right foot (see Fig 7-8b), landing heel-toe, then pick the back foot up and resume the en garde position (see Fig. 7-8c). When you're finished, the toe of the rear foot and the heel of the front foot should be between twelve and eighteen inches apart—the same lateral distance used in the basic en garde stance, as if you were straddling a railroad track). Be sure to keep your hips and chest turned forward (that is, don't go into the "fencer's profile") and keep your center low throughout—don't dip as you extend that leading foot. The distance advanced should be appropriate for that moment of the fight. Remember you are advancing toward the enemy's blade, so don't be too aggressive or over-extend.

From this position, pass forward (into the left-footed en garde) and try an advance on the "weak" side. Since most people are right handed, which means "right legged," too, a left-footed advance may feel awkward. The important thing here, regardless of which leg leads, is *balance*. Don't over-commit yourself to the advance, leaving your weight mostly on your front leg when you stop. Cover ground by reaching out with that leading leg, not by throwing your center too far forward.

Practice strong- and weak-side advances awhile before moving on to the next section.

7-8a.

7-8b.

7-8c.

RETREATS A retreat is an advance in reverse. Extend the back leg to gain distance from your opponent, landing toe-heel (see Fig. 7-9b), then draw the front leg back and resume the en garde stance (see Fig. 7-9c). Just as the advance is quicker than a pass forward, the retreat is faster than a pass to the rear. Again, make the size of the retreat proportional to the threat at that moment of the fight.

Practice both strong- and weak-side retreats and advances awhile before continuing on to the next section.

7-9a.

7-9b.

7-9c.

LUNGES A lunge begins like an advance, but the back foot stays in place. This doesn't mean, however, that it will cover any less ground; in fact, it covers more. In the days of dueling, a very deep lunge (the passata sotto as you practiced in the triangle stance stretches) left a fighter so extended that the free hand was needed on the ground to keep from falling over. A more important distinction between an advance and a lunge is that the lunge is always accompanied by a thrust. In a real duel it was a killing attack, not a maneuver to gain ground.

To practice the forward lunge from the basic en garde position (see Fig. 7-10a), bring your sword arm back, right hand in pronation and approximately level with the hips—this is the prep for a thrust (see Fig. 7-10b), extend your right hand forward as far as you can—the completion of the thrust (see Fig. 7-10c), then step way out on your right foot, allowing your right knee to bend as your weight sinks down behind it (see Fig. 7-10d). Throw your left hand back for balance and to assure maximum extension. Keep your body upright. Be sure to keep the heel of your left foot on the ground, too, as you lunge, as this prevents you from over-extending—throwing yourself off balance and, perhaps, injuring your knee. Just think of distance (the length of the lunge) and height (how far you sink down) as always going together: the farther you lunge, the deeper you must sink to stay balanced. In no case, however, should the right knee hyper-extend, going past the toes, or you will put undue stress on your knee.

There is no "weak-side" counterpart to the right-footed lunge. A right-handed thrust with the left foot forward just doesn't make sense, although some rapier & dagger techniques call for weak-sided lunges, because in those instances the left hand, too, is armed and dangerous.

Words such as coupé, disengage, lunge and beat are all words borrowed by ballet from sword-fighting. . . . The Italian Catherine de Medici (when Queen of France) imported fencing masters from Italy to help develop fencing in France. As part of this development, fencing masters had to document a methodical classification of attacks and parries. This lead to the development of choreography and is why fencing was referred to as a "Deadly Dance."
James R. Gleich
"Fencing vs. Ballet: 'To the Point'—Modern Dualism"
The Fight Master

7-10a. *En Garde.*

7-10b. *Preparation.*

7-10c. *Extension.*

7-10d. *Lunge.*

REVERSE LUNGE This doesn't mean thrusting backward; it simply means that instead of throwing your leading leg forward to achieve the end position, you throw your trailing leg further back. A reverse lunge is one of those "fence tricks" decried by early theorists who thought swordfights should be straightforward, stand-up affairs. As a subtle form of offense hidden in what appeared to be a defensive move, the reverse lunge turned out to be an excellent way to skewer an over-aggressive opponent. The passata sotto frequently took the form of a reverse lunge where the defender lunged under the extended arm of the attacker; also known as a stop thrust.

To perform the reverse lunge from the basic en garde position (see Fig. 7-11a), prep and extend your sword arm as described above (see Figs. 7-11a and b), then throw your left leg back, planting your heel firmly, while sinking down behind a deeply bent right knee. You should end up in the same position as a forward lunge only you will have moved your center down and back instead of forward and downward (see Fig. 7-11d). You may or may not extend your left arm back as you did in the forward lunge since balance here, while still important, is easier to keep. Besides, originating as a defensive move, it's just as natural and realistic for a fighter to keep that left arm forward in case the opponent's blade gets through.

RECOVERY FROM A LUNGE As you've undoubtedly noticed, returning to en garde from a lunge can be a little awkward, especially if the lunge was deep. At the Academy of the Sword, we teach both forward and backward recoveries, since choreography can require either an offensive or defensive posture after a lunge.

To recover forward, swing the left hand (particularly if it has been extended to the rear) upward and forward. Move the rear foot forward and rise to the basic en garde stance, leaving the front foot in place throughout the movement. Allow the movement to come from your center as you did in recovering from the triangle stance stretching exercise.

To recover to the rear (employed often after a reverse lunge), push off with the leading (right) foot and, as you rise, bring the right foot back to the basic en garde stance, leaving the left foot in place throughout.

Practice lunges and reverse lunges, with both forward and rearward recoveries, awhile, before moving on to the next section.

Late sixteenth century Italian swordmaster Ridolfo Capo Ferro in his "Great Simulacrum of the Use of the Sword" defines two new measures (the distance between the point of the sword and the adversary's body): "Misura Larga," when it is only possible to hit the enemy by lunging and "misura stretta" when this can be done by merely pressing the body forward. He also says the length of the sword "should be as long as the arm twice." Capo Ferro is very in favor of the straight line; he looked upon "passing" as a loss of time which might be avoided by closing the measure before lunging. But it is his contemporary, Nicoletto Giganti, who was the first to clearly define the "lunge."

Egerton Castle
Schools and Masters of Fence

7-11a. En Garde.

7-11b. Preparation.

7-11c. Extension.

7-11d. Reverse Lunge.

DESIGNING CUSTOM FOOTWORK DRILLS

Practice makes perfect, and few things pay off more quickly in swordplay than mastering basic footwork. When foot and body placement, including balance, are under control at any given moment, sword cuts, thrusts, and parries—and the acting that goes with them—become much easier.

To perfect your ability to maneuver effortlessly in a swordfight, try assembling the elements of footwork into custom footwork drills—the variety, and challenge, is virtually endless. Here's a sample to get you started.

Perform the following in exactly this sequence, depending on the space available, and pause in the en garde position briefly at the end of each movement:

1. En garde.
2. Pass forward (five times).
3. Pass to the rear (five times).
4. Double pass forward (three times).
5. Double pass to the rear (three times).
6. Fleche forward (two times).
7. Fleche to the rear (two times).
8. Advance (six times).
9. Retreat (six times).
10. Double pass forward, advance (three times).
11. Double pass to the rear, retreat (three times).
12. Fleche forward, advance, pass to the rear (two times).
13. Fleche to the rear, retreat, pass forward (two times).
14. Double pass forward, advance, lunge, recover forward (three times).
15. Double pass to the rear, retreat, reverse lunge, recover back (three times).

As you can see, with two directions and five basic movements, the combinations and sequences are virtually endless. Arrange and change your own drills to keep the challenge fresh, or execute specific moves at random to keep your reflexes sharp. Even after you've achieved competency with a sword, practice footwork (armed or unarmed) often as a swordfighting ritual—a reminder that, no matter how good you become, there is always room for improvement.

John Florio said of Italian Fencing Master, Vincentio Saviolo: "There is no man that teacheth with more dexterity and nimbleness. He hath skill in every kind of weapon. He dances very well both galliard and pavane, he vaults most nimbly and capers very loftily."

J.D. Martinez
"A Tale of Jealousy, Swordplay, and a Certain Italian"
The Fight Master

8

DEFENSIVE RAPIER FORMS

At the start of his lessons, a student asked his swordmaster, "Where is the best place to be in a swordfight?" The veteran answered, "Anywhere else will do."
Anonymous

8-1. *Leonard Whiting as Romeo and Michael York as Tybalt fight it out in the town square in Zefferelli's "Romeo and Juliet." Fight Director: William Hobbs. (The Everett Collection.)*

This chapter explores the basic principles of sword defense. After completing it, you'll:
- Know how body and blade work together to defend against sword attacks
- Be able to perform the nine basic parries and their variants
- Perform a complete defensive sword form including footwork
- See how to begin a rapier fight from a variety of historical wards and stances

Most people associate the term "fencing" with the entire realm of swordplay, although it originally meant *the art of defense*: using the blade as a substitute for armor.

SWORDPLAY BEGINS WITH DEFENSE

Historically, even skilled swordfighters were careful about picking fights. Most duels ended one of three ways, two of which were bad:
1. You were killed or wounded
2. You and your opponent wounded each other, sometimes fatally
3. You escaped injury and wounded or killed your opponent

Because of this, medieval tournaments gradually became more defensive or fencing-oriented. Rules were devised that rewarded good swordplay, especially tactics that foiled, or spoiled, an opponent's attack. When gunpowder completed the obsolescence of plate armor, defensive swordplay took on an even more important role. On the battlefield as in the street, less armor or protective clothing (such as the heavily padded garments worn in the Renaissance and in Elizabethan times) meant more dependence on the blade for protection. By the eighteenth and early nineteenth centuries, duels were fought essentially in street clothes.

To the actor-combatant or fight director, this increasing reliance on defense has a big impact on how fights are performed today. Combat involving medieval broadswords and early rapiers should still be very physical and aggressive, as the victory often went to the strongest. Duels portraying a later period should emphasize the increased reliance on technique.

THE PHILOSOPHY OF DEFENSE

The shift in swordfighting strategy from all-out attack to skillful defense was encouraged by a parallel development in European culture. By the late Middle Ages, alchemists were searching for the philosopher's stone—a substance that would turn the baser metals into gold. Such a substance never existed, but the systematic methods developed for that search led not only to the scientific method and modern chemistry, but to a general belief that any goal could be achieved given enough thought and experimentation.

The philosopher's stone of early swordmasters was the idea that one perfect form of attack could be devised that would kill any opponent. Indeed, any fencing school worth its salt advertised a "botta segreta"—an attack for which there was no possible form of defense (except, perhaps, that same master's so-called "universal parry"), to be revealed only to paying students for a great price. It came with a money-back guarantee, even if the refund had to be paid to their heirs.

Secret forms varied from school to school and their details are less important than the simple fact that they existed. Sometimes actors and directors attribute a character's willingness to fight solely to passion, pride, or some other dramatic reason that has nothing to do with the practical expectation of winning. This botta segreta factor—the simple and erroneous idea that a particular school had the best of all possible methods—was one of the things that put the swagger into swashbuckling and encouraged even beginners to engage in duels they would have otherwise avoided.

A BOTTA SEGRETA FOR SAFE, EFFECTIVE THEATRICAL SWORDPLAY

One mental trick we employ at the Academy of the Sword, is the "box of safety." Although we don't advertise it as a surefire way to win applause or eliminate all chances of accident, it *is* the best way we know to keep both actor-combatants as safe as possible while they concentrate on the action and their acting.

8-2.

MEASURING THE BOX OF SAFETY Hold your arms straight out in front of you, chest high, and point your fingers in toward each other. Now imagine that the rectangular volume of air enclosed by your body, arms, and hands extends from the floor to a foot or so above your head (see Fig. 8-2). As a defender, your job is to make sure the aggressor's weapon (or hands or feet or anything else that could harm you) never penetrates this space. In a real swordfight, a blow that failed to enter the box would never land on you. In stage combat, the same principle applies—although the goal of *both* partners is to keep the box clear, except for those instances when the choreography calls for closer contact.

Marozzo (fencing master, 1536) accordingly binds his scholars upon a cross hilt, "as it were God's Holy Cross" never to take part against the master, and also never to teach any other person without his permission the secrets he is about to impart.

Egerton Castle
Schools and Masters of Fence

POINT AWARENESS Perhaps the biggest danger in most stage fights comes from the point of the sword. While an accidental cut from a dull stage-combat rapier can scrape the skin, raise a welt, or leave a bruise, a puncture (always more serious than a cut) can severely damage the eyes or another part of the body. Because this very real danger is one we share with historical swordfighters, we'll borrow another practical technique from their book, a mental trick called "point awareness."

Point awareness means that you know both consciously and intuitively and at all times where the point of your sword—and the point of your partner's sword—is located in the space around you. This subtle but important skill is developed by a combination of direct observation, peripheral vision, proprioception (the body's own knowledge of its position, including the position of the limbs), and other knowledge of sword-arm dynamics gained through experience. In real swordfights, point awareness allowed combatants to accurately evade or parry with lightning speed, as well as avoid wounds from weapons being wielded around them in a melee. In stage combat, this same skill is used to avoid injury to yourself, your partner, and others sharing the stage.

You'll begin developing this swashbuckler's sixth sense as you explore how the sword is used to keep the walls of the box of safety clear, beginning with the basic parries.

USING THE BLADE AS A SHIELD

Real swordfighters learned quickly that, if a shield or buckler was unavailable, the best way to avoid a cut or thrust was simply to step out of the way—to evade it by ducking, jumping back, twisting away, or otherwise removing the targeted part of the body from the path of the blade. This also reduced the chances of a missed parry or broken blade—both possibilities in real combat.

However, as shields, bucklers, and defensive armor became less practical or went out of fashion, sword parries became more important. Indeed, many early swordmasters spent their entire careers searching for the universal parry—a single move that would block any form of attack. Capo Ferro (in the conclusion to his *Great Simulacrum of the Use of the Sword*) offers a "universal" parry, especially useful, he says, in a melee or after dark. It is a sweeping parry beginning from the right shoulder and traveling to the right hip, traveling past the left shoulder, left hip, and clearing all points in between.

Through generations of trial and error, a number of standard parries were developed and accepted as the most efficient ways to stop cuts and thrusts aimed at various parts of the body. In this book, we'll use nine basic parries, with variations on several, all based on historical practice (see Figs. 8-3a through 8-3i, in order: parry 1, or prime: parry 2, parry 3, parry 4, parry 5, parry 5A, [sometimes called parry 9] parry 6, parry 7, and parry 8). In moving toward the end position of each parry, you must remember to use the forte of your blade to "sweep out" the box of safety: catching any sword that might have penetrated it and moving it *away* from the target area.

8-3a. Parry 1.

8-3b. Parry 2.

8-3c. Parry 3.

8-3d. Parry 4.

8-3e. Parry 5.

WARNING:

Sword stances, movements, exercises and drills demand adequate clearance between the student and objects to the front, rear, sides, and overhead. Indoors, never swing a sword near an object you're not prepared to see broken. Indoors or out, never swing a sword close to people or animals. Never attempt partnered swordplay without the instruction and supervision of a qualified teacher.

8-3f. Parry 5A.

8-3g. Parry 6.

8-3h. Parry 7.

8-3i. Parry 8.

WHICH PARRY SHOULD I USE? The sequence of parries named above gives you practice in moving smoothly between parries that guard the *high line* (arm, shoulder, and chest on either side); the *low line* (abdomen, hips and thighs on either side); and vertical cuts to the head, which require two variations on basic high line parries. This training sequence may seem unrealistic (you'll make many defensive moves in succession in order to learn proper technique and build up muscle-memory) but stick with it. In a stage fight, the choreography will be much more varied and require you to switch often between attack and defense. Your ability to do this—and act at the same time—will depend largely on how well you master these early drills.

WHAT MAKES A GOOD SWASHBUCKLING PARRY? In real swordfights, a good parry was anything that worked. In the fashionable fencing schools of the fifteenth and sixteenth centuries, where theory was held in as high esteem as practice, students were praised for mastering form, even if that form never quite proved itself in combat. One self-described "English gentleman," George Silver, criticized his countrymen's enchantment with the florid "schoole trickes and jugling gambolds," of the Italian rapier masters in his 1599 book, *Paradoxes of Defence*, where he boasts: "Bring me to a Fencer, I will bring him out of his fence trickes with good downe right blowes!"

Silver was a passionate advocate of what we might call the "English brawling" style of swordfight, where both defensive and offensive moves were simple, straightforward and powerful—emphasizing the cut of the broadsword over the thrust of the slimmed-down, stretched-out continental weapons. His advice undoubtedly worked well in the street, where most fights were between half-trained drunkards who promptly forgot their swordmaster's formulas once tempers flared and steel began to ring.

We make this point early to remind you that: a/ any system of parries is arbitrary—its value lies mainly as a point of departure for learning swordhandling skills, and; b/ you will be called upon in the course of your career to mimic many styles of fighting—some of which may contradict the elegant moves so loved by modern fencers. In these cases, remember stage combat's prime directive: do justice to the style that best applies to your character, your production, and the needs of a particular fight.

THE NINE BASIC PARRIES

In real swordfights, good parries were characterized by economy of motion. A skilled swordfighter could tie a foot-long string from belt to wrist and make all the basic parries (except the overhead variants) without breaking the string. On stage, such control would be appropriate only to the most expert fighter—and then, only in situations where that character felt little threat. Usually, you'll want to convey both good swordsmanship *and* the drama appropriate to a life and death struggle.

Those who are good in defense are as invisible as the lowest underground.

Those who are capable of good defense will win when they are ready to attack.

Sun Zi, translated by Leong Weng Kam
The Art of War

A curious point about all books of fence written during the sixteenth century is that although the word "parry" is continually used, not a single parry is ever defined. The principle on which the masters of that period founded their practice, was evidently that all attacks, if they could not be warded off by a buckler, a cloak, or a dagger, were to be met by a counterattack, or avoided by a displacement of the body.

Egerton Castle
Schools and Masters of Fence

The main thing to remember about any stage parry is to hold the sword well out in front of you on the appropriate "wall" of the box of safety, receiving the attacking blade on the true, or cutting edge of your own. Although historically, a couple of special-use parries involved the false, or back edge of the blade, these were considered awkward for a rapier and, according to the sixteenth century swordmaster de Grassi, dangerously weak. Never parry with the sword held out stiffly at arm's length with your elbow locked, since this makes your sword hard to control and easy for an attacker to knock away. Instead, keep the parry at a comfortable distance (perhaps a foot or so) from your body, with the blade angled forward at about forty-five degrees, elbow slightly bent, ready to cushion the shock.

Obviously, a blade held too close to one part of the body may leave some other part exposed. Less obvious is the danger of making a parry with the sword held too far back from the attacker, where some part of your body (ahead of your blade) may have entered the box of safety. In stage combat, parries like these encourage some attackers to over-extend in an effort to strike steel-on-steel, making the attack unbalanced. An over-extended, out-of-balance attack can easily put the tip of the attacker's sword in distance, threatening contact with your body, or injure the attacker through a pulled muscle or even a fall. Either way, your ability to position a parry properly and consistently will be one measure of your sword-handling competence. Unless your routine calls for an amateurish, comic, or desperate defense, make your parries in a relaxed, controlled manner.

CATEGORIES OF PARRIES

Like fencers, most stage combat teachers define parries in terms of their end positions—that is, the arm, hand, and sword positions you assume when the parry is finished. This is useful as far as it goes, but end position is only half the story. Since a parry is also a *movement to intercept* the attacker's blade at a certain point in space, it helps to note the path the sword must take to reach its end position. The categories used to describe these paths of movement are direct, semicircular, or circular. The path depends on the distance the defender's blade must travel to reach its destination. The shorter the distance, the more efficient the parry. For example:

DIRECT PARRY Moves the sword quickly between the left and right sides of the body along the high line (above the waist) or low line (below the waist), but never between the two. This makes a direct parry the fastest and most efficient of all.

SEMI-CIRCULAR PARRY Shifts the blade between the high and low lines, and is named for the half-circle, or 180-degree arc, the blade travels. Because of this extra distance, a semi-circular parry is less efficient and takes longer than a direct parry. Skilled attackers often vary their attacks between high- and low-line targets precisely for this reason.

The dagger in combination with the sword is a different weapon in combat. We have seen that in the rapier fight it was used as the principal weapon of defense, and that it also had attacking possibilities. Silver, admittedly, thought it "an imperfect ward," preferring the buckler to it, but he had no doubt about its lethal possibilities. When two rapiers are in engagement, he says, "it is impossible to uncrosse, or get out, or to avoid stabbes of the Daggers. And this hath falne out manie times amongst valiant men at those weapons." The stab with the dagger is lethal, "wherein there lieth no defense."

Arthur Wise
The Art and History of Personal Combat

CIRCULAR PARRY Sometimes called counter-parry, this is one in which the blade tip inscribes a full circle from the beginning of the move to its end position. This is the least efficient of all parries, but it has its uses. In a real swordfight, a circular parry had a good chance of catching the attacker's blade at least somewhere, although it may not have been the best parry for the situation and could even have guided the attacker's sword toward the target, rather than away from it, if the defender misjudged the attack. Circular parries were also used when parries made directly didn't connect, and had to be repeated, or against simultaneous attacks from multiple opponents. In stage combat, a circular parry (sometimes called "the actor's parry") is lovely to look at (lots of flashing steel) and conveys great energy. It's used often by choreographers to show that a defender has been caught by surprise, been deceived, or has had an attack interrupted and must now scramble to defend him- or herself.

"All movements—instead of being as small as possible, as in competitive fencing —must be large, but nevertheless correct. Magnified is the word. The routine should contain the most spectacular attacks and parries it is possible to execute while remaining logical to the situation. In other words, the duel should be a fight, not a fencing exhibition, and should disregard, at times, classically correct guards and lunges. The attitudes arising naturally out of the fighting instinct should predominate. When this occurs the whole performance will leave the impression of strength, skill, and manly grace."

(Attributed to Fred Cavens, Fight Choreographer of Jose Ferrer's *Cyrano de Bergerac*)

Jeffrey Richards *The Swordsmen of the Silver Screen*

8-4a.

8-4b.

PARRY 1, OR PRIME Pronounced "preem" after the French, the end position has the hilt held on the left edge of the box of safety, tip down, in pronation (knuckles up), with the sword's true, or cutting, edge on the outside, ready to receive a cut or deflect a thrust aimed along the low line to the defender's left leg, hip, or left side of the abdomen. This parry was named "number one" because it was considered the first defensive move a fighter could make when attacked and was caught in the process of drawing the sword from its scabbard (see Fig. 8-4b).

8-5a.   8-5b.

From the basic en garde position, reaching prime requires a semicircular blade motion beginning with an outward and downward roll of the blade before sweeping the box of safety from right to left along the low line. As you'll see, this rather awkward way to guard the body's lower left quadrant leaves the defender with few practical options for a counterattack. Another parry, useful for thrusting ripostes (counter-attacks), was developed later for this area (see parry 7).

PARRY 2, OR SECONDE From prime, it is a short, direct parry along the low line to seconde. In the end position of parry 2, the hand is in pronation, tip down with the true edge out, hilt held at about the level of the stomach, on the right edge of the box of safety, ready to deflect a low-line cut or thrust to the defender's right leg, hip, or right side of the abdomen (see Fig. 8-5b). A sword moved from prime to seconde "sweeps out" the box of safety from left to right along the low line.

PARRY 3, OR TIERCE From parry 2, the next most efficient parry is a semicircular parry to parry 3 which guards the right arm, shoulder, and right half of the chest against a cut or thrust along the high line. Simply move your blade clockwise (inward, then upward—clearing the box of safety from left to right) keeping your sword hand in pronation, until the tip points up and slightly leftward, true edge facing out (see Fig. 8-6b).

The move from parry 2 to parry 3 is a good place to pause and examine the difference between good technique and bad: that *how* you make a parry is as important as the end position itself. If, when moving from parry 2 to parry 3, you rotate the blade the other way—outward instead of inward, or counterclockwise instead of clockwise—you could easily trap the attacking blade with your sword, forcing it toward your body rather than away from it. This would be dangerous in stage combat and suicidal in a duel. However, if you think of each parry as a move to clear the box of safety prior to arriving at the end position, the chances of this happening are remote.

8-6a.

8-6b.

PARRY 4, OR QUARTE From parry 3, simply move the sword (tip still up) in a direct parry across the chest to arrive at parry 4, sweeping the box of safety from right to left, ending with the hilt held at the same level as parry 3, but this time in supination (fingers up, knuckles down), true edge facing outward ready to receive a cut or deflect a thrust aimed at the upper left quadrant of the body (see Fig. 8-7b).

These first four parries provide a complete defense for all four body quadrants against all attacks except vertical overhead cuts.

8-7a.

8-7b.

8-8a.

8-8b.

PARRY 5 This parry was developed to protect the head and shoulders from an overhead cut arriving more or less vertically. It is a very strong parry that ends with the sword being held above the head, a foot or so in front of the body, blade parallel to the ground, hand in pronation with the true edge tilted toward the attacker at about a forty-five degree angle ready to receive a downward cut.

To reach parry 5 from parry 4 (see Fig. 8-8a), imagine that the point of the sword is "tacked" or fixed in midair and sweep the hilt in a gentle arc from lower left to upper right, ending in pronation above your head (see Fig. 8-8b). The tip should be pointing left, blade parallel to the ground, cutting edge angled up at about forty-five degrees toward the attacking blade. Whatever you do, though, never try to reach parry 5 by lowering the blade into place, from right to left (counter-clockwise), since this could trap the attacker's sword and force it onto your head. As with any other parry, think of reaching the end position *only* after the sword has swept through the box of safety.

8-9a.

8-9b.

8-9c.

PARRY 5A Sometimes called parry 9. Parry 5 is not always the most convenient or desirable way to block an overhead cut. A variation, its mirror image, was developed wherein the hilt is held in supination on the left side of the body, blade parallel to the ground but pointing to the right. This end position leaves the defender looking through the crook of his or her own right elbow, at the attacker—a heroic, crowd-pleasing stance, but not especially strong as parries go. Still, if time or the logic of the fight does not permit assuming parry 5, parry 5A works well.

To reach parry 5A from parry 5, lower the forte of the sword to the waist, roll the wrist from pronation to supination while bringing the point of the blade from left to right, then raise the hilt to the upper left corner of the box of safety, about a foot in front of your head, blade pointing right and parallel to the ground with the true edge angled slightly toward the attacking blade (see Figs. 8-9a through 8-9c). Again, make sure you assume parry 5A by *raising* the blade, not lowering it into place.

8-10a.

8-10b.

PARRY 6, OR SIXTE A variation on parry 3, parry 6 uses the blade's false edge (instead of the true, or cutting edge) to guard the defender's upper right quadrant from a high-line thrust (see Figs. 8-10a and 8-10b). This means that the defender's hand is in supination, not pronation, which on this side of the body makes for a very weak parry, suitable mostly for deflecting the thrust of a very light weapon, such as a smallsword; or when the defender was equipped with a "backsword" which had a thick, or blunted, false edge.

8-11b.

8-11a.

PARRY 7, OR SEPTIME Another way (other than parry 1) to defend the lower left quadrant of the body is parry 7. Like prime, it clears the box of safety from right to left and ends with the true edge of the blade catching a cut or deflecting a thrust, but with the hand in supination. It is a bit easier to reach from the basic en garde position than prime because instead of having to end in pronation, which requires an initial roll of the sword and rotation of the hand before lateral movement can begin, the hand can begin moving toward the end position in supination as soon as the blade is dropped. Just as important, parry 7 leaves the blade pointed generally toward the attacker, making an immediate thrust in reply (riposte) a real possibility.

To reach parry 7 from parry 4 (where our previous four-quadrant, or box drill ended), keep the hand in supination while bringing the blade inward then downward in a clockwise, semi-circular arc until the sword is on the lower left side of the box of safety (see Fig. 8-11b). Never try this in the opposite direction, since a counterclockwise movement would "scoop" the attacking blade in toward your body rather than force it away.

If you wish, you can now incorporate parry 7 rather than parry 1, as the starting point of your defensive box drill, going from en garde to 7, to 2, to 3, to 4.

8-12a.

8-12b.

PARRY 8, OR OCTAVE This is a variation of parry 2. Unlike that strong, true-edge parry, however, parry 8 is a false-edge parry that leaves the hand and wrist in a very weak position to guard the lower right quadrant—especially from a powerful rapier cut. To assume parry 8 from parry 7, simply move the hilt in a direct parry across the low line, leaving the hand in supination, until you've reached the end position (see Fig. 8-12b). Like other false-edge parries, octave is used mostly with smallswords, much lighter, thrusting weapons; or with the backsword's thicker false edge forte.

CIRCULAR PARRIES To turn any direct or semicircular parry into a flashy circular parry, simply put the sword in motion in the direction of the desired parry, but carry it *past* the usual end position in a loose, exuberant fashion for a complete circle, then snap the sword crisply into the proper end position.

To execute a circular parry 2 from en garde, allow the tip of the blade to fall through center to the lower right. Then swing the blade exuberantly counterclockwise in a full circle, allowing your hand to resume pronation as the tip passes the top of the arc and continues to the end position for parry 2.

Although most circular parries can be made simply by rolling the wrist, they read much better to the audience when performed in a showy manner. To add energy to such a parry, choreographers often ask you to make hand and arm movements wider than usual and combine the parry with similar desperate looking footwork, such as a frantic flèche to the rear.

COMPLETE SWORD PARRY DRILL By adding parries 5 and 5A (and the hanging parry variants you'll learn about shortly) to your basic box drill, you can practice all eight (or nine, if you begin with prime) direct and semicircular parries used in most theatrical swashbuckling. When you feel comfortable with this basic drill, repeat it using circular parries to arrive at each end position. Although the circular parries will feel awkward at first, practicing them increases the strength of your hand and the flexibility of your wrist and, ultimately, your ability to control the sword.

USING HANDS AND FEET IN DEFENSE

Even in knightly tournaments where chivalry was on display, the rules of courtesy extended mostly to horses, where the penalty for killing an expensive charger was death. Beyond rebated (blunted) swords and lances, it was "anything goes." Well into the age of rapiers, no swordfighter was considered trained without some rudimentary instruction in wrestling.

Because of this, you'll often be asked to incorporate at least a few unarmed combat moves into swordfighting routines. As always, don't practice them with a partner until you can be supervised by a qualified teacher.

EMPTY HAND PARRIES   When a shield or buckler was unavailable or lost in battle, a swordfighter often held his empty, gauntleted hand even further out in front of himself than we do in the basic en garde stance—particularly when faced with an opponent armed with a shield. This allowed him to grab the shield or blade (yes, it's possible to hold even a sharpened blade if you grip it tightly) or bat down cuts and thrust. The palms of some gauntlets were lined with chain mail expressly for this purpose. If the attacker was reckless and moved too close, the defender's free hand could deliver a punch or seize the opponent by the throat, hair, clothing, or the wrist of the sword arm to immobilize him, or wrestle him to the ground.

In practice, the risk to the free hand was minimal. Eyewitness reports and swordmaster manuals say blows were seldom aimed at an empty hand because it could quickly be pulled away, leaving the attacker vulnerable.

DEFENSIVE KICKS   In addition to conventional footwork, swordfighters used their feet to gain any advantage they could, from tripping an off-balance opponent to kicking that opponent in the knees, groin, or belly while parrying an attack. Review Chapter 6 to get a sense of how backhand slaps, punches, and kicks can be used defensively in an armed routine. Again, don't try any of these techniques without the supervision of a qualified teacher.

> The "Grype" is the seizing of the sword-hilt with the left hand—for this purpose a "guanto da prase," or gripping gauntlet with the palm protected with fine mail, was sometimes used.
>
> George Silver
> *Brief Instructions on My Paradoxes of Defence*
> 1599

EVASIONS

Theatrical swordfights involve a lot more ringing steel than the real thing. Throughout history, evasions were favored over parries whenever possible. In stage combat, we may reverse this preference, but we still invest all evasions with the intensity of life-or-death decisions—making them some of the most athletic and physically demanding of all swashbuckling moves.

DUCKING   If someone swung at your head with a pool cue or golf club, your instinct would be to duck, perhaps covering your head for insurance. A roundhouse attack with a sword (which we call a swipe) demands a similar

8-13a.

8-13b.

Avoidance or evasions were in common practice in early rapier play, and can be theatrically effective in part of a sequence. When they were in use, the idea was to avoid the oncoming attack, while at the same time stretching out the sword arm in the direction of the adversary to run him through. For our purposes the latter is not at all a good idea.

William Hobbs
Fight Direction for Stage and Screen

instinctual response—although in theatrical swashbuckling, we'll augment that instinct with trained reactions.

First, never duck just by bending at the waist, as in a bow. When you bow, your head goes down and you risk losing sight of the attacking sword—something you'd never do in a real fight. Instead, drop down quickly into a squat, in the manner of a deep knee bend. By dropping to your haunches you can remove the target (your head) from harm's way *and* watch the sword as it passes, adding realism to the move. Dropping down this way also helps you remove your sword from the path of the swipe (don't let the blade stick up like a periscope), avoiding an accidental clash (see Fig. 8-13b). Above all, stay balanced. Don't land on one or both knees or roll backward onto your buttocks—any of which leads to an awkward recovery, at best; or at worst, a blown routine or an injury. When the attacking blade has safely passed, rise quickly, re-establish eye contact, and go on to the next move.

As with all stage combat, a swipe executed on target but safely out of distance looks far more threatening than it is. The illusion of danger the audience feels comes mostly from your reaction as the defender, not from the attacker's swing.

8-14a.

8-14b.

JUMPS When the swipe is aimed low, the choreographer may ask you to jump to simulate the blade passing beneath your feet, although in reality it is safely out of distance. This move has become a cliche in movie sword-fights, but it probably really happened from time to time when a fighter was "down but not out," and swung a sword desperately to keep an opponent at bay. From the defender's viewpoint, parrying a swipe aimed at the feet or lower legs would be foolish. Not only would the distance be hard to judge; but even if the attacking blade were met, the parry would be caught on the defender's foible, the weakest part of the blade. Either way, a jump would have been easier, more natural, and safer—so that's what we do in stage combat.

Jumps are easy if your legs are already bent in the usual springy horse stance. Whatever you do, though, don't stoop before jumping, while the attacker is preparing the swipe—this just telegraphs the move to the audience. If you need some help to get off the ground, throw both your arms into the air, sword and all, as you start up. This extra momentum makes the jump easier, look higher, and gives the impression that your escape was much narrower (see Fig. 8-14b).

STOMACH EVASION When a swipe is aimed at your stomach, your instinct is to pull the target back. In stage combat, we can do this in one of two ways.

If the choreography calls for you to hold your ground, you can simply suck in your stomach and bow your back out. The illusion of increased physical distance can be achieved by throwing one or both arms, sword and all, forward and up at the same time—just make sure your blade is up high enough to avoid contact with the attacker's sword (see Fig. 8-15b).

If the routine calls for you to give ground, a realistic reaction would be to flèche or double pass to the rear, leading with hips and stomach, trailing with upraised arms to increase the illusion of a narrow escape—but be sure to keep your balance and avoid any obstacles behind you on the stage, including other actors.

DIAGONAL EVASIONS If the swipe is on a diagonal line from high to low at an angle across your chest, the choreography will probably call for you to make a diagonal evasion in the direction from which the attacker's blade is coming. This may sound like an unnatural reaction (and will probably feel strange the first time you do it), but its logic is inescapable—one of those instances where trained reactions can save you and instinct can get you hurt. Let's take a moment to see why.

When the attacker preps by raising the sword, say, above his or her left shoulder for a diagonal swipe across your body from your upper right to lower left, your natural impulse is to run from the blade, or evade *away* from the direction the sword is coming. If you actually did this and angled your body to the left, away from the prep, and the attacker was in distance, you would not only fail to evade the swipe, the sword would cut you in half.

Now, suppose you see the same swipe coming, but evade to the right, *into* the direction of the prep. Now, the angle of your body will parallel the path of the blade, but remain *below* its plane of motion, allowing it to pass harmlessly above you even if the attack is in distance. Of course, no stage combat swipe is planned to take place in distance, but if it happened accidentally, you would certainly want the same safety margin demanded by real swordfighters.

8-15a.

8-15b.

8-16a.

8-16b.

8-16c.

To evade a diagonal swipe originating on your right, step out and slightly to the rear on your right foot while leaving your left foot in place. Be sure to take your sword with you by holding it downward and to the right, or leave it behind by letting it trail, blade down, along the leg that remains in place—a gesture many actor-combatants feel is more natural for a sword held in the right hand (see Fig. 8-16b). Whatever you do, though, don't let your blade wander into the path of the swipe and cause an accidental clash.

To evade to the left, do the same thing, but on the left foot, leaving the right foot in place (see Fig. 8-16c).

Finally, unless otherwise instructed by the fight director or the necessities of your character, let your head tilt in the same direction as the evasion. This keeps your neck aligned with your spine, avoiding possible injury due to muscle strain or accidental contact with the attacking sword, and looks committed to the danger of the moment.

HANGING PARRIES As you've learned, the overhead parries 5 and 5A are intended to stop a vertical cut, the same way the four basic parries are intended to stop horizontal cuts against the body. You'll recall, too, that real swordfighters usually preferred to evade attacks rather than risk parries. This was especially true for vertical cuts, which are inherently powerful, fight-stopping attacks.

A hybrid parry that combines the elements of an evasion with elements of a parry 5 or 5A is the "hanging parry." To perform one, the defender steps to one side and slightly to the rear, angling the body to evade a vertical or diagonal overhead cut, while interposing the sword in a parry 5 (if the evasion is to the right) or parry 5A (if the evasion is to the left) as extra insurance. In terms of end position, the chief difference is that, in both cases, the blade parallels the defender's angled body (not the horizon) so that the attacking sword glances off, sparing the blade the stress of full impact. In a real swordfight, this move often had the additional advantage of leaving the attacker off balance and vulnerable to immediate counterattack.

- A hanging parry 5 is made by evading to the right and moving to a modified parry 5 (see Fig. 8-17a). As your body moves downward, back, and to the right on the evasion, raise the hilt to just above and in front of your head, hand in pronation, blade extending with the true edge up along a line parallel to your torso, protecting your head, left shoulder, and left arm like a shield.

- A hanging parry 5A is the mirror image of hanging parry 5, with the sword held in a modified parry 5A (see Fig. 8-17b). As your body moves downward, back, and to the left in the evasion, bring your hand up in supination to just above and in front of your head with the blade extending down and to the right, true edge up, to protect your head, right shoulder, and right arm.

Sometimes, the attackers' blades may miss the defenders' blades completely, and aside from the loss of ringing steel, that's fine. The historical reality here is an evasion "with insurance"—a very real and frequently used combat move.

COMBINING PARRIES AND FOOTWORK

Opponents maneuvered constantly in real swordfights, seeking the advantage for attack and defense. Many of the swordmasters tried to organize this footwork into idealized patterns which they sketched in their manuals and painted onto salon floors. Some were so intricate and complex they seem to defy logic, let alone memory. Others looked more like the courtly dances that formed the gentler half of the swordfighter's world.

While theatrical swashbuckling has no real need of such systems, the idea behind them is sound. There are many advantages to practicing footwork and parries simultaneously—not the least of which is reinforcing a basic defensive stage-combat principle: move the body first, then the sword.

For example, from the basic en garde position, suppose a routine calls for your partner to attack with a cut to your right hip. Under the guidelines for re-creating historically accurate moves, your first reaction as a trained swordfighter would be to remove the targeted body part, then to interpose your blade. Thus, you would pass to the rear while moving to parry 2 (see Fig. 8-18b, then 8-18c). The same thing is true for other defensive moves. If your partner followed up this failed attack to your right hip with a new

In the fencing school as visualized by Thibault there are geometric patterns on the floor for the practice of accurate foot movements. The geometric nature of the Spanish style gives the swordplay something of the quality of a dance.

Arthur Wise
The Art and History of Personal Combat

8-17a.

8-17b.

8-18a.

8-18b.

8-18c.

attack to your left shoulder, you would now remove that target area again by passing to the rear. As the leg goes, so goes that side of the body, so your targeted left shoulder would now be further out of distance; though you would still move your sword to parry 4.

The point here is not to reduce all swordplay to a set of mechanical motions, but to have you begin thinking about the essential connections between hands, feet, and head—trained reactions versus instinct. By practicing all the defensive moves—parries and evasions—in combination with all the possible footwork combinations (as well as standing your ground and using no footwork at all) you will increase your ability to learn the choreography of any particular fight quickly and perform it with maximum drama and safety.

PARRY DRILLS WITH FOOTWORK To begin, make sure you can perform the nine basic parries, with hanging variants (5 and 5A), comfortably, from a position of en garde with either the left or right foot forward. Practice the parries not only in numerical or functional sequence, but in random order so that you won't depend on that sequence alone to find a particular end position quickly. After that, combine the parries with appropriate defensive footwork, mainly rearward passes and retreats, but also rearward double-passes and fleches—experimenting with circular parries.

Initially, make sure parries protecting a particular side of the body (the way parries 2 and 3 protect the right side, for example) accompany a rearward displacement of the leg on that side. Parries 5 and 5A, being guards against vertical head cuts, are not as closely associated with either the left or right side of the body, although most people feel that 5 is a stronger parry for the right side and 5A is a stronger parry for the left—giving as a reason the left or right side location of the forte of the blade. Hanging parries make this a moot point. You *must* evade right for a hanging parry 5 and left for a hanging parry 5A. Other than these, you should practice all parries with both the left and right foot forward—a parry 3, for example, with the right foot forward, or a parry 7 with the left foot forward. Competence in such difficult stances will only increase your ability to coordinate or isolate upper and lower body movements at will, increasing your movement choices, control, and safety in any stage fight.

HISTORICAL WARDS AND STANCES

A "ward" is a guarding or initial position for beginning a fight. The basic en garde position we use in this book is only one of many wards and stances developed by swordmasters over the centuries. The criteria for evaluating all wards were the same: Did they give the fighter a fighting chance at the beginning of a duel? Did the defensive benefits of a given ward preclude or encourage a quick and effective attack?

Figure 8-19 shows some typical single rapier wards taught by Marozzo, a sixteenth century swordmaster. They are precursors to those used by Saviolo and Carranza, two Italian swordmasters known well to Shakespeare and whose methods were undoubtedly reflected in the performances of his day.

As an actor-combatant, you should feel comfortable in any stance, ward, or en garde the choreographer assigns, understand how it contributes to your character's attitude and actions at the beginning of a fight, and be able to make a smooth transition from it to the first defensive or offensive move of the routine.

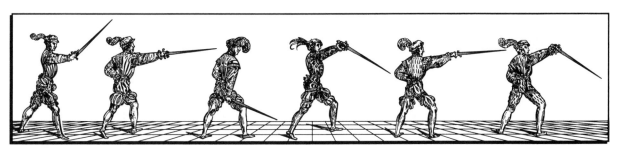

8-19. *The positions recommended by Marozzo for the fight with the single sword.* *(Re-rendered by Alex Daye.)*

• Early wards were designed primarily to guard against cuts; later wards were designed more with the thrust in mind. This paralleled the evolution of the rapier from a heavier military-style weapon to the lightweight versions favored by civilians. Your technique in performance should reflect these historical differences.

• The selection of a particular ward was based on a fighter's aggressiveness and knowledge of the ward his opponent was using. Thus, real duels involved a lot of preliminary posturing as the combatants "tried on" various stances, then switched them, depending on their opponent's reactions. Changing wards a few times at the beginning of a fight adds realism and builds tension, as long as the fight doesn't become a ballet.

• Different stances and fighting styles were associated with different nations, although fighters of one nationality often trained with masters of another. Spanish fencing schools of the fifteenth and sixteenth centuries emphasized technique and theory, and insisted upon total devotion from their students—qualities that made Spanish or Spanish-trained duelists feared throughout Europe for their steely nerves and precision. In his 1630 book, *The Academy of the Sword*, Girard Thibault catalogued a Spanish system "wherein are set forth by mathematical rules, on the basis of a mysterious circle, the true and heretofore unknown secrets of the use of the weapons on foot. . . ." The Spanish master, Narvaez, on whom Thibaust based his work, taught his students to dodge about, avoid some hits and parry others, so as to try and gain on their adversaries.

The antithesis of the Spanish fencer was the English fighter, who trusted physical strength and a few simple moves—learned well and performed aggressively—to end a fight quickly. Germans and Italians ranged somewhere in between. Unless your script or director tells you otherwise, you can always tap into these styles and techniques to add vitality and accuracy to the fighter you portray.

R.L.

8-20a. En garde!   8-20b. Pass back, parry 2.   8-20c. Pass back, parry 7.

SINGLE RAPIER DEFENSE FORM

Wards and stances, parries and evasions, footwork and free-hand defenses can all be combined into fun and instructive solo practice routines—workouts that not only teach and consolidate technique, but begin conditioning you to the demands of a typical stage fight.

Figures 8-20a through 8-20h show one such defensive form. Learn it move by move; then as each phrase is mastered, go on to the next. Work very slowly at first, then increase your speed as your precision and confidence increase. Don't just mimic the moves, *think* about their significance to the fight and the fighter as you perform them. After you've read Chapter 9, try to visualize an attacker pressing you as you continue your defensive drills, imagine the preparations, then move accordingly. As with any stage combat routine, safety should never be sacrificed for speed. The time you spend now, mastering yourself, will reward you greatly when you work with a partner and a qualified teacher.

In the next chapter, you'll see what all this parrying and evading has been about as you learn the other half of the theatrical swashbuckler's dance of life and death: the art of sword attacks.

8-20d. Pass back, hanging parry 5.

8-20e. Pass back, hanging parry 5A.

8-20f. Pass back, parry 3.

8-20g. Pass back, parry 4.

8-20h. Retreat, parry 1.

Agrippa (a fencing master who published his work seventeen years after Marozzo) reduced the number of useful guards from seven to four. As a practical man (architect, mathematician, engineer), he wisely considered the first guard to be assumed in the act of drawing the sword: men did not then stand on much punctilio in matters of fighting, and, in a quarrel, to draw and to be on guard had to be one action. A long "rapier" could not be whipped out as deftly as a court sword; before the point had left the scabbard the hand was above the head. Accordingly, the position of a man who had just drawn and turned his point to his adversary's face, was Agrippa's first guard.

Egerton Castle
Schools and Masters of Fence

9

ATTACK RAPIER FORMS

> It sounds so obvious, but if I had to list the single most important
> ingredient in a good knife fighter it would be courage. It doesn't take
> courage for a mugger or purse snatcher to pull a knife on an unarmed
> civilian. It does take a special kind of courage for one man to face
> another, both armed only with a knife.
>
> Harold J. Jenks and Michael H. Brown *Bloody Iron*

9.1. *Milady (Faye Dunaway) attacks D'Artagnan (Michael York) in "The Three Musketeers"*
(1975). Fight Director: William Hobbs. (The Everett Collection.)

Like a knife, the sword is primarily an offensive weapon. In this
chapter, you'll learn:

- How the psychology of attack differs from that of defense
- How all the parts of the sword—including the pommel and quillons—
  can be used for attack
- To perform safe yet convincing stage combat thrusts, cuts and swipes
- Flashy techniques like moulinets and pris-de-fer—the "taking of the
  blade" that turns defense into offense
- To combine attacks with footwork in a solo rapier form

Combat with blades is an inherently aggressive act. All other things being equal, the swordfighter most motivated to win (to take the fight to the opponent) usually did. Actor-combatants hoping to achieve the illusion of this violent intent should keep this in mind as they work through the attack sword forms presented in this chapter.

A SURVEY OF SWORD ATTACKS

Basic sword attacks consist of cuts, thrusts, and swipes—all made with the blade. More advanced attacks, such as moulinets and pris-de-fer, also use the blade, but for slightly different reasons: usually to gain some advantage before delivering a blow. The hilt of the sword can be used in attack, too, often as a battering weapon. In the past, most real fights also involved a bit of wrestling, so unarmed techniques are used in many stage swordfights as well. Here's an overview of the sword attacks you'll learn to perform in this chapter:

CUTS   Until the late Renaissance, the cut was the basic method of sword attack. Intended mainly to wound or disable an opponent in preparation for a killing blow, a cut is nothing more than a controlled slash to a specific part of the body. Since stage combat targets are usually at some distance from the actual parts of the body, the way you'll know when you've performed a cut properly is from the sensation you feel in your forearm as you stop the blade after extending its point beyond the target.

THRUSTS   A thrust is a stab made by pushing the sword point forward, often augmented by the legs during a forward pass, advance, or lunge. In terms of muscle feedback, you'll feel a properly made thrust first in your lats—as if you're trying to extend your forefinger an impossible distance across the room. More than any other attack, a thrust is an exercise in balance and recovery.

SWIPES   A swipe is an exuberant, roundhouse swing in either direction made against a high-, low-, mid-line, or diagonal target. It's used out of frustration or desperation (to reverse the course of a losing fight, for example), or when an opportunity suddenly presents itself. As a result, swipes in stage combat should look a bit ragged, though they will always be controlled and follow the eye contact, preparation, reaction and action safety sequence.

OTHER BLADE ATTACKS   Over time, a wide range of techniques were developed to help an attacker deliver cuts, thrusts, and swipes to maximum advantage. A "moulinet," (pronounced moo-lihn-ay, French for windmill), is nothing more than a fancy windup to increase the power of a vertical cut or diagonal swipe. "Pris-de-fer" (preez-day-fair, French for "taking of the iron") refers to a variety of techniques for immobilizing an opponent's blade after a parry. A "glissade" (glee-sod) is a simple slide down the opponent's blade in order to knock it back in the direction from which it came, opening a path for counterattack. A "bind" (rhymes with "blind") carries the

Marozzo is generally looked upon as the first writer of note on the art of fencing, the first edition of his *Opera Nova* appearing in 1536. After the invocation to the Holy Virgina and the 'Cavaliere San Giorgio' the 'Maestro' places a sword into Disepolo's hand and explains the various ways of holding it. The master then draws on the wall a diagram illustrating all the cuts, from the right and left sides— "mandritti" and "reverso." When the pupil, who, it seems, generally took his first lesson in private, was proficient in the variety of cuts, he proceeded to learn his guards, no special attention being paid to the thrust.

Egerton Castle
Schools and Masters of Fence

opposing blade on a corkscrew, semicircular path between the low and high line, or vice versa. A "croisé" (kwah-zay) carries the opposing weapon from a high line to a low line, or vice versa, but on the same side as the engagement, not across the body as with a bind. An "envelopment" (usually pronounced as it appears in English) is a long, circular bind that carries the opposing blade 360 degrees back to the original position. The purpose of all pris de fer is to reverse the impulse of an attack and create an opening for a counterattack.

The "countercut" occurs when two fighters simultaneously attack each other along the same line, aiming at roughly the same targets. This was used widely in all historical periods, but is seldom employed in stage combat—and for good reasons. First, theatrical fights are supposed to tell a story, and countercuts tend to be ambiguous: just who is attacking who? Second, they occur very quickly, making them hard for an audience to follow. Finally, they must be flawlessly timed—either to succeed (as in a real fight), or to avoid injury on stage. As a result, this move is best left to the history books or Hollywood films where clever editing can preserve both the drama and the safety of the fight.

Even though they start with parries, we classify every pris-de-fer as an attack on the blade—turning defense into offense in a single, bold move.

HILT ATTACKS Occasionally, situations arise where different parts of the sword can be used for attack. If you drop the sword, for example, and don't have time to find a new grip, you can still grasp the blade, parry, and use the hilt as a club. (The quillons make an intimidating "war hammer" when aimed at the head.) Similarly, the pommel can be used to bash an opponent; and a rapier's knuckle bow makes a good set of brass knuckles.

In stage combat, attacks with the hilt can be extremely dangerous and all targets of such attacks must be safely displaced from the defender. These techniques should not be tried without the advice and supervision of a qualified fight director.

HAND AND FOOT ATTACKS If a dagger, buckler, shield, cloak, or other object is not used in the fight, one hand is left free to slap, punch, or grapple, while the feet are free to kick and trip. Combining unarmed and armed attacks is beyond the scope of this chapter, but the better you become with each, the easier it will be to use them effectively in the same routine.

THE PSYCHOLOGY OF SWORD ATTACKS

In real swordfights, combatants sought to inflict as much harm as possible on their opponents while minimizing or avoiding harm to themselves. In close-quarter combat, this created a serious paradox: to win, one had to be aggressive; but being aggressive meant risking injury. In other words, gain often brought pain. Successful fighters were bold, but not stupid—and certainly not suicidal. Swordmasters put a lot of thinking into creating ways to

More important than esthetically picking and choosing from the multitude of historic combat techniques... is the process of "weeding out" unsafe techniques.

J.D. Martinez,
Fightmaster
The Fight Master

deliver cuts and thrusts with minimal risk. In stage combat, we recreate this studied aggressiveness by simulating both the swordfighter's technique (swordplay and footwork) and violent intent; but the two must work together.

USING TARGETING, TIMING, AND DISTANCE   To really hurt someone, you must strike a vulnerable area. Thus, historical swordfighting targets tended to be those parts of the body that were *not* naturally or artificially protected. For civilians, these included the face, neck, shoulders (upper arms), hips (including thighs) and groin. For armored soldiers, targets were places where chinks, or gaps, occurred in armor or padded clothing. Breastplates, gorgets, vests, and doublets—even heavy coats—made the chest and abdomen resistant to cuts, but the point of a sword could sometimes get through, making thrusts a constant danger. Hands were seldom targeted, except when fighters' wrists presented tempting targets for disarms. Legs made better targets: wounds there could cripple or slow fighters down, making victory a matter of time.

To keep from hurting someone on stage, you must avoid vulnerable areas while giving the illusion of attacking them. This paradoxical goal is achieved partly by targeting. Recall that a stage combat target is related to, but slightly removed from, the corresponding part of the body (see Fig. 9-2). We don't attack the shoulder, for example, but a point in space a few inches from the shoulder. And even if we fail to stop our cut in time, the out-of-distance margin should prevent accidental contact. Just as important is our hard-and-fast rule that *no stage combat blade ever passes in front of soft tissue*: face, throat, groin, or women's breasts. Through the discipline and precaution of keeping proper distance, throwing the energy of the blade *past* the target, and allowing the defender's reaction to control the timing, a stage combat attack always looks more threatening than it truly is.

SAFD Fightmaster J.D. Martinez puts actor-combatants into four categories, based on body type and strength. Each class has its own special characteristics, which affect performance. To achieve maximum realism in stage combat, these descriptions should be studied and taken into account.

Longer and Stronger. These tall, athletic fighters should avoid wasteful attacks, maintain wide fighting stances, and go directly at their opponents. They shouldn't try to keep up with smaller, faster fighters, but rather close off their avenues of escape. When attacked, they should defend with strong counterattacks, keeping opponents at weapon's length. If their adversaries get inside their guard, they should rely on their own superior reach and strength to disarm them or wrestle them to the ground.

Longer and Weaker. These thin and rangy fighters should keep their distance from stronger opponents and stay on the move, attacking from all quarters. They should wait for openings, then strike quickly. Opponents trying to close with them for in-fighting should be kept at arm's length by aggressive counterattacks, shoves, and evasions.

Shorter and Stronger. These muscular, bullish fighters would do well to stay out of range of longer-reaching opponents until they're certain of success. They should create openings by feinting, drawing attacks, then slipping away, sidestepping, and counterattacking with intentions of wounding and weakening. Close in, they're aggressive in-fighters capable of effective grappling, wrestling, and disarms.

Shorter and Weaker. These physically less imposing fighters must use brains—mobility and patience—as well as muscles and weapons. They should stay out of the range of longer reaching, stronger opponents and never try to grapple and wrestle. Instead they should use footwork to draw opponents off balance. They can't afford to waste opportunities, so their attacks must be accurate and fast. For their characters, space and mobility mean life.

R.L.

9-2. *Cuts should send energy past the target areas, rather than cutting into the body, and thrusts, while directed on target, should stop well before reaching the body (out-of-distance, or, if fighting in-distance, off-line).*

THE ATHLETIC SIDE OF ATTACK

Most actor-combatants find offense more tiring than defense. One reason is that attacks generally call for more movement and extension (including thrusts that require the weapon be held continuously at arm's length). When fatigued, both partners face the risk of self-inflicted injury, such as pulled muscles and sprains, as well as accidents with their swords.

Stretching and warming up before each training session, rehearsal, and performance go a long way toward preventing such problems. If you have little upper body strength you should also add a set of standard pushups at the end of your Chairman Mao exercises—especially if you envision going on to broadswords. Begin with one or two pushups a day and add a few more each week until you can comfortably manage a dozen. Be sure to perform them properly: lie on your stomach, palms down on the floor directly below your shoulders, and push yourself (back straight) up to full arm's-length, with your legs straight, then lower yourself gently back to the ground (the slower the better) and repeat.

9-3a.

9-3b.

9-3c.

9-3d.

9-3e.

9-3f.

9-3g.

PERFORMING SWORD ATTACKS

All attacks follow the same eye contact–preparation–reaction–and action sequence you've learned. Breath control is especially important in attack, since it is easy to get winded (huffing and puffing is fine if it's your character, not you). Try making a sharp exhalation (a battle cry or martial-arts style "ki-ai") when you make a cut or thrust. Vocalizing this way can increase the energy and perceived power of your blow.

PERFORMING CUTS From the basic en garde position, to prepare for a cut, raise the hilt to your shoulder, point up, on the same side of your body on which the cut is to fall; to your left for a cut to your partner's right, and look directly at the targeted area (see Fig. 9-3b). When your partner reacts to the prep and begins moving to the proper parry, you are free to continue the action.

There is no question of the superiority of the thrust over the cut since the point has the advantage of time and distance over the edge. As early as the fourth century the Roman writer Flavius Vegetius Renatus. . . pointed out that the right arm and flank were exposed when cutting, while during a thrust the body was guarded and the adversary was wounded before he perceived the attack.

Linda McCollum
The Fight Master

McCollum's article goes on to offer a number of reasons why the English were so slow to see the wisdom of this ancient advice. Some had to do with quasi-scientific theories of swordfight physiology. Sir Richard Burton, in his *Book of the Sword* (1884), claimed that burly Anglo-Saxons took more naturally to a side-to-side swinging action than their wiry Mediterranean cousins, who preferred to poke—although *all* human beings, he believed, had a predisposition to cutting and had to be taught to stab. Other English experts complained that the rapier and its thrusting technique spoiled the hacking and bashing reflexes needed for war; a weak argument at best, considering that soldiers in mass formations always had less, rather than more, room to swing edged weapons.

The best explanation is xenophobia and professional rivalry. The English never cared much for continental ideas, no matter what the topic; and traveling Italian fencers took jobs away from English swordmasters.

R.L.

Cutting to your partner's right, keep your hand in pronation, bending your wrist slightly and leading with the hilt (see Fig. 9-3c), and extend your sword toward the target, finishing the cut (snapping the blade into its final position, cutting edge toward your partner) with a crisp whipping motion as if you were trying to fling a drop of water from the tip *past* the target area (see Fig. 9-3d). Your elbow should be straight and your wrist aligned with the blade. To keep the cutting edge against the target, cuts on your right side (to your partner's left) are made with the hand in supination (see Figs. 9-3e through 9-3g).

Certain dueling techniques of the sixteenth century used the false or reverse edge of the blade for very quick, snapping cuts controlled by the wrist. These cuts were intended to inflict "showcase wounds," generally to the face, whose scars were marks of honor; a duel ended with no real damage to the defender. Techniques like these are difficult to master and their effectiveness on stage, where subtle moves can be lost on an audience, is questionable. Cuts delivered with the flat of the blade caused no life threatening damage—the proverbial "dry beat" decried by Mercutio in *Romeo and Juliet*.

Obviously, for solo practice, you'll have to use an imaginary partner; but it still helps to imagine eye contact, and visualize the targeted area, as well as the defender indicating the proper reaction before you make the cut.

9-4a. En Garde.

9-4b. Preparation.

9-4c. Extension.

9-4d. Lunge.

PERFORMING THRUSTS A thrust may be made from a lunge, reverse lunge, advance, or forward pass. To illustrate, let's make a thrust from a lunge at an imaginary defender's left hip, which he or she will deflect with a parry 1, or prime. From the basic en garde position, prepare by lowering the sword point and pulling the hilt back to your right hip, keeping the blade horizontal and pointed toward your imaginary partner. Now, look directly at the imagined target area, your partner's left hip (see Fig. 9-4b). Next, extend the sword toward the target to full arm's length, keeping the blade low (see Fig. 9-4c). Imagine that your partner reacts and begins the move to prime, freeing you to complete the attack. Letting the point of the sword draw you forward, push off into the lunge, keeping your arm at full extension (see Fig. 9-4d). *Never combine the arm extension with the foot movement of the lunge*, since this would ruin the defender's timing and possibly put you in distance, risking an accident. Done correctly, the prep and extension are inconspicuous while the action of the lunge looks spectacular but remains quite safe.

Thrusts can also be made from the extreme left (inside line) or right (outside line) sides of the attacker's body in an attempt to outflank the defender. "Punto" is Italian for point. A thrust from the left with the hand in supination is the "punto reverso;" from the right, in pronation, it is the "punto mandritte." In the past, these were considered gutsy as well as clever attacks, since the awkward final stance left the attacker open to a variety of counterattacks.

To execute a punto reverso from the basic en garde position, prepare by turning the sword into supination and pull the hilt back to your left hip. The purpose here is to wound the defender behind the right thigh. Extend the tip out toward your imaginary partner's right hamstring—yes, all the way around behind the leg—and lunge, allowing the sword to pull your front foot slightly to the left. Done properly, the reverso lunge will make a graceful circular pattern, heaving your chest out toward the left, causing your blade and sword arm to make a gentle arc back toward the right.

In all attacks, be careful not to throw the thrust with too much violence and not to over-reach.

Salvatore Fabris, Italian Swordmaster 1600

Egerton Castle
Schools and Masters of Fence

A punto mandritte proceeds in a similar fashion, but with the preparation and extension on the right (thus angling the lunging foot out slightly on that side), with blade and sword arm circling back gently to the left, targeting the back of the defender's left thigh.

Whether your target is on the high or low line, left or right side of the body, or accompanied by a lunge or a pass, thrusts *always* follow the same pattern: eye contact, preparation, extension, reaction, action (lunge, advance, or pass).

PERFORMING SWIPES Prep for swipes just as you did for cuts, but with a bit more gusto, bringing the sword back to the left or right shoulder and looking directly at the targeted area (see Fig. 9-5b). The defender's reaction (the beginning of an evasion) will depend on where the swipe is targeted. If it's a horizontal swipe at the head, the defender will start to squat, taking his or her own sword down as well, to prevent an accidental clash. If the swipe is at the feet, the defender will begin to rise in anticipation of a jump, often throwing his or her arms upward to gain momentum or create a fearful

9-5a.

9-5b.

9-5c.

9-5d.

9-6a.

9-6b.

effect. If the swipe is at the stomach, the defender will begin to raise both arms and bow the back in anticipation of a stomach evasion, with a backward pass or fleche to the rear.

When you've seen the beginning of the desired reaction, keep your eyes locked on the point in space where the target *originally* was (if it is a head swipe, for example, you will be looking at the place in the air where the defender's head was before he or she ducked) and perform the swipe by making an energetic, roundhouse swing through the targeted area, leading with the true edge of the blade (in pronation for swipes from left to right—[see Fig. 9-5c]; in supination for swipes from right to left). Most of the energy of the swipe should come not from your arm, but from your shoulders, connected to the torsion of your rotating chest while using your hips as an anchor. Think of yourself rooted as a tree in a windstorm, with your torso as the trunk and your limbs as the branches. With this image in mind, you'll commit to the swipe with the right amount of energy and control.

End the swipe with your sword still in view from the corner of your eye—don't let it drift behind your body where it can tangle with props or bystanders, or leave you looking defenseless (see Fig. 9-5d).

A diagonal swipe (which the defender evades left or right, depending on the path of your blade) is similar to the swipe above, but with adjustments to the prep and the cutting path itself. A diagonal swipe from your high left to lower right would be targeted to simulate a cleaving blow from the defender's right collarbone through the bottom of the lower left ribs. Prepare as if for a cut, by your left shoulder, but hold the hilt slightly higher (see Fig. 9-6b). Remember, an evasion is always made to the side which you, the attacker,

9-6c.

9-6d.

have prepped. In this case, when the defender has begun an evasion to his right, begin your exuberant swipe (see Fig. 9-6c) from upper left to lower right. Imagine you are slicing through where the defender *had been* before the evasion, ending with your own sword still in view on the lower right (see Fig. 9-6d).

Performed properly, a healthy swipe gives the illusion that the defender has just evaded a powerful and dangerous slash, even though the attack was out-of-distance and the defender well-removed from the path of the blade.

PERFORMING MOULINETS You've undoubtedly seen movie swashbucklers twirl their sword flashily at the wrist, first on one side of the body and then on the other. This snazzy maneuver, a moulinet, (performed to the right, on the outside line, is an "outside moulinet," and to the left, on the inside line, an "inside moulinet"), was taught to real swordfighters, often in combination with footwork drills. It was used to make the wrists limber and strong, and to give the fighter more confidence in handling the sword. It is also an efficient way to begin a vertical cut, particularly as a cut to the head from parry 1, by increasing the momentum of the blade with minimum arm motion.

To practice, let's try an inside moulinet leading to a vertical head cut, which your imaginary partner will block with a parry 5. From the en garde

9-7a.

9-7b.

9-7c.

9-7d.

9-7e.

9-7f.

position, prepare for the moulinet by bending the wrist (see Fig. 9-7b) and thereby dropping the tip of the sword. Now bring the hilt across your chest, sword point down, as if you were trying to read a watch on your right wrist. You should feel a similarity between this position and parry 1—only now you are attacking (see Fig. 9-7c). When you see the defender begin to react, continue the leftward motion until the blade is clear of your body, then bend your wrist so the leading edge of the blade is facing behind you. Now let the blade rise and come up past your left ear, leading with the cutting edge (see Figs. 9-7d and 9-7e). Stop the sword crisply when you've reached full extension, snapping your wrist as if you were trying to fling a drop of water off the point, and sending it *past* the target area: the space about a foot above the defender's head (see Fig. 9-7f). You should be able to stop such a cut at

9-7g.

9-7h.

9-7i.

9-7j.

9-7k.

precisely this position—at full extension with your arm and sword making one continuous line—each time, whether the defender's sword reaches the parry position or not.

Prepare for an outside moulinet by dropping the sword's point to the right (see Fig. 9-7g), rolling your wrist and hand into supination as you raise your arm. As you do this, the defender will react by beginning a move to parry 5A. As soon as you see this reaction, let the momentum of your blade carry it down and back around your right shoulder, then forward, cutting edge first (see Figs. 9-7h through 9-7j), until you've completed the vertical head cut described above (see Figs. 9-7f and 9-7k). The end positions of the inside and outside moulinets are identical.

Diagonal head cuts, or swipes beginning high on one side and finishing low on the other, are often performed from moulinets. To make a diagonal swipe from your high right to your lower left, modify the last part of your outside moulinet so that the blade, instead of coming up directly behind you, flares out a bit to the right on the way up. The momentum will help the blade travel down at an angle across your chest to the left. As with any swipe, do *not* complete the cut until you see your partner react with the proper evasion—in this case, an evasion to the defender's left (your right).

A diagonal swipe from your high left to low right is done the same way, only this time it's from an inside moulinet. Let your blade flare out slightly to the left as it comes up before descending from high left to low right.

Moulinets, performed continuously on one side, or alternated quickly from one side to the other and then terminated with a single, crisp, overhead cut, make great exercises for strengthening the wrist and increasing your ability to the control the sword. If a fight begins with a running attack, one or two moulinets are a sure crowd-pleaser, giving you something to do with the sword as you cross the stage, adding energy to the attack and increasing the sense of danger.

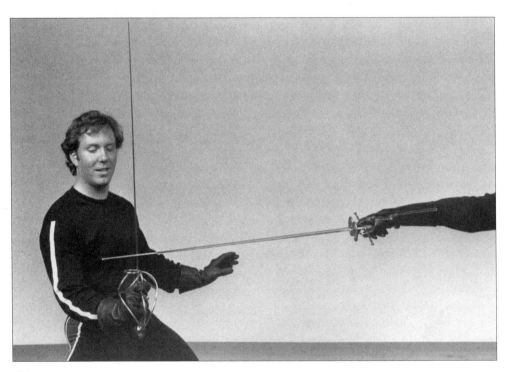

9-8a.

COUNTERATTACKING WITH A PRIS-DE-FER

Attacks on the blade are a historically accurate and dramatically useful way to shift the momentum of a fight. They're also a good way to get the actor-combatants in distance for punches, chokes, or slaps because the swords are in contact with each other and immobilized, thereby reducing the chance for injury.

Of course, you can't practice a complete pris-de-fer by yourself—only your half of it; but you can get a feel for its dynamics by parrying a cut from your imaginary partner and going through the motions. This will help you learn the technique more quickly under supervised instruction.

PERFORMING A GLISSADE AND CROISÉ A "glissade" is simply a brisk sliding motion along the opponent's blade from the point of contact in a parry back towards the defender's quillons. It is intended to knock the attacking sword back along the same line from which it came, and perhaps expel it off line by forcing the blades to break contact. A "croisé" is a glissade that knocks the attacking sword back, but changes the line from high to low, or vice versa, with or without an expulsion.

To get the feel of a glissade with an expulsion, parry 3 and imagine you've caught the foible of your partner's blade about a foot or so above your quillons (see Fig. 9-8a). Now, briskly extend your arm toward and beyond the attacker's left shoulder, angling it slightly to your right (this helps keep the blades in contact), and then flick your wrist outward sharply. The combination push-flick, will drive the other blade back and outward to the right, in the direction from which it came (see Fig. 9-8b).

9-8b.

Although a glissade or croise can be performed satisfactorily with both partners standing still, the counterattacking impulse can be enhanced if you advance or pass forward using the leg on the side of the parry. If your partner remains stationary while you move, you can easily come in distance for a punch or other action with your free hand.

The most common problem with any pris-de-fer is what we call "noodling;" that is, your partner does not keep the sword arm extended, but lets it go loose, like a wet noodle. This causes your partner's sword to drop or sail away the instant you exert pressure, leaving your blade with nothing to push against. This is irritating in a glissade or croise, but in other pris-de-fer techniques, it can be dangerous.

PERFORMING A BIND   A "bind" takes your partner's blade from low to high, or high to low, and across each partner's center line, where it can be held in a corps a corps or expelled. It shows a lot more flashing steel than a glissade and, because it releases more energy, it works best when footwork is involved.

To practice the bind from the en garde position, pass to the rear and parry 2, picturing the foible of the imaginary blade in contact with your forte (see Fig. 9-9a). Now, maintaining the relative sword-wrist position of the parry, begin raising your arm. Exert a little outward pressure to make sure the two blades stay in contact. When the hilt is about head-high, begin extending your arm as you would for a thrust, keeping the tip of your sword well above your imaginary partner's head (see Fig. 9-9b), and begin passing forward. Move the sword to your left, reaching full extension as the hilt passes the center of your body in its pass forward. At this point in the pass, your right foot should also be crossing parallel to your left. Continue this motion with your arm and body until your sword reaches roughly the ten o'clock position and you've completed the pass. You should now have your right foot forward with your sword at just past the parry 4 position (see Fig. 9-9c).

Performed correctly, the hilt will have inscribed a corkscrew pattern through the air, from low right (parry 2) to high left (parry 4) for the distance of your pass. Fight choreographers often describe binds by referring to the parries from which they begin and end, such as "a bind from two to four," or "a bind from three to seven." These binds always cross the high-low line and follow the cork-screw pattern.

Although the entire two-to-four bind you've just completed can be performed with the hand in pronation, some people maintain that rolling into supination at some point feels more natural and increases the power of the bind. If you intend to expel, or force the other blade away, this supinated end position also allows you to flick your blade outward more easily, flinging the other sword backward with a flourish. If you'd like to try this supinated technique, be sure to stay in pronation *at least* until your hand has passed overhead, then roll your wrist and flick away as your body comes to a stop.

A high to low bind works much the same way. To bind four to two, start with your right foot forward in a parry 4 and let your hand roll into pronation as the blades pass your centerline, going left to right. Binding three to seven, start left foot forward in parry 3 and let your hand go into supination naturally as the blades pass your centerline traveling right to left. Just be sure both blades have moved *past* your centerline before your active leg moves forward in the pass.

9-9a.

9-9b.

9-9c.

9-10a.

9-10b.

9-10c.

9-10d.

PERFORMING THE ENVELOPMENT

An "envelopment" takes both swords on a 360-degree trip. Why would a swordfighter want to do this? First, when performed with footwork, an envelopment eats up a lot of space, requiring at least a double pass for the attacker, and often three passes for the defender. Second, it's the most powerful of all pris-de-fer techniques—it literally takes over the opponent's blade and keeps it under your control as long as you keep moving forward. For this reason, the envelopment on the move is sometimes called a "traveling envelopment."

To demonstrate this technique from the en garde position, pass to the rear and parry 2 (see Fig. 9-10a). Now bind your imaginary partner's blade toward the parry 4 position (see Fig. 9-10b), but instead of stopping or tossing it off at the parry 4 position keep rolling your sword counterclockwise (see Fig. 9-10c);

Do not draw your sword, but to serve your king, preserve your honor, or defend your life.

M. L'abbat
The Art of Fencing or the Use of the Smallsword
1734

continue into a double pass—making sure that your pronated hand/hilt has passed your body's centerline before you put your left foot forward to complete the second pass. When your sword has returned to the parry 2 position, stop. If you wish, you can also give the imaginary blade a final flick to the right (see Fig. 9-10d). If you have done things correctly, your hilt will have inscribed a 360-degree corkscrew through the air and your left foot will once again be forward.

Noodling becomes increasingly troublesome—and potentially dangerous— the longer the blades are in contact. Beginners sometimes think they're helping their partner when, as defenders, they bend their elbows and pull back their swords as the pris-de-fer progresses. Losing contact between the blades this way not only spoils the rhythm and effect of the move, it puts two bodies in motion around a pair of loose swords—an easy way to get hurt.

COMBINING FOOTWORK AND ATTACKS

In solo practice, your main concern is synchronizing upper and lower body movements until every cut, thrust, swipe, and pris-de-fer can be performed with virtually any combination of footwork.

A cut is generally made while passing forward or advancing with the foot on the same side as the cut. That is, from the basic en garde position (with your right foot forward), a cut to your imaginary partner's right hip would be made on the left side of your body while passing forward with your left foot. A subsequent cut to your partner's left hip would be made by prepping to your right shoulder, then passing forward on your right foot as the momentum of the blade pulls you along. Remember, the prep always comes first, then the defender begins to react; after that, the blade is put in motion; and *then* comes the pass as the blade begins to extend and pull you forward.

Thrusts are usually made from lunges, advances, or forward passes although historically, clever swordfighters would occasionally thrust from reverse lunges or backward passes to catch over-eager opponents, as in a passata sotto. Remember to prepare and extend *before* moving your feet in any of these maneuvers.

Swipes look best when they appear to be spontaneous—even a little hurried or over-committed. They're often used at the ends of phrases, where exchanges have just finished and the fighters are moving to new positions, when the momentum has shifted and one fighter is getting desperate or, to open the attacker for a simulated surprise kill by the defender.

Moulinets can be performed on the pass or with an advance. "Baronial hall advances" (so called because they can be performed even in narrow hallways) are fine hand-foot coordination drills in which moulinets on both sides are synchronized with a series of overhead cuts and strong-side (right foot) heel-to-heel advances. Just make sure you bring your trailing left heel up to your leading right foot while you moulinet, then step forward on your right foot as you deliver the overhead cut.

Close reading of Di Grassi's *The True Arte of Defence*, Saviolo's *His Practice*, and Silver's *Paradoxes of Defence* reveal an Elizabethan rapier fighting style significantly different from what we usually see re-created on stage. Cutting, to a rapier man, was controlled from the elbow and wrist, swinging the arm was out of the question. The Elizabethan masters used cuts only in addition to thrusting attacks. Using the dagger also influences the squared-off look to the torso. In considering footwork, it would have been common in Shakespeare's day to see fencers simply pace or run (right-left-right) at each other in attempting thrusts. Saviolo and Di Grassi go into considerable detail to list the varieties of traverses and slips. This dodging, weaving, and pivoting is central to the technique of the best of the rapier fighters. Circular fight patterns must have been common with skilled rapier specialists. There are a number of rapier techniques that may be impossible to re-create for stage. For instance, in every example from Di Grassi and Saviolo there is a specific understanding that the preferred technique in rapier fighting is to simultaneously parry and return thrust against the opponent. There is no hesitation, or more accurately, separation between defense and attack.

Craig Turner
"Notes from the Elizabethan Swordplay Masters"
The Fight Master

9-11a. En garde!

9-11b. Prep to left shoulder for a cut to defender's right hip.

9-11c. Cut to the defender's right hip and pass forward.

9-11d. Prep to right shoulder for a cut to defender's left hip.

9-11e. Cut to defender's left hip and pass forward.

9-11f. Drop sword tip to begin inside moulinet for a diagonal (left to right, high to low) swipe and "look at your watch" as you draw the blade back.

9-11g. Begin the high left to low right diagonal swipe.

9-11h. Complete the diagonal swipe and pass forward.

A SINGLE RAPIER ATTACK FORM

This single rapier attack form combines cuts, moulinets, swipes, and thrusts with forward passes and a lunge. It is the reverse, or complementary part of the single rapier defense form you learned in the previous chapter: the moves of the one should shed new light on the moves of the other.

As you practice, visualize a partner reacting to your preps before you complete each action. Fully extend all cuts and thrusts, and throw your energy from the tip of the sword *past* the imaginary target. This will not only help you include these vital steps automatically when you move on to supervised, partnered training, it will keep you focused on the purpose of the form: an entertaining, staged *sword fight*—not a ballet or set of calisthenics.

In the next chapter, you'll put your defensive and attacking skills together in an integrated stage combat form.

9-11i. *Supinate—begin prep for outside moulinet and drop point with cutting edge behind you, leading to a swipe in the other direction.*

9-11j. *Begin the diagonal swipe from your high right to low left.*

9-11k. *Complete the swipe and pass forward.*

9-11l. *Prep to your left shoulder.*

9-11m. *Cut to defender's right shoulder, pass forward.*

9-11n. *Prep to your right shoulder.*

9-11o. *Cut to defender's left shoulder, pass forward.*

9-11p. *Begin prep for a thrust.*

9-11q. *Extend, and...*

9-11r. *Lunge!*

It can be argued that the last French duel of chivalry was the encounter between Jarnac and La Chataigneraye in 1574, which not only partook of all three institutions (trial by combat, duel of chivalry, and duel of honor) but was one of the most famous duels in history. Chataigneraye was a skilled swordsman and wrestler and Jarnac, a less skilled swordsman, sought assistance from the Italian master Caizo. Caizo proceeded to teach Jarnac the cut at the knee. Although accounts differ as to the length of the duel we do know a few things for certain: Both men were clad in demi-armour reaching only to the knees, and were fighting with swords. Suddenly Jarnac, parrying a thrust, returned a riposte, which, gliding past his opponent's guard, slid downward to the unarmoured leg of his adversary, cutting the ham. Staggered and confused by this unusual stroke, Chataigneraye had no defense ready, and in another moment Jarnac, doubling the stroke, succeeded in cutting also the ham of the right leg. Upon this Chataigneraye fell, helpless, to the ground, his sword dropping from his nerveless grasp [other accounts indicate Chataigneraye actually swiped at Jarnac from the ground]. In a moment Jarnac was upon him, calling that now his life was "at his discretion," but that he would spare it willingly "if he would restore his honour, and acknowledge his offense to God and King." Chataigneraye answered nothing, whereupon Jarnac turned to the King, and kneeling, prayed. But the King made no answer. Upon this Jarnac returned to his bleeding antagonist, and finding him still prostrate, and in a half-fainting condition, raised his hands to heaven with the cry: "Lord, I am not worthy; not to me, but unto Thy name be thanks!" Undoubtedly a gentleman with an eye to the gallery!

Lewis Melville and Reginald Hargreaves
Famous Duels and Assassinations

Chataigneraye died later of his wounds and the victory feast that he had planned before the duel went uneaten. It was said that he died more of anger than of loss of blood but either way he was the first to fall to the "Coup de Jarnac," a term that has come to mean any kind of treacherousness or underhanded action.

R.L.

10

A SOLO RAPIER FORM

The concept of *kata*, a set of formal exercises containing the essence of the art being taught, is the basic method of teaching used in all Japanese arts, including acting. The *bujutsu kata* not only contain the essence of the martial specialties being explored, they serve to maintain the original essence of the style, provide a margin of safety in training, and hide the essence of the technical repertoire from the casual or uninitiated observer.

Dr. Robert W. Dillon, Jr. "Classical Japanese Martial Art" *The Fight Master*

10-1. Errol Flynn fights one-against-many in "The Sea Hawk" (1940). Fight Director: Fred Cavens. (The Everett Collection.)

Practice makes perfect, but *how* you practice makes a difference. In this chapter, you'll learn:

- How attack and defense are integrated in a typical stage fight
- Why a swordfighting form or a solo martial arts kata, can improve your physical conditioning and acting ability as well as your sword handling technique
- To perform a custom solo rapier form—a mini-drama—demonstrating the theatrical swashbuckling moves you've learned so far

To gain a higher rank, an Asian martial artist learns a variety of complex forms, or "katas," that display his or her technique and martial spirit. The formats for these exercises are often miniature dramas, similar to stage fights, where the candidate being tested defends him- or herself against numerous imaginary opponents attacking from all sides.

In theatrical swashbuckling, our tests tend to come on opening night; although (as you'll see in Part III), SAFD-trained candidates can earn acknowledgment as Recognized or Recommended Actor-Combatants following a performance-oriented examination by an SAFD Adjudicator. For now, you will learn to combine the techniques you've studied so far into an integrated sword form that closely reflects the ebb and flow of a choreographed stage fight.

BENEFITS OF THE SOLO SWORD FORM

Difficult techniques become easier through practice—by building up muscle memory and cultivating the proper mental attitude. In stage combat, familiarity with attack, defense, and partnering techniques *before* you're called upon to fight means you'll perform much better when you work with a choreographer. But the benefits of practice don't stop with technical proficiency.

If you're a performer, your ability to act while in action and focus on what a character is thinking and feeling, as well as doing, in a fight will increase as you master the techniques. The less you have to think about moving and doing, the more time and energy you'll have to express your character. In the solo sword form below, which is based on a dramatic one-against-many scenario, you'll have a chance to begin acting the fight—while cultivating new skills.

Physically, regular form practice improves your sword-wielding strength, your stamina, and coordination, making the physical demands of acting easier.

THE ONE-AGAINST-MANY SCENARIO

The single rapier form presented below simulates a fight between a lone swashbuckler (you!) and two assailants. Encountered often in fiction and drama, such heroics really occurred in history.

On one occasion, a certain Count Claudio, a man more valiant than wise, was strolling alone through the glades when he came upon four men preparing to fight, two to a side. Appalled by the double duel, Claudio tried to prevent the fight, but antagonized the combatants so badly that all four turned their blades on him. When the dust cleared, Claudio alone was left standing, having killed three of the men and seriously wounding the fourth.

In swashbuckling films, the one-against-many scenario has become a cliche. Virtually any swordfighting movie will provide examples, but particularly good ones may be found in Errol Flynn's classic *Adventures of Robin*

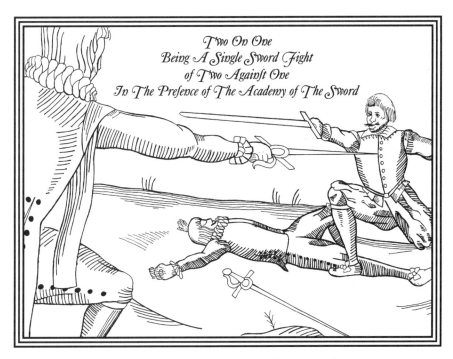

Two On One
Being A Single Sword Fight
of Two Against One
In The Presence of The Academy of The Sword

10-2. A two-on-one fight in the style of George Silver's "Paradoxes of Defence."
(Art by Alex Daye.)

Hood, Michael York's *The Three Musketeers*, and both the Jose Ferrer and Gerard Depardieu versions of *Cyrano de Bergerac*. The one-against-two solo rapier form you'll learn here has a similar heroic outcome—guaranteed.

HOW TO GET THE MOST FROM YOUR PRACTICE

As with all stage fights, you'll begin learning this one slowly, then speed up as your skills, stamina, and confidence increase. Rehearse each phrase by itself until you feel comfortable with its moves before going on to the next. Try to coordinate sword motions and footwork in a natural manner, blending moves, sections, and phrases smoothly; avoid jerky, stop-start movements. One way to do this is to focus on breath control: inhaling when you gather energy in a prep, exhaling when you expend that energy in action. And don't forget to stretch and warm-up before each rehearsal session.

When the solo form feels fully controlled, fluid, and graceful, begin to focus on the acting. Visualize your attackers as real people—partners in your performance—and respond accordingly, imagining the proper reactions to your preps before continuing with the action. The more vividly you create this alternate reality, the easier it will be for you to submerge yourself in future roles while keeping yourself and others safe.

Finally, don't wear yourself out by over-rehearsing. Your body and your brain will benefit more from a few half-hour workouts a week than from daily marathon sessions. And after you've mastered the form, work in some variations to keep the process fresh. Add some new moves or change the old ones around, but always strive for maximum artistic expression.

A SINGLE RAPIER SOLO FORM

This is the principal part of a three-part (protagonist versus two assailants) fight. The weapon is a single rapier of the type commonly used for personal defense in the fifteenth through seventeenth centuries—from the age of Shakespeare through the era of *The Three Musketeers*.

The fight features thirty individual moves and is broken down into six brief phrases demonstrating all the basic attack and defense moves in a dramatic theater setting, yourself against two phantom partners. The moves required for your part are in the roman typestyle and the moves of the two phantom partners are in italic. Although you'll gain more from the form by practicing on stage, it can be performed anywhere within the space of a few hundred square feet—roughly the size of a modest living room or a two-car garage.

Begin facing stage left, en garde position, left foot slightly forward (see Fig. 10-3a).

PHRASE ONE/ THE FIRST OPPONENT ATTACKS, YOU RESPOND.
The first opponent runs at you from the downstage right, sword raised to attack

1. Pivot, turning one-quarter of the way around clockwise, and make a left-to-right stomach swipe; pass back, and end facing the imaginary opponent downstage right (see Fig. 10-3b).
   Opponent One stops, evades the swipe, and faces you, en garde.

2. Pass forward, cut to opponent's left shoulder (see Fig. 10-3c).
   Opponent One passes back and parries 4.

3. Pass forward, cut to opponent's right shoulder (see Fig. 10-3d).
   Opponent One passes back, parries 3.

4. Pass forward, cut to opponent's left hip (see Fig. 10-3e).
   Opponent One passes back, parries prime, then attacks with a diagonal swipe, going from your high right to lower left.

5. Evade right using a hanging parry 5 (see Fig. 10-3f).
   Opponent one runs past you traveling upstage left.

6. Turning counterclockwise to face stage left, pass back on your left foot, and carry your blade from the hanging parry 5 around your head into a stomach swipe going from your right to your left (see Fig. 10-3g).
   Opponent One evades, runs past you to upstage left.
   End facing upstage left, ready for the second attacker.

10-3a.

10-3b.

10-3c.

10-3d.

10-3e.

10-3f.

10-3g.

PHRASE TWO/ YOU RESPOND TO OPPONENT TWO.

Opponent Two runs at you recklessly from upstage left.

7. Pass forward, using an inside moulinet, make a diagonal swipe from your high left to low right (see Fig. 10-3h).
Opponent Two stops, evades to the right.

8. Pass forward, making a diagonal swipe from your high right to low left (see Fig. 10-3i).
Opponent Two evades to the left, then counterattacks with a cut to your right hip.

9. Pass back, parry 2 (see Fig. 10-3j). Keeping pressure against Opponent Two's blade, you immediately...

10. Pass forward, bind the blade from parry 2 to parry 4 (see Fig. 10-3k).
Opponent Two falls back, up-stage left.

PHRASE THREE/ OPPONENT ONE ATTACKS AGAIN— NOW THINGS GET PHYSICAL!

Opponent One runs downstage from stage left and attacks you with a moulinet ending in a vertical head cut.

11. Pass back on the right foot, turning counterclockwise slightly, facing stage left and parry 5 (see Fig. 10-3l).
Opponent One holds the blade in place while you. . .

12. Advance on the weak side and grab the wrist of Opponent One's sword arm with your left hand (see Fig.10-3m).
Opponent One's momentum carries him or her forward—then you. . .

13. Throw Opponent One downstage right, then pass forward with your left foot (see Fig. 10-3n).
Opponent One continues, again momentarily out of the action.

10-3h.

10-3i.

10-3j.

10-3k.

10-3l.

10-3m.

10-3n.

PHRASE FOUR/ NOW IT'S PERSONAL—IN YOUR FACE, OPPONENT TWO!

Opponent Two attacks with a cut to your left shoulder from upstage left.

14. Pass forward and then, turning counterclockwise, pass back on left foot (facing upstage left), parry 4 (see Fig. 10-3o).
   Opponent Two passes forward and attacks with a cut to your right hip.

15. Pass back, parry 2 (see Fig. 10-3p).
   Opponent Two holds the blade in place.

16. Beginning with your left leg still forward, double pass forward and throw your left elbow up toward the imaginary partner's left shoulder (Opponent Two's arm has crossed the chest after the cut to your right hip), simulating an elbow strike to Opponent Two's face (see Fig. 10-3q).
   Opponent Two knaps, left hand against the thigh, bends over to the left, cradles his or her jaw with the left hand, and cries out in pain.

17. Touch Opponent Two's right shoulder lightly with your left hand and simulate pushing as Opponent Two staggers back, stage left (see Fig. 10-3r).
   Opponent Two stumbles away a step or two, dazed.

PHRASE FIVE/ KEEP OPPONENT ONE AWAY, WHILE YOU KILL OPPONENT TWO.

Opponent One attacks with a cut to your left hip.

18. Turn clockwise to face downstage right, double pass back and parry prime (see Fig. 10-3s), then immediately. . .

19. From prime, make a diagonal swipe, your high left to low right, passing forward (on left foot) after the swipe is completed (see Fig. 10-3t).
   Opponent One evades downstage right (to your left—in the direction of your prep).

20. Let the momentum of your swipe carry you around 180 degrees to the right, into an extended punto reverso (stepping into the lunge on your right foot), which kills Opponent Two, still staggering from your elbow strike (see Fig. 10-3u).

21. Remove your blade from Opponent Two, pivot 270 degrees to the right (see Fig. 10-3v), and end facing downstage right.
   Opponent Two falls forward between you and Opponent One.

10-3o.

10-3p.

10-3q.

10-3r.

10-3s.

10-3t.

10-3u.

10-3v.

PHRASE SIX / ONLY ONE OPPONENT
NOW!

22. Fleche forward (downstage right) over the "slain" body in pursuit of Opponent One. End with left foot forward, en garde, facing downstage right (not shown).
   Opponent One recovers to en garde to meet you.

23. Make a diagonal swipe from your high right to low left, passing forward after the blade has passed (see Fig. 10-3w).
   Opponent One evades left and back.

24. Cut to Opponent One's right hip, passing forward downstage right on your left foot (see Fig.10-3x).
   Opponent One parries 2.

25. Cut to left shoulder, pass forward (see Fig. 10-3y).
   Opponent One parries 4, then immediately swipes from your right to left at your head.

26. Duck (see Fig. 10-3z).
   Opponent One pauses at end position of the swipe.

27. Staying low, enter a reverse lunge, thrusting to center (slap sword under One's left armpit upstage), killing Opponent One (see Fig. 10-3aa).

28. Remove blade from Opponent One, pass back on right foot (see Fig.10-3bb).
   Opponent One collapses and dies.

29. Pivot clockwise on right foot and bring left heel to right heel, stand erect and salute (see Fig. 10-3cc).

30. Turn clockwise following swipe and exit downstage left—smiling.

10-3w.

10-3x.

10-3y.

10-3z.

10-3aa.

10-3bb.

10-3cc.

11

SWASHBUCKLING WITH BROADSWORDS

Let you opinions be what they will, but that the thrust cometh a nearer way, & is sooner done than the blow, is not true: & for thereof read the twelfth Paradox. . . . Again, the force of the thrust passeth straight, therefore any crosse being indirectly made, the force of a child may put it by. . . I have known a Gentleman hurt in a Rapier fight, in nine or ten places through the bodie, armes and legges, and yet hath continued in his fight, & afterward hath slaine the other, and come home and hath been cured of all his wounds without maime, & is yet living. But the blow being strongly made, taketh sometimes cleane away the hand from the arme, hath manie times been seene. Againe, a full blow upon the head or face with a short sharpe Sword is most commonly death. . . . He that giveth the first wound with a strong blow, commandeth the life of the other.

George Silver *Paradoxes of Defence* 1599

11-1. Timothy Flanagan evades a swipe from Eric Zivot in Marin Shakespeare Festival's "Macbeth."

The European crosshilt is among the most physically demanding of all stage combat weapons. After completing this chapter, you'll:

- Understand how broadsword and rapier fights differ in intention, technique, results, and dramatic possibilities
- See how body and brain must adapt to strenuous broadsword dynamics
- Perform a special broadsword form using attack and defense, as well as unarmed techniques

You may wonder why we started your stage combat training with rapiers when broadswords came first historically.

If you do, you'll probably answer that question yourself as soon as you pick up a broadsword. This hefty weapon fills the hand as no rapier can. It's heavier, more awkward, and intimidates many beginners. Starting swordplay with broadswords is a little like asking novice target shooters to start "plunking" with a 44-magnum—the hand cannon made famous by Clint Eastwood's Dirty Harry. Such a thing may be possible, but most people don't want to try it.

Stage combat with broadswords also includes many modern techniques that historians have not documented in the centuries before the rapier. This doesn't necessarily mean that these techniques weren't used in medieval times; only that we have no written proof that they were. From a teaching standpoint, it's easier for a novices to practice these basic techniques with a lighter, more manageable weapon like the rapier, and then see how these techniques *differ* when the older, heavier weapon is used. For this reason, too, we'll continue to use certain rapier-related terms (such as "true" and "false" edge even though most crosshilts had two cutting edges) since it helps us to orient the sword properly during a given maneuver.

WHAT MAKES A BROADSWORD A BROADSWORD?

"Broadsword" is an all-purpose term that means different things to different people. To most fight directors, sword makers, and historians, a broadsword is any weapon of the European crosshilt variety. A "crosshilt" is a sword that looks more or less like the stereotypical knight's sword: with straight or slightly drooping quillons, a generous pommel, and a fairly wide, longish blade—though any and all of these things can and did vary during the crosshilt's long reign: from approximately 800 to 1400 C.E.

During this period, personal combat was dominated by impact weapons: those that required strong arms to do the damage their designers intended. Cutting weapons included crosshilts and battle axes, poleaxes, falchions (oversized medieval machetes), and halberds. All of these used impact to rend mail, leather, scale, and quilted armor in order to get at, and slice, the flesh and bone underneath. Percussion weapons like blunted crosshilts and maces, morningstars, war clubs, and war hammers used impact mainly to crush muscle and bone, even through armor, stunning defenders and knocking them off balance. Thrusting weapons (like highly tapered crosshilts and all lances, spears, and pikes) concentrated the impact on a very small area, to penetrate armor (through chinks or punctures) and stab the victims.

Thus crosshilts come not only in the honed and unhoned variety, but with various blade shapes and lengths, depending on the designers' intentions. Historically, long, broad-bladed swords with honed parallel edges were used mainly for cutting. Square or round-tipped swords were used

I refuse to use "broadsword" to mean anything but the highland basket hilt sword or heavy cavalry sword of the Baroque period. Medieval crosshilts were never called "broadswords"; there were no "narrow swords" during that time. More confusion arises with swords of the two-handed variety. None of the stage weapons available today really resemble the true medieval hand-and-a-half or two-handed sword. The true two-hander is too heavy and too long for unskilled actors to wield on stage. In its place is the hand-and-a-half crosshilt, usually designed for an artificial edge-to-edge fighting style. "Hand-and-a-half" is probably a Victorian term; more accurate would be "bastard sword," on the heavy end of the spectrum, and "arming sword" on the light.

Dennis Graves, Swordcutler
"A Brief Discussion of Sword Nomenclature"
The Fight Master

exclusively for cutting; many executioner's swords taking this shape. All types made formidable battering tools. Tapered blades gave up some cutting power for increased maneuverability and the ability to thrust. The greater the taper, the more the center of balance shifted back toward the hilt and the sharper the point, the more effective the thrust. Indeed, the *estoc,* a needle-bladed crosshilt with no cutting edges at all, was designed exclusively to thrust.

In early medieval times, about the time of the First Crusade, most European crosshilts were of the single-handed variety, with moderately tapered blades. As plate armor was perfected and used more widely, the cut went into decline and thrusting and percussion weapons became more important. With longer blades came the longer handles, wider quillons, and bigger pommels needed to balance the blades. This led to the heavyish "bastard" (and lighter "arming") hand-and-a-half swords, as well as the genuine two-handers like the Scottish Claymore. Toward the end of the Medieval period and the beginning of the Renaissance, five- to six-foot "Zweihanders" (German for two handers), many with serrated or "flame" (Flamberges) blades and leather-covered ricassos, appeared. These latter monsters were wielded only by elite troops and eventually assumed mostly training and ceremonial roles. Two-handed swords were often wielded with one hand on the blade, producing a thrust-oriented bayonet, or spear-type, fighting style.

WHAT WERE BROADSWORD FIGHTS REALLY LIKE?

Arising from a warrior culture that prized individual combat but often made its weapons with inferior materials, the typical European crosshilt was much more prone to break than its modern theatrical counterpart. As a result, despite its value as a symbol of rank, it was usually viewed on the battlefield as an auxiliary weapon to be used when lances, polearms, battle axes, and hardier percussion weapons were lost or damaged.

Even so, the cut-and-thrust fighting style depicted on medieval tapestries and described in the records of the time, reveals that a battle with crosshilts was a brutal, physically exhausting affair. Even if the profusion of severed limbs, split heads, and decapitated bodies were poetic exaggerations, the power of the properly wielded crosshilt must have been awesome.

BROADSWORD VS. RAPIER: INTENTION, TECHNIQUE, RESULTS

Figure 11-2 shows an array of single-handed, hand-and-a-half, and two-handed theatrical crosshilts. They all have things in common—with each other and with the rapier—but they also have their differences. Generally, the heavier the sword, the slower and more difficult it is to wield. This creates opportunities for, and the necessity of, a more physical style of fighting: using hands for grappling, fists for punching, feet for kicking, and shoulders for barging an opponent.

Claymore is a corruption of the Scottish claidheamah mor, meaning "great sword." Originally a two-handed sword used by the Scots through the 1400s and 1500s. It had a heavy, straight blade up to sixty inches long. The quillons (cross guards), slanting toward the blade, were straight. The grip, often bearing an interwoven Celtic pattern, was also straight. The weapon was noted for its fine balance.

By the 1700s, the two-handed sword had passed into disuse. The name "claymore," however, was now applied to the basket-hilted broadsword that became Scotland's national weapon. The name transference probably occurred because many of the old-style claymore blades were simply cut down and converted into basket-hilted weapons.

Nick Evangelista
The Encyclopedia of the Sword

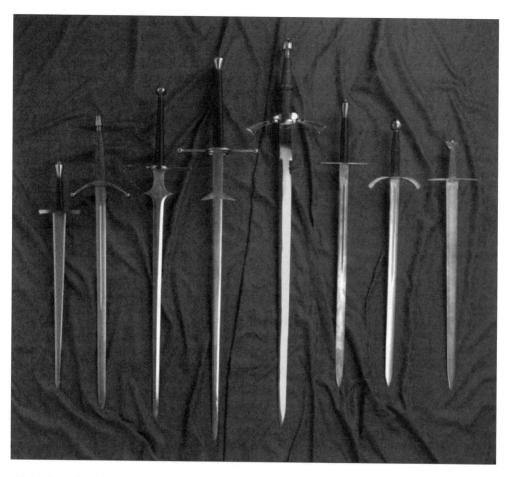

11-2. *Swordmakers (from left to right): Lewis Shaw, American Fencers Supply, Colonial Armory, American Fencers Supply, Oscar Kolombatovich, Dennis Graves, Dennis Graves, Museum Replicas.*

SIMILARITIES AND DISSIMILARITIES   As you've seen, the historical rapier is intended for thrusting, with cutting as a secondary possibility. The honed, gently tapered crosshilt (the model for most stage combat broadswords), reverses this: cutting predominates and thrusting is saved for targets of opportunity, or for the final kill. Because the rapier was lighter, the techniques developed for it encouraged a wide array of feints, deceptions, and ripostes impossible with a heavier weapon. In those more fencing-oriented fights, a defender could never be quite sure of the attacker's true intention: was it to cut, thrust, disarm, wound, or kill? With the broadsword, the intention was obvious: most blows were fight-stopping cuts and swipes, with the occasional deadly thrust thrown in.

11-3.

The amount of misconception on the subject of ancient sword-play often displayed by some historical painters and novelists is truly incredible. Even in the works of such writers as Dumas, Ainsworth, and even Walter Scott, very seldom guilty of anachronism on any other subject, one reads of duels in the seventeenth century, details of which are evidently borrowed from a modern fencing school.

Egerton Castle
Schools and Masters of Fence

BASIC BROADSWORD TECHNIQUE Because of the weight of most crosshilts, when wielding one you must keep your center of gravity low by using a somewhat squatty en garde stance. Your feet should be wider apart and your knees more deeply bent than when using a rapier. This helps you keep your balance on defense while adding the additional power of your legs and torso when you attack.

The broadsword is customarily held with both hands, using the grip shown in Figure 11-3, right hand in front of the left, with the web of the right thumb positioned just below the quillons, over the false edge of the blade. Single-handed broadswords are also held in this manner. In this case, just tuck the pommel into the palm of the left hand and use it to help guide and steady the blade. Don't loop your right forefinger over the quillons or you're liable to lose it—or get it sorely mashed. (Witnesses of medieval battles said the grounds were littered with forefingers—one reason pas d'anes were invented.)

USING BROADSWORDS IN DEFENSE

Figure 11-4a shows the basic broadsword en garde stance used by most actor-combatants. Hold the sword comfortably with both hands, right hand over left, in front of the centerline of your body, using your back and shoulders (not your arms) to support most of its weight. Hold the hilt no higher than your navel with the sword tip pointing up at the opponent. Since the extra weight of the broadsword tends to pull you forward, adjust your stance by stepping further back on your left foot and lower your center of gravity until you feel stable. (A heavy blade in motion will also tend to pull you off-line, so CG control is even more important after the action starts.) Keep your back straight, head up, with your body balanced.

Two-handed parries with a broadsword follow the basic forms you already know, though they'll take a little more effort. Be sure you clear the box of safety as you move between parries and don't inadvertently scoop an attacking blade in toward your body. Working our way around the familiar defensive box drill:

PARRY SEVEN   Parry 7 is much more comfortable and natural with broadswords (and much quicker to achieve with two hands) than is parry 1, or prime, so that's what we use for a basic low-line defense on the left side (see Fig. 11-4b). Parry 1 can be useful, though, to riposte with an inside moulinet and vertical cut to the head.

PARRY TWO   Broadsword parry 2 is similar to rapier parry 2. Use the left hand to adjust the angle of the blade, which should point slightly leftward as well as down (see Fig. 11-4c).

PARRY THREE   Parry 3 is similar to rapier parry 3—just make sure you continue to hold the true edge out to receive the attacker's cut and not the flat of the blade (see Fig. 11-4d).

PARRY FOUR   Parry 4 is similar to rapier parry 4, but the addition of the left hand below the right makes it even stronger (see Fig. 11-4e).

PARRY FIVE   This takes a bit of getting used to, since you must now extend your left arm across your body while raising your right hand to a rapier-style parry 5 (see Fig. 11-4f). Keep that left hand securely on the handle or pommel; don't let it slip away to become a useless finger grip. It's also easy to let the hilt creep to the left, which exposes your right side to attack. Also be careful not to hold the hilt directly overhead. Make sure you hold it slightly to the right and a foot or so in front of your body, so that attacks to your head are parried with the forte of your blade.

Unlike the "bastard" sword, which may be wielded with one hand or with both, the two-hander was of such a ponderous nature that it was no easy matter for even a stout fellow to maneuver it well, and that was of necessity always with both hands. It approached six feet in length from pommel to point. It does not appear to have possessed any scabbard, but the soldier carried it naked at the "slope," with the flat of the blade resting on his shoulder. From its immense weight, it could only be entrusted to the biggest and strongest men-at-arms, some of whom used often to be detailed to act as escort to the Auncient, or Standard-bearer.
Alfred Hutton
The Sword and the Centuries

11-4a.

11-4b.

11-4c.

11-4d.

11-4e.

11-4f.

11-4g.

11-4h.

PARRY FIVE A This is similar to rapier parry 5A, but stronger due to the inclusion of your left hand (see Fig. 11-4g). Again, be sure to hold the sword comfortably in front of you with the forte (not the hilt) guarding your head.

HANGING PARRIES Perform broadsword hanging parries 5 and 5A as you would the corresponding rapier parries, keeping your left hand on the handle or pommel (see Figs. 11-4h and 11-4i). For hanging parry 5, don't let your left arm, elbow, or shoulder block your view of the attack, or allow the fingers of your left hand to slip. For both parries, don't let the tip of the sword drift back to expose the trailing leg. Keep the blade aligned with, and out in front of your body, and angled down at about forty-five degrees.

REINFORCED PARRIES To reinforce any parry (except parries 7 and 5A, where the blade is inaccessible to the left hand) place your left hand on the foible (fingers *over* the blade) while the right hand grips the handle normally and holds the sword at the proper end position. This makes the sword more rigid and conveys the image of strength—or desperation, depending on where in a fight it occurs.

To apply this system of clearly defined parries to the use of crosshilts would appear to be anachronistic—especially the further one goes back into their history. Single-handed crosshilts were primarily military weapons intended for use with shields, so blade parries of any kind were probably few and far between. When true hand-and-a-half and two-handed swords

11-4i.

came into widespread use, countercuts were the favored method of defense and, as you've learned, those are best left to the movies, and not used in live theatre, where safety is paramount. Besides, the Middle Ages encompassed the "Age of Faith," when a systematic approach to anything except religion was not encouraged. Still, we must base our broadsword play on something, and it's possible that many of the standard defensive moves documented later, appeared first as devices employed by successful broadsword fighters.

SOME HISTORICAL BROADSWORD STANCES USEFUL ON THE STAGE

Even as rapiers gained in popularity, the old swordmasters continued to teach their students the art of the broadsword as a complement to their training. Part of this was undoubtedly due to tradition; but it had practical aspects, too. The great two-handers were still being used by select troops in many armies, so no "manly" nobleman considered his training complete without some experience with these larger weapons. Two-handed swords used by civilians were somewhat shorter and lighter than their military counterparts, with more highly tapered blades (though they often retained the "flukes," or steel spikes, on the forte to protect the hand when gripping the ricasso for close-in thrusting).

This weapon, sometimes known as the old English "long sword," as a fighting arm stands by itself; it was the favorite weapon of our King Henry VIII in his athletic days, and he proposed its use in the tournaments at the "Field of the Cloth of Gold," but Francis I objected to it on the ground that there were no gauntlets then made sufficiently strong to guarantee the hands against its powerful strokes. . . . The best manner of carrying the two-hander is taken from Alfieri. It is borne point upwards in the left hand, which grasps the grip about the centre, with the flat of the blade resting against the shoulder; it must be remembered that this sword is double edged.

To Salute:

1. Pass the right hand across the body and seize the grip close to the quillons.

2. Bring the sword perpendicularly in front of the body with the quillons in line with the mouth.

3. Carry the sword over to the right side, and lower the point to the front about four inches from the ground, and draw back the right foot about six inches.

4. Raise the sword to a perpendicular position at the right side.

5. Carry the sword over to the left side, and resume the marching position.

Alfred Hutton
Old Sword-Play: the Systems of Fence in Vogue During the XVI, XVII, and XVIII Centuries
1892

In *The Fight Master*, September, 1985, Charles Daniels surveyed three sixteenth century swordfighting manuals (Boeheim, *Kriegbuch*, 1573; Lichtenauer, *Kunst des Fechten*, circa 1600; and Mener, *Grundliche Beschreibung der freihen Ritterlichen und Kunst des Fechtens*, 1600) which revealed how standardized the two-handed technique had become by this period—a time when Italian swordmasters had already begun to write their own treatises on rapiers. The wards shown in Daniels' survey were designed to facilitate delivery of five "master cuts" (*Meistershiebe*), four types of cuts to the head (top, left side, right side, and chin) as well as stealthy inverted cuts, rising from low to high. According to Daniels, Mener's advice to novices included, "Try to be the first on the fencing floor. When your opponent comes into the area, try to hit him before he gets into a stance,"—an interesting commentary not only on the effectiveness of a proper stance, but the state of chivalry in the late Renaissance.

Did medieval broadsword fighters ever use these stances? The visual records from tapestries and other artwork is scanty, and medieval texts, such as the legends of King Arthur, are historically unreliable. It seems likely, though, that these later techniques were based at least in part on practices handed down by military and knightly traditions. Certainly, in stage combat, we should feel free to incorporate the spirit, if the not the letter, of such techniques into our fights, particularly when the precise details may never be known.

USING THE TWO-HANDED BROADSWORD STANCES   The basic broadsword stance used in this book (and by most theatrical fight directors) is what the old German masters called "pflug": a multipurpose guard with the sword held low in front of the body's centerline. This gave the fighter a variety of defensive options, although it was less useful for a quick attack, since the sword had to be brought back (prepped) considerably to build momentum. Because victories with the broadsword often went to the quickest and strongest, holding a given stance for too long was not recommended. Other en gardes were probably used when an aggressive fighter planned a rapid attack: an effect we can easily duplicate on stage. To do this (keeping in mind our general rule that a sword should be pointed at the opponent to convey a sense of maximum threat), we've adapted six of the traditional two-handed stances to use as alternatives to the basic en garde stance (described above) at the beginning of a theatrical broadsword fight (the gist of each term, in English, follows each German name):

11-5a.

11-5b.

11-5c.

1. OLBER (HIGH OR ABOVE) To enter the stance from the basic broadsword en garde, pass back, (left foot is now forward) letting your chest face right, and raise the hilt to at least shoulder-height, right hand in pronation and left shoulder pointed forward. The blade should be pointed forward, tip downward at about a thirty-degree angle, with the true edge (the edge on the same side as the fingers) facing up (see Fig. 11-5a). This stance looks best when the grip is clearly visible to the audience.

2. LANGORT (EXTENSION) To assume this stance from the basic en garde, raise the hilt from hip level to just above the level of your eyes, keeping the blade pointing forward at the same relative angle. You should now be looking at your opponent through the space between your wrists below the pommel. Be sure to hold the sword well forward, but not at full extension (see Fig. 11-5b). This stance can be used facing either stage left or stage right with equal effect.

3. HANGETORT (HANGING EXTENSION) From the basic en garde, raise the hilt to your left shoulder, as if you were about to make a cut, but let the blade fall until its tip is pointed forward. (This stance is similar to parry 5A except the sword tip and your right shoulder are now pointed at the opponent—see Fig. 11-5c.) Again, this stance looks best if the audience can see your grip.

11-5d.

11-5e.

11-5f.

4. SCHLÜSSEL (KEY) This stance employs a body position similar to Olber, with left foot forward, except that a/ the flat of the blade, not the true edge, faces up (right hand in pronation), b/ the blade is parallel to the ground (the tip does not tilt down); and c/ the hilt is held lower, no higher than the chest. In other words, to find this stance, simply move to Olber and drop the hilt, flattening the blade as you go. This lower, flattened stance looks particularly menacing, as if a deadly thrust is imminent (see Fig. 11-5d).

5. EYNHORN (UNICORN) From Schlüssel, simply raise the hilt to your head. This looks very much like parry 5, except your left shoulder and the tip of the sword face the opponent. The blade is still parallel to the ground, but the true edge now faces up (see Fig. 11-5e).

6. SCHRANKHUT (CLOSED GUARD) From Eynhorn, let the sword fall forward in a gentle arc until the blade reaches about a forty-five degree angle to the ground. Your left elbow will be almost touching your ribs and your right arm will be at nearly full extension (see Fig. 11-5f). If your sword is very long or very heavy, or if you are shorter than average), the sword tip may tend to touch the ground, but keep it "alive"—at least a few inches off the floor and pointed in the general direction of your partner. Remember, a sword pointed at the floor kills the tension, so you want to display that menacing cutting edge. This stance is effective when you face any direction on stage.

PERFORMING BROADSWORD ATTACKS

Two-handed cuts look powerful and convincing if you keep your center low and strive for full extension. Don't over-exaggerate your prep by leaning backward before you swing, but *do* let the sword pull you forward when cutting on a pass.

CUTS To demonstrate cuts on both sides from the basic en garde position, draw the hilt back to your left shoulder as you did with the rapier, targeting your imaginary partner's right shoulder. Keep the tip of the blade up and out of your partner's face as you prep (see Fig. 11-6b). Begin the cut, leading with your wrist, right hand in pronation, then snap the blade forward at the end of the cut, as if you were trying to fling a drop of water *past* the target. Don't begin the forward pass with your left foot until the sword has passed your body and it feels like it wants to pull you forward (see Fig. 11-6c).

11-6a.

11-6b.

11-6c.

11-6e.

11-6d.

Next, draw the sword back at once, to your right shoulder (see Fig. 11-6d) and repeat the cut in the same manner to your imaginary partner's left shoulder, only this time with your right hand in supination (see Fig. 11-6e). Strive to really feel that extension and remember, you don't have to hit hard to make a broadsword cut look hard-hitting.

THRUSTS Because they add variety to a fight, we use broadsword thrusts on stage more often than they were probably used in real combat. To get the feel of a two-handed thrust on a forward pass, start in the en garde position and prep to your left side by bringing the hilt back to your left hip, right hand in supination (see Fig. 11-7b), then extend the tip toward the target, which is your imaginary partner's right hip, keeping your feet in place (see Fig. 11-7c). When you've read the defender's reaction (suppose your opponent is moving to parry 2), pass forward on your left foot, letting the blade draw you forward (see Fig. 11-7d). It's easier to lose balance with a broadsword than with a rapier, so be sure to keep your trailing right foot flat on the floor and your body upright during the pass.

11-7a. En Garde.

11-7b. Preparation.

11-7c. Extension.

11-7d. Passing lunge.

11-8a.

11-8b.

11-8c.

11-8d.

MOULINETS Two-handed moulinets can feel a bit awkward, but because of the extra weight of the broadsword blade, the moulinets are very efficient for beginning overhead vertical or diagonal cuts and swipes.

To perform a stationary inside moulinet from the en garde position, (see Fig. 11-8a) drop the tip to the left and "look at your watch" on your right wrist (see Fig. 11-8b) as you pass through parry prime. Make sure the cutting edge of the blade continues twisting back until it faces the rear (see Fig. 11-8c) then begin the blade's upward and forward motion (see Fig. 11-8d). End with full extension (your left arm and sword making a straight line—(see Fig. 11-8e), snapping the blade smartly into position about a foot or so above and in front of the head of your imaginary partner. This process should feel like a moulinet with a rapier, and may even be easier, given the extra weight of the blade. Use your left hand to help balance and steady the weapon.

Now try an outside moulinet. Let the tip drop to the right (see Fig. 11-8f) and roll your wrists, bringing the blade back until your knuckles (and the true edge) face behind you (see Fig. 11-8g), then begin the blade's upward and forward motion (see Fig. 11-8h). Reach for full extension—your right arm and the sword being perfectly aligned as you snap the blade into position a foot or so above, and in front of, the head of your imaginary partner. Again, keep your left hand on the handle (or the pommel) throughout, to steady and control the blade (see Fig. 11-8i).

11-8e.   *11-8f.*   *11-8g.*   *11-8h.*   *11-8i.*

PRIS DE FER The basic techniques for rapier glissades, croisés, binds and envelopments apply to the broadsword, except, of course, that your grip is two-handed and the sword is a lot heavier. These two factors are assets when it comes to attacking another blade. If you transmit most of the strength from your legs and body through your right arm, and use your left hand to help steady and direct the blade, you may find all "taking of the blade" maneuvers much easier with a broadsword. And, since the broadsword moves a bit slower than the rapier, you'll generally find it easier to avoid entanglements with your feet during binds and envelopments that involve a forward pass.

COUNTERCUTS Like a countercut with the rapier, this technique was widely used, historically, but is seldom seen on stage. Combining defensive and offensive moves into one, a defender performing a countercut with a broadsword (provided it was timed correctly) had an advantage over the attacker because the impact of the parry tended to drive the attacker's sword away and helped push the counterattacker's sword in *toward* the target. On stage, countercuts like these are hard to control because there is no predetermined or safe end position. Because it is also difficult to tell who is attacking and who is defending, there is little dramatic payoff.

POMMEL AND QUILLON ATTACKS The broadsword's heavy hilt was used often in attack. To simulate a pommel attack on an opponent's stomach from the en garde stance, release the handle with your right hand and drop the tip to the right until the blade is parallel to the ground (tip pointing right), grab the foible of the blade with your right hand in pronation (fingers *over* the blade) and cover the pommel with your left palm. Now prep by passing back with your right foot into a narrower, deeper, springier horse stance (see Fig. 11-9b). Continue the prep by drawing the sword back like a battering ram until the hilt is next to your hip and look directly at the stomach of your imaginary partner (see Fig. 11-9c). Complete the action by driving the sword forward, hilt first, with your hand safely covering the pommel, blade parallel to the ground, until you're just short of your imaginary partner's stomach. Accompany the pummeling action with an advance on the weak side (left foot first, landing heel-toe, then bring the right foot after it—see Fig. 11-9d). Your partner should respond with a suitable groan and double over, completing the illusion.

You must never strike your partner with the pommel, which should always be covered by your hand for added protection.

Broadsword quillons make an excellent war hammer when the weapon is swung by the blade. To get the feel of an overhead "smash," start at the en garde position and pass to the rear, narrowing your stance as you did for

11-9a.

11-9b.

the pommel attack. Take your left hand off the handle and bring the hilt back to your right hip, blade pointing forward, as if you were preparing for a thrust. Now grip the foible of the blade with your left hand (fingers *over* the blade) and supinate your right hand, seizing the forte (with the flat of the blade against your palm), and look at the target—the air a foot or so in front of and above your imaginary partner's head. When your partner reacts (begins to parry 5 or 5A, or evade—all common defenses against this move), swing the hilt overhead like a sledge hammer, passing forward after the hilt has crossed the centerline of your body. It's permissible to let your right hand slide down the blade a little, but keep it somewhere on the forte. The closer your right hand stays to the quillons, the more control you'll have over the sword. Stop the hammer blow higher than you would stop an overhead cut, for the ends of your quillons will extend down below your partner's parry: about eighteen inches above and in front of the imaginary defender's head. This is the same relative area where your attack would be parried, on your forte, between hand and quillons. Extend fully, as you would for an attack with the blade—that's what sells the power of your blow to the audience.

Hilt attacks can also be made as swipes, although this desperate-looking maneuver works best when the story of the fight gives you a reason to be holding your sword by the blade; such as having to recover the sword hurriedly after a disarm.

11-9c.

11-9d.

REVERSE GRIP ATTACKS Once the blade is stable, it's fairly simple to assume a "reverse" grip on a sword, where the quillons are against the heel of the hand rather than the web of the thumb. The easiest way to reverse your grip intentionally is to move the sword to the scabbard position on your left hip (don't insert it into the scabbard if you're wearing one; just hold it blade-down against your hip with your left hand) and switch the grip with your right hand. You can now return the sword to play by making diagonal swipes, such as inscribing an X in the air in front of you as you pass forward.

To make a right-handed reverse-grip swipe (left to right) with such a weapon, it's best to steady the blade with your left hand on the ricasso, thereby increasing your control. To reverse-grip swipe from right to left, a one-handed grip is permissible as long as the forte rests securely under or along your forearm because, in this grip, where your forearm goes, the blade will follow.

To make a reverse grip thrust (that is, to thrust at an opponent attacking from behind), always stabilize and guide the blade with the free hand. A reverse thrust on the left side, for example, positions your right hand in a reverse grip on the handle (heel of the hand near the quillons) and your left hand on the forte or somewhere near the middle of the blade at the "point of percussion." A reverse thrust on the right side has your right hand grabbing the forte with your thumb near the quillons and your left hand on the pommel. If you use this move in supervised partnered work, your instructor or fight director will give you cues for the eye contact, preparation, reaction, action sequence needed to keep it safe.

11-10a.

11-10b.

11-10c.

USING HANDS AND FEET IN ATTACK Although the basic broadsword grip requires two hands, either hand may freed to punch, slap, or grapple at close quarters. To get the feel of this combination of armed and unarmed moves, we will practice delivering a backhand slap to a shared knap while wielding a broadsword—a move that might be required in a typical stage fight.

From the en garde position, open your stance to the left (step back farther on the left foot to enter a shallow drop stance) taking the sword with you in your left hand, letting the tip drop and move backward as you release the handle from your right hand. Prep for the slap as you did in unarmed combat by moving your right hand across your chest and down to your left hip (see Fig. 11-10b). When your imaginary partner reacts by placing the knapping (left) hand onto the chest (palm facing the direction of the blow), deliver the back-hand slap as described in Chapter 6 (see Fig. 11-10c). Make sure your right hand and your body continue to the right and your sword stays to the left, as your imaginary partner reacts by pivoting away and cradling his or her jaw in pain.

To demonstrate a combat kick (see Figs. 11-11a through 11-11c) imagine your opponent has been knocked down on all fours during the fight and you want to kick the vanquished defender in the ribs. Approach the victim from the side, with his or her head to your right. From the en garde stance, pass forward while transferring your sword to your right hand, moving it safely out of the way (down, to the right, and a bit behind you. Do not bring your sword anywhere near your partner's head—see Fig. 11-11b). You should now be about one step away from your partner's side. From a left foot forward stance, pass forward, raising your right knee sharply. Extend your lower leg gently until the soft pocket of your upper foot (between the arch and the toes) gently contacts your imaginary partner's external obliques on the left side (see Fig. 11-11c). Upon contact, snap your foot back while your partner reacts by falling over and groaning, completing the illusion (see Chapter 6 for more details on kicks and knaps).

Other unarmed techniques can be applied safely during swordfights, depending on the choreography. In a real fight, the attacker sometimes kicked the defender's groin while performing an overhead cut, and the defender kicked back at the groin or knee during parries. Whatever your fight calls for, though, just be sure both the aggressor's and victim's swords are discreetly removed, clear of the paths of moving bodies, hands, and feet.

11-11a.

11-11b.

11-11c.

"I have this intensity in me, it makes the audience believe in what I do because I do believe in what I do"– Bruce Lee.

David Chow and Richard Spangler
Kung Fu: History, Philosophy and Technique

A SOLO BROADSWORD FORM

Here is a broadsword form to help you develop your technique, get a better feel for crosshilt dynamics, and cultivate your ability to act while in action. Like the solo rapier form, it simulates a lone swordfighter being beset by multiple attackers and incorporates moves from unarmed combat. Your twenty-one move, six-phrase part is given in the roman typestyle; the moves and reactions of your imaginary opponents are in italic.

Begin slowly, learning the routine move by move, then phrase by phrase. Your goal is to achieve a fluid and realistic combat rhythm. Don't forget to breathe!

When you feel comfortable with the moves and have memorized your part of the routine, try visualizing your imaginary partners as real actors in a stage production. Express the feelings your character would have at each stage of the fight, and experiment with vocalizations. In forcing you to be extra physical, the broadsword is an excellent weapon for cultivating the release of combat energy through an exhalation as you strike—similar to the "ki-ai" portion of the Swans in the Chairman Mao warmups (see Chapter 5).

PHRASE ONE/ "WHERE'D THEY COME FROM?"
TWO OPPONENTS ATTACK

1. Face the audience in a relaxed, open stance, right foot slightly forward, holding the sword in your right hand only, outstretched downward and to the right, as if in prayer or supplication (see Fig. 11-12a).
   The first opponent attacks with an overhead cut from stage right.

2. Step out diagonally on your left foot, downstage left, and perform a hanging parry 5A (see Fig. 11-12b).
   Opponent One runs past you on the right.

3. Bring your sword clockwise over your head and pivot around until you're facing upstage left, following Opponent One, who continues to run stage left (see Fig. 11-12c). However, Opponent Two has now entered upstage left. Continue to pivot, pass forward on your left foot and cut to Opponent Two's right shoulder (see Fig. 11-12d).
   Opponent Two parries 3.

4. Pass forward on your right foot, cut to Two's left shoulder (see Fig.11-12e).
   Opponent Two parries 4.

5. Balancing on your right foot, kick Opponent Two in the stomach with your left foot (see Fig. 11-12f). Put your left foot down in front of your right.
   Opponent Two doubles over and falls back.

11-12a.

11-12b.

11-12c.

11-12d.

11-12e.

11-12f.

11-12g.

11-12h.

PHRASE TWO/ OPPONENT ONE ATTACKS AGAIN

Opponent One now runs at you from downstage left, moulineting for an overhead cut.

6. Turn to the right to receive the attack, pass back on your right foot facing down left and parry 5 (see Fig. 11-12g). You drive this attack away with a glissade (see Fig. 11-12h).

7. Pass back on your left foot and make a horizontal stomach swipe. *Opponent One evades back* (see Fig. 11-12i).

Opponent Two now re-enters the fight from stage left, with an overhead cut.

8. Pass back on your right foot, parry 5 (see Fig. 11-12j).

Opponent One now moves in beside Opponent Two, sword raised for an overhead cut. Their stomachs are exposed, making them tempting targets.

9. From the parry 5 position, pass back and swipe at their stomachs from right to left, 360 degrees—making one complete turn counter-clockwise (see Figs.11-12k and 11-12l).

Both opponents jump back to evade your swipe.

Finish facing the audience, your right arm across your chest with the sword to your left, pointing in the general direction of your two opponents. Now, take your left hand off the handle and put it over the blade at the forte, just below the quillons (see Fig. 11-12m). Pull the blade crisply down into its scabbard position.

The two opponents continue to eye your blade (pointed at them) warily, even though you're facing away from them.

11-12i.

11-12j.

11-12k.

11-12l.

11-12m.

PHRASE THREE/ OPPONENT THREE ENTERS THE FIGHT FROM DOWNSTAGE RIGHT

Opponent Three now confronts you, entering in the en garde position from downstage right.

10. Take your right hand from the sword then put it back on the handle, gripping it from underneath, putting the heel of your hand against the quillons in a reverse grip. Make a diagonal swipe from high left to low right holding the sword in a reverse grip and pass forward on your left foot (see Fig. 11-12n). As the momentum of the blade carries the sword past your right side (see Fig. 11-12o), raise the handle and swipe in the other direction, high right to low left, then pass forward on your right foot (see Fig. 11-12p).

Opponent Three jumps back to evade your double swipes, but the two behind you run forward to attack.

11. Let the momentum from your last swipe help pivot you around to face the two attackers coming at you from the rear and carry the sword to your left side (see Fig. 11-12q). Your sword blade still points behind you in the direction of Opponent Three, downstage right.

Opponents One and Two, startled to see you facing them, stop suddenly—confused. Opponent Three, now recovered from the evasions, runs at you from the rear, sword raised for an overhead cut.

Still facing Opponents One and Two, perform a backward thrust from your left hip, reverse lunging (simply step back on your left foot and sink down lower into a deeper horse stance). This thrust impales Opponent Three.

Opponent Three dies.

11-12n.

11-12o.

11-12p.

11-12q.

11-12r.

11-12s.

PHRASE FOUR/ OPPONENT ONE GETS KNOCKED OUT OF THE FIGHT

Opponents One and Two attack again, simultaneously.

12. Release the handle with your right hand and, with your left hand holding the sword by its forte just below the quillons, make a diagonal swipe (left to right) and then pass forward on your left foot (see Fig. 11-12r). *Both opponents jump back.*

13. As the swipe carries the sword to your right side, take the handle with your right hand in the normal forward grip and return your left hand to the handle behind it (see Fig. 11-12s). Pass forward stage left on your right foot, making a two-handed swipe at your opponents' stomachs, right to left (see Fig. 11-12t). *Both opponents jump back again. Opponent One, from downstage left, attacks, with a cut to your right shoulder.*

14. Pass back on your right foot and parry 3 (see Fig. 11-12u), then immediately "beat up" the attacking blade by raising your hilt sharply, banging Opponent One's blade with your quillons, driving it upward (see Fig. 11-12v). *Opponent One, startled, watches the blade bounce up to a vertical position, leaving One's stomach open to attack.*

15. Take your right hand from the handle and, letting the blade drop to your right, place your fingers over the foible in pronation. Prep back horizontally to your right, covering the pommel with your left hand, and make a pommel attack on Opponent One's stomach accompanied by a weak-side (left-footed) advance (see Fig. 11-12w). *Opponent One collapses downstage left and is out of the fight.*

11-12t.

11-12u.

11-12v.

11-12w.

PHRASE FIVE/ "CUT 'EM IN HALF"
Opponent Two attacks your exposed left side from stage left.

16. From the end position of your pommel attack (full extension from the weak-side lunge), move your left hand up to the handle just below the quillons, face upstage right, and pass forward upstage right on your left foot (see Fig. 11-12x). Leaving your right hand on the blade, continue to spin around to the right, clockwise, by pivoting your hips to face stage left and pass back on your right foot. End in a *left-handed*, reinforced parry prime, protecting your right side from Opponent Two's cut. You are now facing stage left again with your left foot forward (see Fig. 11-12y).
Opponent Two with sword against your blade, is amazed at how quickly and inventively you were able to recover from your awkward lunge and foil the attack.

17. With Opponent Two's blade still against yours, push the tip of your sword upward with your right hand into a one to three bind. (Remember, your grip is now left handed, so the references to the parries are now reversed: prime is on your right side, and so on) As both blades pass overhead, pass forward on your right foot facing upstage center (see Fig. 11-12z.) Finish the bind with an expulsion, shoving the opposing blade up and away sharply. Release your right hand from the blade and let the sword travel to your left hip.
Opponent Two's sword is thrown violently back to the right, leaving the stomach open to attack.

18. From the end position of your bind (left hand holding the sword in a normal forward grip with the hilt near your left hip, and extended to your left, prep for an elbow to the stomach. Raise your right arm high over your right shoulder— (see Fig. 11-12aa) then drop your right elbow smartly to your right hip (see Fig. 11-12bb).
Opponent Two doubles over and staggers backwards slightly downstage simulating an elbow to the stomach.

19. Put your right hand below your left on the sword's handle. Pass back on your right foot and pivot to face downstage center. Deliver a crushing two-handed vertical cut to Opponent Two, effectively "cutting 'im in half" (see Fig. 11-12cc).
Opponent Two, cleaved in twain, dies.

11-12x.

11-12y.

11-12z.

11-12aa.

11-12bb.

11-12cc.

There is an account of the use of two-handed swords from as early as the time of the First Crusade, when the crusaders were defending themselves in a small fort into which the Saracens had succeeded in penetrating. With two-handed swords they managed to drive off the invaders. It was only when the besiegers lit a fire at the gates of the stronghold that they finally succeeded in destroying the courageous defenders.

Eduard Wagner
Cut and Thrust Weapons

PHRASE SIX/ "WHERE'D EVERYBODY GO?"

Opponent One, disheartened and shaken, holds the sword out toward you in a tentative en garde.

20. Still in a left-hand, forward grip, raise your sword from the body of Opponent Two and swing it, false-edge first (see Fig. 11-12dd), right to left, spinning with it for one complete circle (see Fig. 11-12ee).

Opponent One, seeing your deadly sword approaching, scampers from the stage.

When your spin has ended with you facing the audience, stop and release your right hand from the handle. Continue to swing the sword overhead in the same direction for one more revolution.

21. When the second sword-spin is finished, assume your original position—arms out and slightly down (but now with the sword in your left hand), legs slightly apart in a horse stance—this time with a triumphant smile on your face, as the spotlight focuses on you (see Fig. 11-12ff).

This ends the fight, and the form.

11-12dd.

11-12ee.

11-12ff.

For those who want an extra challenge, try re-staging the entire fight beginning with the sword in your left hand: *all moves will be mirror images of those in the original fight.* Such exercises are common in the martial arts, and left-handed swordplay is encouraged by some masters as a means to improve coordination and build weak-side strength—an important asset if a character's right arm was wounded in a fight.

In the next and final part of this book, you'll see how everything you've learned will come together when you start working with other actors, directors, and fight choreographers—and how stage combat training can add depth and bring more opportunities to any theatrical career.

PART III

THE COMPLEAT
SWASHBUCKLER

WORKING WITH FIGHT DIRECTORS

With an emphasis on historical swordplay, the thought that stands out the most was a comment Paddy Crean attributed to Errol Flynn. What Flynn wanted in a fight was "good, fast action." Paddy pointed out that "one fits the historical accuracy in where you can and when you can."
Linda McCollum "Special Workshop Report" *The Fight Master*

12.1 Fight Director Richard Lane giving direction to Aloysius Gigl (top) and Michael Degood on the set of A.C.T.'s "The Royal Family."

It takes two to fight, as well as to tango, so your perspective on stage combat will change when you work with a partner. In this chapter, you'll discover:

- How a fight director differs from a stage director: what you can expect from each
- Tricks for learning complex fight choreography quickly and safely
- Practical tips for acting while in action—and how to safely cover up mistakes

SAFE FIGHTS ARE NO ACCIDENT

Competence and confidence go hand in hand, but they're only the beginning of theatrical swordplay. For most performers, a swordfight isn't a swordfight without an audience and ringing steel. The best way to blend your personal skills with professional showmanship is under the tutelage of a qualified fight director, also called a fight arranger or fight choreographer. Unlike stage directors, who know about acting technique and drama but are sometimes untrained in stage combat, professional fight directors devote their entire careers to bringing intense, physical conflict to life theatrically. Among the many benefits they bring to your ensemble are:

- *Increased safety.* Fight directors are, first and foremost, masters of illusion They know how to make a move look dangerous while keeping it safe. If you've studied stage combat with amateurs or entirely on your own, they can help you break bad habits.

- *Feedback on performance.* Fight directors are skilled observers. They advocate the best fight possible—one that does justice to the story—not simply one interpretation over another. They help you find and realize the best your character has to offer.

- *Diagnosis and resolution of problems.* Fight directors help confine the conflict to the fictional characters. If you're having difficulty communicating with your partner, verbally or non-verbally, the fight director can usually spot the problem and help you find the right solution. This is especially helpful when actors with different backgrounds, experience, and stage combat skills must perform together.

- *Customized instruction.* People have different learning styles—particularly when it comes to the multiple demands of movement, coordination, and vocalization. Good fight directors are also good teachers, and like all good teachers, they are aware of individual differences and tailor their instructions accordingly.

- *Tips, tricks, and shortcuts for saving time and money.* Because each production is different, no two fights are ever the same. The actors' skills and physical capacities, the stage director's artistic values and intentions, the physical resources of the set and setting, and the production's budget must all be considered. Good fight directors use these raw materials creatively to get the maximum bang for the buck, sharing trade secrets that enhance the illusion and keep the action moving. They also collaborate with stage directors, shortening the fights when they run too long, re-staging them to accommodate problems with lighting, even re-choreographing the routines should the demands of the fights exceed the strength of the sets and costumes.

So essential have professional fight directors become in today's world of naturalistic theater that the Actors' Equity Association and the American Guild of Musical Artists (AGMA, the singers' union), now require that fight directors

. . .anyone attempting to teach fence in [fifteenth century] Germany was offered the alternative of fighting the one captain and five masters in turns or together, or of entering the association under their rule.

Egerton Castle
Schools and Masters of Fence

By the middle of the fifteenth century, it was probably safe for a man to admit that he ran a school of fence, though legislation of the thirteenth and fourteenth centuries forbidding such schools was still in force. But the professional fencing teacher was still classed with "rogues and vagabonds"— and actors!—and such a classification did not encourage lively, analytical discriminating minds into the profession.

Arthur Wise
The Art and History of Personal Combat

be retained whenever weapons are involved in a production. AGMA rules, in particular, require:

- That they be engaged during rehearsals to work with artists and understudies, in collaboration with the choreographer or stager, and that no artist shall be issued a weapon until he or she has received instruction in its safe use.
- That when questions of safety arise, the decisions of the fight director will prevail.
- That rehearsals shall be preceded by appropriate warmup periods.
- That a fight director be present for at least one on-stage technical rehearsal of the fight, and supervise any re-staging (such as that made necessary by smaller stages found on tour).

Last but not least, the rules require that, to be considered qualified, the fight director must be certified by the Society of American Fight Directors or have similar qualifications. This is a long-delayed but significant step toward better and safer fights.

HOW SOLO AND PARTNERED SWASHBUCKLING DIFFER

No matter how well you master solo swordplay—that is, your half of the fight—the fact that you are now part of a team whose members are responsible for each other's safety, as well as for a good performance, means you'll have to expand your thinking.

THE NEED FOR GREATER CONTROL The biggest and most obvious difference between solo and partnered stage combat is that you now have a very

> . . .beware of false Teachers of Defence, and how they forsake their owne naturall Fights. . .
>
> George Silver
> *Paradoxes of Defence*
> 1599

> Someone once said that a teacher is like a needle and the students are the thread: the thread follows wherever the needle goes. If a teacher is wrong, the students will be wrong, too. Nobody has all the answers. Learning is not a career-long, but a lifelong process.
>
> R.L.

12-2. Actor-partners working in a studio setting. Fight Director Richard Lane rehearsing with Kit Wilder and Bob Borwick. (Photo by Chely Simon.)

real, flesh-and-blood person standing in front of you. The target areas, preps, and reactions you've been imagining are now real, so your ability to observe these details quickly and accurately—then act in concert with your observations—will now be greatly tested. This boils down to one thing: the need for control. If you've become careless about targeting in attacks, or if you've let your footwork wander, you'll have to correct these problems in order to make progress.

Fortunately, your fight director/teacher will start your partnered training *very* slowly, working through all the basics—diagnosing and helping you correct any bad habits you've developed, before letting you move on to a choreographed fight. When you begin a partnered form, such as the simple attack-defense box drill, you'll do so at a constant rate of speed, making sure you don't start slow, for example, and finish fast, or vice versa. Although the fight you actually perform may (and probably will) change rhythms often, those variations must be by choice and not by chance.

Most importantly, the rhythm of the prep-reaction-action cycle that works best for you and your partner in a given move must stay constant—and remain under perfect control, no matter how much lunging and leaping, fleching and falling the rest of the routine demands. Such control is possible *only* if you stay focused on (and in) the moment.

THE NEED FOR MUTUAL TRUST This is probably the toughest idea for novice swashbucklers to accept. Acting is a competitive business, but those competitive urges must be dropped if stage fights are to be successful. There are no stars, winners, or losers in stage combat—no matter what the script says—only actors who are easy or difficult to work with, producing good or bad experiences. If you want to look great in your role, the very best way to achieve this is to give your partner your complete cooperation. If you're the hero, it's your partner's reaction that makes you look good. If both partners cooperate fully and commit themselves to the moment, the risks diminish and new possibilities open up.

Trust is personal, and reciprocal. It can't be mandated by an instructor or developed with one partner and then simply transferred to another. It must be cultivated through practice with the same person who will perform with you night after night in the actual fight. One-to-one experience, in this case, is the best and only teacher.

Begin building trust by constantly re-establishing good eye contact throughout the fight. Partners who know you are in the moment are more willing to trust your actions. And as trust increases, so do the pace, credibility, and safety of the fight.

Trust also means you both know what to do when you "don't know what to do"—when a mistake is made, but the show must go on. During training and rehearsal, the fight director can stop the routine after a mistake (or even before one happens), explain what went wrong, then show you ways to prevent it from happening again. In performance, this diagnosis, troubleshooting, and correcting must be instantaneous and is entirely up to you and your

"Thoughts fast, blades slow, points low, fight light"
Paddy Crean

David S. Leong
"Teaching Stage Combat, Helpful Hints"
The Fight Master

partner. Since you can't plan for every contingency, mutual trust born of joint experience is the only tool you can use to smoothly cover errors and get the routine back on track. However, breaking a blade or having an accidental disarm can be practiced during rehearsal so that it's not such a big surprise if it happens in performance.

THE NEED TO MANAGE SPACE JOINTLY You already know the dramatic and safety problems associated with consistently fighting in-distance/on-target, or being too far out of distance, or (even worse) oscillating between the two. Even if you manage to complete such routines safely, poor distance control invariably means poor communication—and that usually means a poor fight, one that lacks either drama or safety.

The best partnering rule here is: If your distance feels wrong, it probably is. In practice or rehearsal, stop the routine, re-establish proper distance, and continue. In performance, learn to communicate with your eyes so that space adjustments can be mutual, instantaneous, and unnoticed by the audience. Many times, errors in preps or reactions—which can lead to broken routines—are traced to poor space management, one of the easiest problems to fix. Additionally, jointly managed space means looking out for your partner's back. If you're attacking, look behind the defender for obstacles on the floor, or parts of the set that might cause an accident—including the edge of the stage. Nothing stops a fight quicker than when one participant suddenly disappears!

THE FIGHT DIRECTION PROCESS

Because many actors lack stage combat training, are worried about being injured, or have had bad experiences with staged fights, they can feel intimidated by the fight director before they even meet. This is unfortunate, because good theater is a positive, collaborative affair; one in which every participant understands and respects the contributions of the others. If you're cast as a fighter, you'll feel better knowing ahead of time what fight directors do, and how they usually do it.

STEP ONE: ANALYZE THE SCRIPT Some stage directors have definite, preconceived ideas about how the fights in a production should go, even before the fight director comes on board. Others stand back and leave everything up to the choreographer. In our experience, the best fights result from a collaboration between stage and fight directors. The former know best how the characters are to be interpreted; the latter have access to more movement and choreographic choices to help bring those interpretations to life.

Either way, in a collaborative or solo effort, the fight director profiles the characters historically and psychologically: how they came to be the way they are in the story, and why they fight. From these motivations come preliminary decisions about the historical and stage combat techniques most appropriate for each character, as well as some general ideas about how the fight should progress, how long it should last, and how it might end.

Using slow-motion improvisation, we started working on the first part of the sequence. Every movement of each actor was performed again and again, until we found a way that looked right for the moment, felt right to the actors, and was safe for them to do ten times out of ten. Then we re-ran the section some more, looking for certain "cues" that would enable the actors to let each other know when they were ready to go on to the next movement in the choreography.

• Always build in alternatives in case something unexpected occurs.

• Always try to eliminate "variables." These are actions that cannot be relied upon a hundred percent of the time.

• If you don't have the time and energy to do stage violence right, you shouldn't be doing it at all.

David S. Leong
"Staging Realistic Violence"
The Fight Master

STEP TWO: EVALUATE THE ACTOR-COMBATANTS No fight is better than its performers, so the fight director carefully weighs the strengths and limitations of each actor cast in a combat role. This includes the actors' previous stage combat, martial arts or sports experience and the other roles they've played, as well as their physical resources for the fight at hand. For example, an athletic, large-framed actor with no previous training in swordplay might successfully carry off techniques in a fight with medieval weapons that a lighter framed, but more experienced, actor may find too difficult. Certainly, if the two were cast as partners, the fight director would take these physical differences into account when choosing specific weapons, moves, and techniques to make the fight as convincing, exciting, and entertaining as possible. Of course, the weaponry and techniques chosen might be inappropriate for the understudy or cover if he or she has significantly different physical characteristics or abilities, so the fight director must take that into account, too. It would be unfair and unsafe to ask any actor to learn two routines for the same fight.

STEP THREE: REVIEW PRODUCTION RESOURCES Big thinking does not always translate into big fights. Besides the actor's ability to perform a fight there are pragmatic limitations to stage combat choreography that, while not necessarily obvious, cannot be ignored. These practical limits will be set by the size of the combatant cast, the time allotted for rehearsal, the number and types of weapons available, costume considerations, any special effects (including fog) that will be used, and so on. For productions with modest budgets, good fight directors get maximum mileage out of the resources at hand, using creativity, artistry, and the audience's imagination to make up for any lack of resources.

The first production resource considered in any fight is the space available. Even large stages can become perilously small when warring armies, scenery, and props are thrown together, forcing actor-combatants to maneuver in a very tight space. Oddly-shaped spaces, highly raked stages, (stages that are inclined for an improved view for the audience), outdoor theaters, and theaters-in-the-round, offer their own peculiar problems and opportunities. Big spaces increase the options for movement, but being a long distance from the audience can hide subtle techniques, and the actors can tire quickly when covering a lot of ground. Raked stages give the audience a better view, but increase the risk of injury when weapon-wielding performers are in motion.

Eventually, enough is known about the fight and its environment for the fight director to specify the weapons, lighting, props and stage dress, special padding in costumes, special effects such as blood, and so on, needed to make it work. This broadens the "fight family" from the stage director, fight director, and actors to include the property managers, set designer, costumers, lighting specialists, and other technicians—increasing the requirement for clear communication and cooperation.

The Cyrano duel (with Depardieu) was rehearsed two to three hours a day for three weeks before filming began. It was shot in four or five days, weeks later. Depardieu began working with Hobbs' assistant, Michelle Carliez, a French fencer, stuntman, and fight director. Depardieu, a former boxer, was uncomfortable with the fencing positions Carliez taught him. When Hobbs arrived he allowed Depardieu to fight in a style more natural to his boxing experience. "Depardieu was delighted."

Charles Conwell
"Of Fights and Film: A Conversation with William Hobbs"
The Fight Master

STEP FOUR: BEGIN TRAINING THE ACTOR-COMBATANTS Since many per-formers have little or no experience with stage combat, training usually begins with the basics. After stretching and warming up, the fight director discusses and demonstrates the basic principles to be observed (eye contact, distance and targeting, and so forth), followed by the preliminary practice of any unarmed techniques required by the fight. If swordplay is involved, instruction begins with footwork—first without a sword, then with the weapon to be used in the fight. Parries, cuts, and thrusts are introduced, then combined with footwork—all on a solo basis, just as you learned in Part II of this book.

When the fight director feels the actor-combatants can handle their swords safely, they begin partnered exercises, like the basic attack-defense box drill. After that, they will probably move on to short phrases that reflect the mixture of techniques and the ebb and flow of an actual stage fight. At this point, the actors needn't be paired as they will be for the actu-al fights. In fact, there's some advantage to working with different partners initially before learning the final routine. First, practicing with more people builds confidence: performers who have had experience with a variety of partners tend to learn choreography more quickly and execute it better. Sec-ond, since students have different skill levels and progress at different rates, changing partners periodically allows them to learn from each other.

STEP FIVE: MAKE A PRELIMINARY SKETCH OF THE FIGHT While the actors learn the basics, the fight director begins detailing the final fight, or fights, required for the production. Although the fight director knows generally how a fight will go, he or she can't finalize the choreography until seeing the performers in action. Only after that, can specific moves be tailored to the strengths and weaknesses of each actor.

When the fight has been laid out, with all moves identified and grouped into phrases and sections, it is reviewed with the stage director. Any new ideas or suggestions regarding storytelling and acting—the continuation of the drama during the fight—are discussed. Due to other demands on the stage director's time at this phase of production, this last step isn't always possible, but in our experience, it's always desirable.

STEP SIX: FINALIZE AND TEST THE FIGHT When all the ingredients are in place: preliminary choreography, actors, set dress, and so on, the fight direc-tor works out the final fight in detail (often with the help of an experienced assistant), from which any last minute problems with movement, stagecraft, or drama are diagnosed and resolved. Rehearsal schedules can now be set with full knowledge of how long and complex the fight will be.

STEP SEVEN: TEACH THE ACTOR-COMBATANTS THE FIGHT By this time, the performers have become accustomed to the feel of their weapons and the basic techniques, as well as the physical movements for any unarmed encounters. The fight director now pairs them with their performance part-ners, with whom they will practice exclusively for the rest of the production.

Steeply sloped Broad-way stages help audiences see better, but they're a risk for causing the sprains and strains that afflict dancers in the nation's hottest musicals. . . .

A study of 313 Broad-way performers in twenty-three shows, from "Les Miserables" to "Phantom of the Opera," found almost fifty-six percent had suffered a perfor-mance-related injury.

That's not surprising, because they race around obstacle-strewn stages in the dark in high heels or seventy-five pound costumes, notes study author, Dr. Randolf Evans of the University of Texas. He reports in the *American Journal of Public Health* that dancers who per-formed on sloped stages had three times the risk of the average performer. . . .

Also at higher risk were performers whose roles included the most physical demands—racing or jumping around the stage or lifting heavy objects—and those who had been in the business longest and were previously injured.

Lauran Neergaard (AP) "Dancers and Actors Raked by Injuries" *San Francisco Examiner* February 4, 1996

The only exceptions are the understudies, who must fight not only with each other, but with the primary cast members they are most likely to face in performance.

As with basic training, fight rehearsals begin very slowly and increase in speed as the partners become more comfortable with the choreography and with each other. Individual moves flow into phrases which, when mastered, are connected into longer sections. Eventually the entire fight can be performed from start to finish, or rehearsed out-of-sequence as the need arises. As soon as the fight becomes second nature, the actors begin to concentrate on acting: the reason they are there. Similarly, fight directors increase their emphasis on the performance value of the fight: is it exciting and believable as well as historically accurate and safe?

STEP EIGHT: APPOINT A FIGHT CAPTAIN By now, the fight has become a minor industry: there are weapons and other fight-related props to keep track of, a rehearsal schedule to keep, performance quality to develop, and safety to monitor. Because it is uneconomical and impractical to keep the fight director around for all this, a resident assistant called the fight captain is appointed. Drawn from the theatrical company (often the stage manager or a more experienced actor-combatant), the fight captain becomes the fight director's deputy, ensuring in his or her absence that:

- Scheduled rehearsals, including the pre-show fight call, are conducted.
- Understudies are available and trained to assume combat roles.
- Weapons are available, maintained, and secured when not in use.
- The choreography is followed and that problems or suggestions for improvement are noted and brought to the fight director's attention.
- All safety measures are enforced.
- First aid is available and immediately rendered in case of accident, and emergency numbers are at hand.

As you might guess, the most important qualifications of good fight captains are responsibility, humility, and tact. Their duties are manifold and often thankless, but even the least of them must be performed professionally. If you're chosen to contribute as a fight captain, begin by recognizing your own limitations and call freely on those with more experience, especially when it comes to safety. In the appendix to this book, you'll find several forms and checklists to help make the fight captain's job easier and more productive.

During rehearsal, fight directors will visit the company from time to time to critique the performances and resolve any problems. Their participation is *essential* at dress rehearsals, where last minute problems with movements, vision-restricting costumes, damaged weapons, even pre-performance jitters—can be dealt with.

STEP NINE: OPENING NIGHT Roman soldiers were so well prepared for action that they called their drills, "bloodless battles," and their battles, "bloody drills." Similarly, first-class fight direction will help make your performances, from first to last—seem like effortless rehearsals.

Of course, magic happens when an audience is present, sometimes not all of it good. Fight directors always try to attend the first performance to critique the results. This is especially useful when a certain move or bit of stage business is designed to draw a specific audience reaction (such as a laugh, gasp, or groan), and doesn't. Praise for success is also important. Good fight directors will acknowledge the performers' diligence and hard work, and take pains to reinforce it.

STEP TEN: MODIFY THE FIGHT AS NEEDED, THEN MAINTAIN IT If audience reaction or performer feedback shows that parts of the fight aren't working, the fight director will modify the routine as needed, adding new moves and changing or deleting old ones, until it achieves the right effect. After that, the fight captain and performers keep the routine on track through regular rehearsals, or fight calls, conducted before each performance.

HOW TO MAKE THE MOST OF YOUR FIRST STAGE FIGHT

While there is usually just one way to get a stage fight right, there are millions of ways to get it wrong. Here are some practical suggestions for making your first, and all your subsequent, stage combat experiences good ones:

1. *Stay in the moment.* Don't think too far ahead in a routine—and never dwell on something you've just done, even if it was a mistake. As one well-trained actor-combatant once said of stage combat, "It's about as moment-to-moment as you can be," and that spontaneity should come through in each performance. Remember, perfection is a direction, a goal— not a final destination. Every performance holds something new— especially in acting possibilities. Your job is to find those fresh elements and deliver them to the audience in polished form.

2. *Always complete the illusion.* Fight directors can show you how to create an illusion, but they can't do it for you. If you begin a move energetically, with lots of panache, be sure you finish it that way, too; don't slump physically or psychologically, between the high points of the fight. Remember, acting is really *reacting*, so give your partner your full attention, even (and especially) when you have nothing specific to do.

3. *Don't let a broken routine stop the action.* The audience expects and deserves a professional performance, even if it isn't completely as planned. If you or your partner forget a move, get a movement out of sequence, react the wrong way, forget to prep, perform the wrong action, or just blank out on the whole routine, it needn't be a disaster if you both agree ahead of time on a few simple remedies:

   • *Vocalizing.* Because actors are used to relying on dialogue for cues, hearing an extraneous or improvised word can have a jarring effect. If you need to get your partner's attention, you can use prearranged yet theatrically appropriate words to signal that something is wrong,

The basic idea behind the Fight Call is twofold:
1. To physically warm up the actors, and
2. To provide them a feeling of "security" by reviewing the fights before performance.

Checklist for setting up the fight call:
1. Check the weapons.
2. Sweep the stage.
3. Set all set and prop pieces in the fight.
4. Use all sound and light cues involved. [This is doubly important when there is music underneath the fight, as in ballet.—R.L.]
5. Provide all requisite costume pieces, including gloves but *excluding blood-packs.*
6. Preset all weapons.

Tony Soper
"Stage Manager's Fight-Call Checklist"
The Fight Master

To this list I would add:
7. Walk the fights (slow motion) to stimulate memory.
8. Run the fights at one-half speed.
9. Discuss any problems with the Fight Captain.
10. Run the fights again at just below performance tempo.
11. Restore the stage.

R.L.

and to trigger an agreed-upon response. For example, you may agree that if one of you yells "Swine!" during the fight, it means one of you has gotten lost, and you will both break off, maneuver a bit, re-establish proper distance, and then begin the current phrase again, from the top.

- *Posturing.* Since fights are about movement, not speech, gestures often work better than sounds as a means of signalling your partner. This is especially true when the dialogue is well-known, as in a Shakespearean play. By "posturing" we mean departing from the choreography, the sequence of which has already been broken, in a manner consistent with your character at that point in the fight. For example, at the beginning of a fight, you might turn your back on your partner and swagger a bit, showing your character's confident, combative attitude, while inside you secretly rack your brain for what comes next. Near the end of a fight, your posturing might involve a temporary retreat to one side of the stage to examine a wound or catch your breath. No matter what signal you use, make sure you and your partner understand that it means the fight is momentarily suspended until you're both ready to resume it at the point where the routine was broken.

- *Maneuvering.* The simplest and easiest device, however, is to simply keep doing what you're doing, but do it away from your partner. That is, if you're attacking and your prep is correct but your partner reacts the wrong way, or fails to react at all, don't complete the action, but maneuver as if it were all a feint: step side to side, step backward and forward—do anything to keep the fight in motion while your partner collects his or her wits. When this has been accomplished, a kind of "Okay, come and get me!" look of relief in your partner's eyes will be a clear signal for you to resume the action.

What can you do if you or your partner continue to go blank on the fight? If all else fails, agree on a signal beforehand that means you will both automatically go to the *top of the next phrase*, no matter how much action is lost in between. However, if you're so rattled that you can't even remember the next phrase, or if your weapon breaks and only half of the swordfight is completed, just treat the fight like any other blown scene, and follow your partner's lead. As long as one of you still functions, it's enough to finish the fight—with skill, as quickly as possible!

In the last analysis, the fight belongs to the fighters—not the fight director, stage director, critics, or even the audience. If you're not getting what you need to do your job from your colleagues, don't be shy about asking for more, whether it is in the form of more technical instruction, more practice time, clearer cues, easier or less risky techniques, and so on. After all, everyone wins when the fight is good. When things go wrong, center stage can be a very lonely place indeed!

Knowing your enemy and knowing yourself, one can go through a hundred battles without danger.

Sun Zi
The Art of War

12-3. *Swordsmen, Guido Crescendo and Dirk Perfect, a.k.a. David Woolley (left)*
and Doug Mumaw (right), have performed their show thousands of times to the wild enjoyment
of tens of thousands. (Photo by Z. Best, 1995 Bristol Renaissance Faire.)

SWASHBUCKLING AND A THEATRICAL CAREER

Between the stages of apprenticeship and mastership there lie long and eventful years of untiring practice. . . . Practice, repetition, and repetition of the repeated with ever increasing intensity. . . . The way to the goal is not to be measured! Of what importance are weeks, months, years?

Eugen Herrigel
Zen in the Art of Archery

13.1 Nathan Gish, a student at the Academy of the Sword, contemplates his future.

If you treat the swashbuckler's art as the serious fun it is, new worlds of opportunity can open up for you. In this last chapter, you'll learn:

- How stage combat training complements your life both in, and away from the theater
- How to avoid career-limiting mistakes related to stage combat
- Ways to advance your skills and credentials, and gain recognition and income as an actor-combatant

THE BENEFITS OF THEATRICAL SWASHBUCKLING

In the original production of *Cyrano de Bergerac*, the actor for whom Cyrano was written for was an excellent fencer. He in turn hired his fencing master for the part of Valvert so the poem/duel would be spectacular. They rehearsed for weeks. Opening night the fight was truly splendid—until the end of the couplet when Cyrano attempted to thrust home: Valvert parried the thrust! Cyrano tried again and was again parried. This went on for some time until Cyrano fenced him into the wings and asked, "Why didn't you let me kill you like we rehearsed?" "There are other maestros in the audience," said Valvert, "I cannot look a fool." Cyrano grabbed the other's sword, clanged it against his, then stepped back on stage alone to declare, "It is done."

T.J. Glenn
"How To Teach Stage Combat to Martial Artists"
The Fight Master

Few careers are as stressful as acting. Even the healthiest egos show strain when years of training lead mainly to numberless auditions, a few good roles, and too many rejections. Prolonged emotional wear and tear like this can turn the sweetest disposition sour. At worst, it leads to low self-esteem, troubled relationships, even health and financial problems.

That's why many actors and others in and around show business turn to the Asian martial arts and competitive fencing for the life-enhancing mental and health benefits such disciplines can bring. To the degree the action roles they play involve these physical arts, this training also provides a useful skill—although, as you've seen, there's a big difference between collaborative stage combat and competitive sports.

Fortunately, theatrical swashbuckling contributes many of the same benefits of health and fitness as these other disciplines, plus a wealth of solid technique directly useful in any acting career. Its unique blend of traditional martial arts goals—improved concentration, self-confidence, and physical conditioning—and training in individual and cooperative theatrical skills make it perfect as a lifelong discipline for self-improvement. Here are some specific improvements veteran swashbucklers have observed in themselves and their colleagues. Which ones seem desirable to you?

IMPROVED VERSATILITY In a business where you're often thought of in terms of your last role, it's easy to be type-cast. Competence in stage combat opens the way to a variety of leading and supporting roles that some production decision-makers are hesitant to give to less trained, less confident talent.

INCREASED PHYSICAL RESOURCES Performers trained in stage combat move with more poise and authority on stage. Their range of motion—and other physical attributes, such as strength, stamina, coordination, and control—are greater than those possessed by unschooled actors. This includes greater control over the conditioned responses useful to any actor, such as the ability to display intense emotions.

BETTER CONCENTRATION Stage combat helps you to focus completely on the here and now, on the challenge in front of you; helps you give a role everything you've got. Once you know that every instant contains a universe of possibilities, you'll find yourself more creative, more intuitive, and more adaptable to the demands of any role or situation.

GREATER IMAGINATION Stage combat requires you to visualize a perfect, finished form—then shape your physical and mental performance toward that end. Creative visualization like this helps you picture the ideal elements of a movement, gesture, or speech and then render it with clarity. At the very least, this ability to visualize helps you accept direction better—even while your castmates are still fumbling—and come up with interpretations that can be startling in their depth and sincerity.

Taken together, these attributes help you make the most of any moment or opportunity. As your success increases, you gain even more self-confidence and poise—a relaxed brand of optimism reflected on stage and off. Just as physical training liberates the body, so does this new attitude liberate the spirit, putting its great energy at your service.

DON'T OVERDO A GOOD THING

Of course, swashbuckling is no panacea. If you're super-competitive or a very insecure person for example, you'll have to resist those tendencies all your life—although swashbuckling will teach you many new ways to cope. Even people who take to stage combat like ducks to water can overdo a good thing.

- *Don't become a swashbuckling junkie.* Self-improvement is not self-sacrifice; cooperation is not capitulation. Even with your more confident, collaborative attitude, acting will still be a competitive business. Nice people who are *too* passive or obsessed with technique can and will finish last in the race for jobs and opportunities. The key here is to stay balanced: focus on the accomplishment, not the contest. Be proud of your achievments.

- *Don't let virtues become vices.* If you're the type to push yourself too hard, too fast, or jump off the high board before you're ready, it's possible to get in over your head. In stage combat, this trouble usually manifests itself in frequent and sometimes serious injuries, bragging about skills not yet possessed, and the unsolicited coaching of fellow performers. Again, *balance* is the key to successful swordplay—and to a happy, healthy life.

- *Don't play with pain.* In America, we tend to glamorize people who sacrifice everything for their art, or to win. Only after a serious illness or injury do we realize that our best asset is our good health, and nobody should sacrifice that—especially a performer who needs a sound body, strong voice, and clear mind to earn a living. If you've got a significant injury (anything from recurring sprains and strains to chronic back and knee problems) don't fight it, or fight, period. You'll come back faster if you heal, and to heal you must rest—a much better plan than making temporary ailments permanent or loading up with pain-killers.

ATTAINING RECOGNITION AND CREDENTIALS

Legendary fight director, Paddy Crean, probably received the highest recognition any theatrical swashbuckler could hope for, when Errol Flynn, for whom he was stunt double and fight choreographer, presented him with an engraved sword and a portrait signed, "Hello, Pat! Thanks a helluva lot, pal, for making me look good!"

For the rest of us, audience applause, good notices, and peer recognition will have to do. Part of this recognition can come through periodic testing

---

Bruce Lee notes that many entertainers (such as Steve McQueen and James Coburn) asked Lee to teach them "not so much about how to defend themselves or how to do somebody in; rather they want to learn how to express themselves through some movement, be it anger, be it determination or whatever. So. . . what they're paying me to show them, in combative form, is the art of expressing the human body."

David Chow and Richard Spangler
Kung Fu: History, Philosophy and Technique

When someone does a good job, applaud; it makes two people happy.
Samuel Goldwyn

with the Society of American Fight Directors, and its awarding of the credentials that mark your passage from Recognized or Recommended actor-combatant, to Certified Teacher, Fight Director, and perhaps, eventually Fight Master.

Founded in 1977, the Society is a not-for-profit organization of theater professionals, educators, and supporters who share an interest in stage combat. Its primary mission is to advance the technical and safety standards of stage fighting in theatre, film, and television through training and the dissemination of information throughout the country. In addition to its annual National Stage Combat Workshop, SAFD offers training through its network of Certified Teachers and Fight Directors at a variety of institutions, including colleges, universities, and private stage combat schools like the Academy of the Sword. Through its semiannual journal, *The Fight Master* and its quarterly newsletter, *The Cutting Edge*, the SAFD publishes information on the latest staging techniques, historical accuracy in fights, and career opportunities for its members. The Society recognizes four levels of competence among practitioners: Actor-Combatant, Certified Teacher, Fight Director, and Fight Master.

13.2 *John Cash-man (left) and Randall Miller (right) in the Academy of the Sword's production of "Duels and Assassination."*

ACTOR-COMBATANT This level is for performers who have received basic training in three to six weapons and have passed a proficiency test adjudicated by an SAFD-certified Fight Master. Like a driver's license in some states, this certificate must be renewed through periodic re-testing, currently every three years.

Applicants passing the test are categorized as either "Recognized," which means they have proven themselves to be safe, competent performers, or "Recommended," which means they have shown superior ability as actors as well as swordhandlers. Neither category, however, qualifies a person to give instruction in stage combat or to perform the duties of a fight choreographer—both occupations require an additional set of skills.

Of the techniques you've learned in this book, the following are currently required of applicants in the actor-combatant skills proficiency test:

- *Unarmed.* Two punches, a stomach punch, an elbow attack, a slap, a blocked punch, three knaps, two kicks, a knee attack, a fall or roll, a throw or flip, a strangle and a hair pull.
- *Rapier & dagger.* Point work (a variety of deceptions and disengagements); three pris de fer; all footwork; a beat attack; corps-a-corps; a circular parry; a moulinet; a punto reverso; head, stomach, and diagonal swipes and evasions; dagger attacks, parries, and cross parries; and a disarm, feint, and simulated wounding.
- *Broadsword.* Attacks along all lines, two thrusts on different lines, a corps-a-corps, head, stomach, and diagonal swipes and evasions, a bind, a moulinet, a pommel attack, a running attack, and a beat parry.

Applicants can also choose to test with smallsword, quarterstaff, and broadsword and shield, although only a total of three weapons need be demonstrated. Unarmed combat and rapier & dagger fighting are mandatory.

To qualify for testing, applicants usually complete a course of study with an SAFD Certified Teacher whose endorsement is required. The SAFD requires eighty contact-hours of instruction before taking the test. While some very gifted students sometimes pass the test after one course with each weapon, most successful applicants put in an apprenticeship of several years with one or more instructors, combining periodic classwork with performance experience before they take the first test.

The proficiency exam takes the form of a mini-drama, or even a comedy, conceived by the applicants with the help of their teacher, during which the required techniques are employed in the course of the story. This allows the SAFD Adjudicator to gauge the level of acting as well as the technical skills and the performance value of the routine.

Although the evaluation criteria for actor-combatant testing are subjective, the Society is moving slowly toward a more standardized set of performance values. SAFD Certified Teacher, former secretary, and author, Mark Olsen, writing in the Fall 1995 *Fight Master*, has proposed the following terms as a common vocabulary for measuring "acting values" in stage combat tests:

- For a rating of *favorable*, a work should be: connected, crisp, haunting, vivid, inspired, safe, visceral, rigorous, hilarious, fresh, imaginative, gritty, generous, powerful, elegant, daring, captivating, unaffected, original, riveting, vicious, layered, relentless, profound, distinctive. It should be performed ed with: finesse, momentum, panache, dignity, immediacy, elan, abandon, resonance, relish, courage, dimension, force, impact, gravity, authenticity, proportion.
- For a rating of *good, but not exceptional*, a work should be: effective, serviceable, safe, funny, competent, exciting, sharp, creditable, clear, honest, engaging, valuable, worthwhile, acceptable, truthful, challenging, substantial, appropriate, accessible, and energetic.
- For a rating of *unfavorable*, a work must be: dry, ineffectual, forced, phony, unconvincing, disconnected, flat, floppy, dangerous, unfocused, derivative, uninspired, lackluster, overblown, lifeless, murky, muddy, unauthentic, inappropriate, inaccurate, gratuitous, awkward, terse, choppy, half-hearted, indulgent, ambitious, distorted, precious, transparent, static, or perfunctory.

This is just one teacher's view, which, while it reflects qualitative judgments more often found in newspaper theater reviews than academic report cards, *does* give you a hint of the values SAFD professionals often use in arranging, performing, and evaluating stage fights. Indeed, the trend in actor-combatant adjudication at this writing has been toward a greater emphasis on *acting the fight* rather than displaying dazzling swordplay, although safety—as always—remains the top priority.

This highlights another issue currently debated in stage combat circles: the career value, if any, of "certificated competency" over competency itself. Jack Young, SAFD certified teacher and artistic director of the The Warehouse Theatre in South Carolina, reports that at least one recent summer festival specifically refused to hire *certificated* actor-combatants, since past experience had shown them to be indifferent actors—however brilliant they were with swords. Rightly or wrongly, the festival authorities had concluded that anyone willing to invest the significant time and energy needed to pass the SAFD test must be more interested in fight directing than acting, a belief shared by several other production companies, and one reason the SAFD continues to put increased emphasis on acting in its tests. Of course, not all theater, film, and TV producers and stage directors share this view, but if you intend to do a lot of acting, you should be aware that this preconception does exist in some people's minds.

CERTIFIED TEACHER This level is for certificated actor-combatants who have had extensive training and additional education in stage combat teaching techniques, historical weaponry and fighting styles, and stage choreography.

FIGHT DIRECTOR A Fight Director is an individual who has completed all requirements of an actor/combatant and a Certified Teacher. Beyond this, he or she must have a strong background in fight choreography. Fight

> All too often in our "instant" society we forget that value of apprenticeship and want to skip immediately to the level of mastership without the necessary repetition, practice, and dedication required to master an art.
>
> Paul Dennhardt
> "Serving Time:
> The Fight Master's
> Apprentice"
> *The Fight Master*

Directors are endorsed by the SAFD to teach, coach, and choreograph fights professionally.

FIGHT MASTER This level is for SAFD members who have strong professional backgrounds and have choreographed a minimum of twenty union productions. To qualify, they must pass extensive oral, written, and practical examinations. SAFD endorses these individuals to teach, coach, and choreograph fights in all media, and to adjudicate certification of applicants seeking recognition at lower skill levels.

A list of current SAFD-Certified Teachers and Fight Masters, as well as schools, colleges, and universities offering stage combat training (some for academic credit), is presented at the back of this book. Many offer one day, weekend, and intensive week-long workshops periodically throughout the year, as well as group classes meeting for one or two hours, once a week, in regular six-, eight-, or ten-week courses.

SWASHBUCKLING IN FILMS

Many actors aspire to careers beyond the stage: in movies or on TV. Certainly, these media offer the potential for fame and wealth impossible in live theater—but only for the annointed few. Here, stage combat training may give you a slight advantage in film or television casting calls, where performers competent in the techniques of stage fighting are sometimes needed for short periods.

On the set, you'll find that unlike a stage fight, where you must learn the entire fight flawlessly, and perform it night after night, film fights are composed of very short takes, some only a few seconds in length. Continuity comes from editing, not just acting, so you'll probably have to repeat the same move again and again, often for days at a time; or sweat for hours in hauberk and helmet, on call for the big battle scene.

Action doubles for stars and supporting players are another possibility for trained actor-combatants seeking to break into Hollywood. These roles give you a lot more screen time and much more to do—but only in long shots, with your back turned, or with your face covered by a helmet. More importantly, many of these jobs require bona fide stunt work (falls and jumps from horses or high buildings, reaction to pyrotechnics, and so on) which is a separate performance specialty, governed by its own safety standards and unions. Unless you seek training and a subsequent career in this area, leave these riskier jobs alone.

The main barrier to breaking into films, though, is statistical, not technical. Out of the hundreds of people qualified, available, and eager to do the work, only a handful are chosen. Among this elite, most have performed on screen before and hold Actors' Equity or Screen Actor's Guild (SAG) cards— the golden pass to more employment, no matter how small or specialized the part. The good news is, once you've broken into this arena through Equity's eligible performers auditions, and shown you can do the job reliably and well, your work may be fairly steady.

We knew that our fight skills would come in handy, but we never deceived ourselves that they would be the deciding factor in getting cast. What got us the audition in the first place was our acting. Having combat experience was helpful; having passed our SAFD Actor/Combatant Skills Test was a bonus. But the real reason any one of us got cast was not because we could perform the last five minutes of a 150-minute show, but that we could make the 145 minutes before it exciting, visceral, vital to watch, and then top it off in the end with a finely wrought and passionately fought fight.

Jack Young
"What Happened to the *Actor* in Actor/Combatant?"
The Fight Master

OTHER HISTORICAL COMBAT AND SWORD-FIGHTING ORGANIZATIONS

If the gale-force winds and driving rain interfere with the audience's ability to hear our act, at least the sword fights can be seen. At such moments, David [Woolley] and I stop and smell the roses. We say aloud how good it is to be swordfighting for a living. Then, with a gleam in our eyes and fear for our knees in our hearts, we draw our weapons.

Douglas (Dirk Perfect) Mumaw and David (Guido Crescendo) Woolley "Battling the Elements" *The Fight Master*

Historical recreation societies—from Renaissance fairs, and the chapters of the Society for Creative Anachronism, to local civic groups who religiously troop out each year to re-fight every battle from Agincourt to Gettysburg—are always looking for new members who want to dress up, dress right, and march to the sound of a different drum. Most of these organizations are filled with well-meaning enthusiasts anxious to trade the latest gossip and arcania from their various meetings, conventions, field trips, and productions. If you enjoy this side of swashbuckling, look into the organizations nearest you—but be careful. Some of their members have had no theatrical training whatsoever to temper their enthusiasm for realistic swordplay or use of firearms. Simulated duels and battles for these people can degenerate into chaotic melees where you may literally take your life into your own hands.

More orderly—and certainly more profitable—are the growing number of theme parks, medieval banquet halls, and other entertainment companies opening up nationwide that employ trained actor-combatants as featured players and stunt performers. Again, be sure your temperament, job objectives, and practical skills are a good match for these employers before you audition.

13-3. *The Albion Schoole of Defense recreates historically accurate stage combat at the Renaissance Pleasure Faire in Northern California.*

SWASHBUCKLING FOR LIFE

In the end, proficiency in stage combat is but one skill among the many needed for success as an actor; and the most important ingredients—talent and good luck—can't be taught at all. As time goes by and fortune separates the stars from the supernumeraries, every performer must make a choice: to continue seeking work as an actor or move on to other specialties—or even to another career. Certainly, non-acting, theatre-related jobs abound—from directing, coaching, and teaching, on the performance side to a myriad of production specialties on the technical and business side—most with pay, prestige, and job security far superior to that enjoyed by most actors. In any of these fields, your experience with stage combat can pay dividends, since you've had an intimate, up-close and personal acquaintance with just what it takes to fulfill that special moment when the dialogue stops and the script demands, "They fight."

Some actor-combatants stick with their stage combat training regimens even after their performing days are over—using the stretches, warmups, drills, and solo sword forms as a way to stay fit and limber, emotionally centered, and mentally sharp—in the manner of a martial art. If you're interested in using swashbuckling as part of a long-term fitness plan, here are some suggestions:

- Perform the stretches every day, preferably in the morning.
- Perform the Chairman Mao exercises every other day, always preceded by stretches.
- Perform footwork drills three times a week, always preceded by stretches and Chairman Maos.
- Perform the sword forms on the days you *don't* do footwork drills, but always complete the stretches and Chairman Maos first.
- No matter what its content, a given workout need last no longer than thirty minutes to provide both physical and skill-building benefits.
- In all the movements, strive for accuracy and full range of motion before you go for speed.
- Variety is the spice of life, so modify your routine from time to time. Add new stretches and warmups as the needs of your body change. Expand your sword forms as you learn new moves and master different weapons. Try varying your rhythms and tempi.
- The coordination, strength, and balance swashbuckling builds will help your performance in other recreational sports. Seek out pastimes that depend on and reward good eye-hand and hand-foot coordination, such as fencing, tennis, racketball, handball, and softball. Consider also the other martial arts, especially aikido, which shares much of stage combat's non-violent, non-competitive philosophy. Make physical activity a regular, integral part of your life—not just a theatrical skill.

Once you're bitten by the swashbuckling bug, you'll find many new horizons opening up for education, recreation, and self-improvement. Fight master,

Many similar movement patterns may be found in both Asian martial arts and historical European swordfighting. Broadsword and rapier-and-dagger techniques lend themselves to the circular patterns found in Tai Chi, Aikido, and Pa-Kua, while on-line attacks of the smallsword are more akin to the movement patterns of Hsing-I. Awareness of such patterns is useful for training and choreography in stage combat. Tai Chi gives you a way of tapping your personal energy center. Aikido lets you meld your own center with someone else's, helping two individuals to move as one. Both provide training in balance and centering, energy sharing, and communication with a partner. This encourages fluid movements that apply equally well to both armed and unarmed fights.

Gregory Hoffman
SAFD Fight
Director and
Certified Teacher
Interview for
The Fight Master

teacher, and author Dale Anthony Girard recommends that actor-combatants follow-up their stage combat training or certification by taking classes in acting, directing, script analysis, music and dance to deepen their knowledge and understanding of theatre arts. Many fights in opera, musical theater, and ballet are accompanied by the score; and general choreography gives you a great new awareness of space-time relationships on stage. He also suggests that serious stage combat students study Shakespeare, period literature, and medieval and Renaissance history—noting particularly how swords affected fashion, social structures, and codes of behavior.

Through these and other experiences, many actor-combatants become experts in period performance, building impressive book and video libraries in the process. Others become weapons collectors, acquiring a sword or two in each class of weapon with which they are proficient. This not only gives them swords for home practice, but weapons whose weight and balance are familiar and comfortable to use in performance.

Most importantly, *all* actor-combatants become more knowledgeable about, and accepting of, themselves, their bodies, and the world around them. That alone is worth the price of admission!

As Paddy Crean's long career has shown, when it comes to swashbuckling, you're only as old as you feel. How far *you* will go with your new art is limited only by your determination, physical fitness, and the imagination that makes it all possible.

Stage combat can teach actors more than competence in their craft. As a martial discipline it can prepare the actor for the encounter with life. It can unify thought, word, and deed. It can become a tool for personal empowerment and a way to survive the stresses of the theatrical life.

Robert W. Dillon, Ph.D.
"Beyond Acting in Fights: Stage Combat as a New Martial Art"
The Fight Master

13-4. *The "Dean" Paddy Crean takes on all comers at the annual Paddy Crean Workshop.*

APPENDICES

SAMPLE FIGHT REPORT FORMS

GLOSSARY OF STAGE COMBAT AND
SWORDFIGHTING TERMS

BIBLIOGRAPHY

FURTHER READING

INSTRUCTIONAL AND EDUCATIONAL VIDEOS

SAFD CERTIFIED TEACHERS, COLLEGES, AND
OTHERS OFFERING STAGE COMBAT TRAINING

THE STAGE COMBAT MAILING LIST

WEAPONS, PROPS, AND COSTUME SUPPLIERS

FIGHT CAPTAIN'S REPORT

Title _____ Producing Organization _____

Union Contract (which one?)_____

Production Dates: Rehearsal Begin _____ Opening _____ Closing _____

Brief Description Of Fight Scenes (style, period, number):

_____

Actors Involved in Fight Scenes ___ # men; ___ # women

Name _____ Union Affiliation _____

Name _____ Union Affiliation _____

Name _____ Union Affiliation _____

Name _____ Union Affiliation _____

Name _____ Union Affiliation _____

Name _____ Union Affiliation _____

Name _____ Union Affiliation _____

Name _____ Union Affiliation _____

Rehearsal Values:

Was A Daily Fight Call Held? _____

Were actors on time? _____
        If not, list names and record how late on Daily Fight Report Form

Performance Values:

Was A Daily Fight Call Held? _____

Were actors on time? _____
        If not, list names and record how late on Daily Fight Report Form

DAILY FIGHT REPORT
(For Stage Manager)

Title _____ Producing Organization _____

Performance Date: _____ Performance Number (example: 1 of 350)_____

Fight Call Start Time: _____ End Time: _____

CONDITIONS FOR FIGHT CALL

Were Actors on Time? _____ Record any lateness:

Name   Arrival Time

_____   _____

_____   _____

_____   _____

_____   _____

_____   _____

_____   _____

_____   _____

_____   _____

Was the stage clean and available? _____

Conditions of unavailabilty? _____

_____

Adequate Lighting? _____

Briefly describe any weapon malfunction that occurred during the run of the show.
Describe type of malfunction and circumstances. Were there repercussions in terms of actor
or audience involvement? _____

_____

_____

Detail any injuries that occurred during performance. Be specific, including circumstances,
actors involved, ability to continue performance/run, treatment required, probable cause, and solution.

_____

_____

_____

FIGHT DIRECTOR'S REPORT FORM

Title _____ Producing Organization _____
Union Contract (which one?)_____
Production Dates: Rehearsal Begin _____ Opening _____ Closing _____
Director _____ Stage Manager _____
Fight Director _____ FD Hiring Date _____
     SAFD Status _____ Fight Director present at audition? _____
Fight Captain _____ FC Hiring Date _____
     SAFD Status _____ Union? _____

Brief Description of Fight Scenes (style, period, number):_____
Weapons:
     Style of Weapon Used: _____
     Rental? From Whom?_____ Original Manufacturer _____
Weapon condition (excellent/good/fair/poor) _____

Special Effects used (blood, breakaways, fog, etc.). Describe briefly:
_____
_____
_____
_____

Number of Combatants Involved In Fights?
     Union _____ # Women _____
     Non-union _____ # Men _____

SAFD affiliation and status of combatants involved (list all combatants and indicate if they hold current status with the SAFD or have any other Stage Combat training):
_____
_____
_____

Rehearsal Process:
    Hours of basic training allotted (if necessary) _____
Number of hours of fight rehearsal allotted during regular rehearsal period (not including basic training):
     Week # 1_____   Week #3_____   Week #5 _____
     Week #2 _____   Week #4 _____   Week #6 _____

Briefly describe your experience with this production in terms of the acceptance of your task as Fight Director by the management of the theatre and staff. Would you consider this experience a positive one in terms of the safety and artistic integrity of the fight work? Any other thoughts?
_____
_____
_____
_____
_____

GLOSSARY OF STAGE COMBAT AND SWORDFIGHTING TERMS

ACTION
The last step of the eye contact–preparation–reaction–and action sequence; that portion of a stage combat move that reveals its intent. For example, the "action" in a sword-cut is the cutting motion itself.

ACTOR-COMBATANT
An actor performing a role requiring stage combat; a performer trained to SAFD standards. When credentialed by an SAFD-administered, performance-oriented proficiency test, the actor-combatant may either be "Recognized" (meets minimum standards) or "Recommended" (shows superior ability).

ADVANCE
A step forward with the leading foot, followed by the trailing foot.

AGGRESSOR KNAP
See "knap."

ARMING SWORD
A lighter version of the hand-and-a-half bastard sword.

BACKSWORD
A broadsword with only one cutting edge, the back of which (false edge) is left blunt until it nears the point.

BALDRIC
A leather strap slung over one shoulder and across the back and chest for wearing a sword.

BALESTRA
A leaping advance followed by a lunge.

BASKET HILT
A broadsword whose handle is almost completely surrounded by protective plates or bars lined with cloth or leather.

BASTARD SWORD
Also known as a "hand-and-a-half" sword, a bastard sword is a crosshilt designed to be wielded with either one or two hands.

BAYONET
A dagger or knife fitted to the muzzle of a firearm.

BEARING SWORD
Oversized, ornate, and very heavy ceremonial sword—carried by officials as a symbol of their rank and power—not used for fighting.

BEAT ATTACK
A feint made from the en garde position by tapping the opponent's blade sharply in order to unnerve the opponent, provoke a hasty attack, or open a line for a thrust.

BEAT PARRY
A sharp parry that not only stops the opposing blade, but knocks it off the line of attack.

BIND
A pris-de-fer that takes the opposing blade from high to low (or vice versa) across the centerline of the body.

BLADE-CATCHER
A special device or feature near the hilt of a sword or dagger designed to trap, hold, and possibly break an attacking blade.

BOAR SWORD
A hunting sword pierced with a bar near the foible, to prevent overpenetration of the prey.

BOWIE KNIFE
A long, broad-bladed knife of American origin; said to have been created by Jim Bowie, a defender of the Alamo.

BREAK FALL
A stage- or martial-arts fall in which the total energy of the body is safely dissipated as it hits the ground.

BROADSWORD
In stage combat, a generic term used to describe a wide variety of single-handed, hand-and-a-half (bastard), and two-handed European crosshilt swords; also applied to basket hilt swords.

BUCKLER
A small, circular shield.

CALENDAR SWORD
Popular in the sixteenth and seventeenth centuries, this broadsword had a perpetual calendar inscribed on the blade, often featuring signs of the zodiac or propitious days for planting, harvesting, and hunting.

CENTER OF PERCUSSION
That exact location on a cutting edge where maximum force is delivered.

CHAIN MAIL
A type of flexible body armor made of interlocking, riveted steel rings.

CHANGE BEAT
A beat attack made after a change of engagement.

CHANGE OF ENGAGEMENT
To remove the blade from contact with the opponent's blade during en garde and establish contact on the other side or in a new position.

CHINK
From Middle English: a small cleft, slit, or fissure in armor, that leaves the wearer vulnerable to attack—expressed as "a chink in one's armor."

CHOREOGRAPHY
Body movements planned to achieve a specific effect; in a fight, the moves of attack and defense that tell the story of the fight from beginning to end.

CIRCULAR PARRY
Also called the "actor's parry;" the blade travels past the intended parry position for a full 360 degrees before making the final parry.

CLAYMORE
A two-handed crosshilt of Scottish origin—later claymores are identified by their distinctive drooping quillons which feature quatrefoil terminals.

CORPS A CORPS
Literally, "body to body;" achieved when two combatants immobilize each other's weapons and move within very close distance.

COUPE

A change of engagement around the point in which the blade is raised quickly above (in the high line), or lowered quickly below (in the low line) the tip of the opponent's blade and brought to the other side.

COURT SWORD

A highly ornamented smallsword worn as a decorative accessory—not for fighting.

COVERED, OR CLOSED LINE OF ENGAGMENT

The line of attack that is made difficult or impossible because of the chosen en garde stance. The basic en garde stance used in this book closes the line of engagement to the upper right quadrant of the defender's body (en garde in three).

CROISÉ

A pris-de-fer that knocks the opposing blade back along the same side of the body from high line to low line (or vice versa). At the end of the maneuver, the blades may stay in contact or the defender may toss off (expel) the opposing blade.

CROSSHILT SWORD

A European sword with a cruciform hilt, featuring a straight blade, with or without a taper; the stereotypical "knight's sword," often called a broadsword.

CROSS PARRY

A parry made by crossing the blades of a rapier and dagger (or double rapier) forte-to-forte in the form of a "V" and catching the attacking blade in the center.

CUIRASS

An inflexible metal breastplate.

CUP-HILT RAPIER

A rapier with a solid, cup-shaped guard over the ricasso, enclosing the pas d'anes and giving extra protection to the fingers.

CUT

A controlled attack made with the edge of the blade.

CUTLASS

A naval saber featuring a short, thick blade; used widely in the seventeenth and eighteenth centuries.

DAGGER

An edged sidearm longer than a knife but shorter than a short sword—usually worn on the right hip.

DECEPTION ATTACK

A thrust that evades the defender's blade by avoiding the parry and changing the line of engagement.

DIAGONAL SWIPE

A cut that moves from high to low (or vice versa) and crosses the centerline of the body.

DIRECT PARRY

The most efficient parry, in which the defender's blade moves across the body left to right (or vice versa) along the same (high or low) line.

DIRK

A long, broad-bladed dagger.

DISARM

Taking away the opponent's weapon.

DISENGAGE
The opposite of coupe: A change of engagement that passes around the hilt (not the tip) of the opponent's sword: below the hilt on the high line; above the hilt on the low line.

DISTANCE
The space separating two actor-combatants: an attack launched "in distance" could make contact with the defender; launched "out of distance," it would not reach the defender.

DOUBLÉ
Continuing a thrusting attack on the same line after deceiving a parry.

DUEL
A pre-arranged and witnessed combat between two antagonists.

ENGAGEMENT
The touching of blades from the en garde position, that is, both en garde stances cover the same line.

EN GARDE
A position of readiness from which to attack or defend.

ENVELOPMENT
A pris-de-fer that takes the attacker's blade from its parried position through 360 degrees back to the original position.

ÉPÉE
A heavier version of the fencer's foil featuring a cup hilt and thicker triangular blade.

ESTOC
Also called the "tuck" in English: a thin-bladed crosshilt designed for thrusting only.

EVASION
A move intended to remove the body from the path of an attack.

EXECUTIONER'S SWORD
See "headsman's sword."

EYE CONTACT
The first step of any stage combat move; nonverbally ascertaining your partner's readiness to continue.

FALCHION
A cutting sword with a very broad, curved, cleaver-like blade.

FALSE EDGE
On a rapier, the top or back side of the blade opposite the true, or sharpened cutting edge. On a double-edged weapon, such as a broadsword, the edge closest to the web of the thumb.

FEINT
A deceptive attack intended to draw a reaction that opens a different line of engagement.

FENCE
Fence, or fencing: from the word *defence*, the art of attacking and defending with a sword; now a competitive sport.

FIGHT DIRECTOR
A theatrical professional who choreographs and arranges stage fights and trains actor-combatants.

FLÈCHE
An energetic double pass in either direction in which the first step is a leap, followed by a second step which stops and stabilizes the body.

FLUKES
Spiked projections extending from the forte in some two-handed swords to protect the hand when it grips the ricasso.

FOIBLE
The top third of the sword blade, nearest the tip; the weakest part of the blade.

FORTE
The bottom third of the sword blade, nearest the hilt; the strongest part of the blade.

FROG
A device (usually leather) for attaching a scabbard to a belt or baldric.

FULLER
The groove running down a portion of the blade, intended to lighten and stiffen the sword; often erroneously called the "blood groove," or "blood gutter."

FURNITURE
The components making up the hilt, which include the pommel, handle, and guard.

GAUNTLET
A swordfighter's glove with features to protect the hand, wrist and forearm; usually made of leather, sometimes reinforced with mail or segmented plates.

GLADIUS
The Roman short sword.

GLAIVE
A polearm with a large, cleaver-like blade.

GLISSADE
Glissade, or "pressure glide" after a parry; a pris de fer that sends the attacking blade back in the direction from which it came.

GREAVES
Armor protecting the shins.

GRIP
The method of holding the sword; the hand is either in pronation or supination, one-handed or two handed.

HALBERD
A polearm: a staff fitted with an axe-like blade, rearward hook, and spiked cap.

HALF SWORD
A technique in which a two-handed sword is wielded with one hand on the handle and the other on the blade, producing a thrust-oriented, spear-type fighting style.

HAND PARRY
A parry made using the free (non-sword-holding) hand to block, deflect, or catch the attacking blade.

HANDLE
The part of the hilt that is gripped by the hand, or hands.

HANGER
A leather accessory for holding and wearing a sword. Rapier hangers often featured a row of buckled straps resting on a flexible leather sheet to carry the rapier on the hip. Back hangers were attached to baldrics for carrying large broadswords on the back. Swords could be carried in hangers with or without a scabbard.

HANGING PARRY
A parry 5 made while evading to the right, or a parry 5A made while evading to the left: in both cases, the blade follows the angle of the body as "insurance" against the cut.

HAUBERK
A chain mail shirt reaching to the thighs.

HEADSMAN'S (OR HEADING) SWORD
A crosshilt designed for judicial executions, usually featuring a square or rounded tip; also called an "executioner's sword."

HEATER SHIELD
The traditional knight's shield, shaped like the bottom of a flat iron.

HELM
Also known as "great helm;" a helmet that encloses the entire head, including the face.

HIGH LINE
Any line of attack above the waist.

HILT
That portion of the sword which is normally held by the hand, or hands. The hilt usually consists of quillons (and other protective furniture, such as knuckle bow, guard, and pas d'anes), handle, and pommel.

INVITATION
A defensive feint; any move intended to provoke an attack.

IMPACT WEAPON
Any hand-held weapon used in personal combat that depends on the momentum of a heavy mass in order to wound (cut or bludgeon) an opponent. Examples: crosshilt swords, maces, axes, war hammers.

JOUST
Combat on horseback between two knights with lances (often mock), as part of a medieval tournament.

KATANA
A slim-bladed, single-edged two-handed Japanese sword used principally for cutting.

KITE-SHAPED SHIELD
Elongated shield of the early Middle Ages, usually associated with the Norman cavalry.

KNAP
The simulation of the sound of a blow landing on the body, performed out of view of the audience. In an aggressor's knap, the attacking partner knaps by striking the passive hand with the active hand, or uses the passive hand to make the sound on another part of the aggressor's body. In a shared knap, the attacking partner's active hand strikes the defender's hand or other part of the defender's body. In a contact knap, the aggressor's active hand or foot (or the victim's concealed hand) contacts a part of the defender's body that is protected by a major muscle group. In a victim's knap, the defending partner performs the knap. In a bystander's knap, a third party (such as an on-stage extra) performs the knap.

KNUCKLE BOW
A band of metal running from the quillons to the pommel, protecting the fingers.

LANDESKNECHT
A sixteenth century German foot soldier, usually a lower-class knight, famed for wielding the giant Zweihander (two-handed sword).

LINE
An axis or plane of movement used for attack and defense. "On line" means the partners face each other directly. (An on-line attack would therefore be targeted directly at the defender's body.) "Off line" means the partners do not face each other directly. (An off-

line attack would therefore be targeted away from the defender's body.) The "outside line" refers to the side of the body on which the sword arm is located (usually the right side). The "inside line" refers to the other side (usually the left).

LISTS
The enclosure used for fighting tournaments.

LONG FORM
Quarterstaff technique in which the staff is held near one end, allowing most of the staff to be used for attack or defense.

LOW LINE
Any line of attack below the waist.

LUNGE
A deep step in which the forward foot steps well out while the trailing foot remains in place, allowing the torso to sink low behind the deeply bent forward knee.

MACE
A short, steel club featuring a flanged head.

MAIN GAUCHE
A parrying dagger with a very wide guard that completely covers the top of the left hand.

MATCHLOCK
An early firearm wherein gunpowder in a pan at the side of the barrel is ignited by the fall of a slow-burning match held in the lock, which fires and then causes a detonation of the powder charge inside the barrel. Misfires in a matchlock gave us the expression, "a flash in the pan."

MELEE
Chaotic combat among an intermingled group of people—as opposed to single combat or combat between soldiers in orderly ranks.

MORNING STAR
A spiked club, similar to mace.

MOULINET
Literally, "little windmill;" rotating the blade along the line of attack before making a cut. Mostly performed on the vertical plane on the inside or outside line before making an overhead or diagonal cut.

MOVE
The smallest unit of a stage fight, a "move" conveys the fighter's capability and intent.

MUSKET
A long-barrelled, smooth bore firearm used in the sixteenth and seventeenth centuries, related to the earlier arquebus, which was fired from a specially-designed rest. Slow-firing and unreliable, "musketeers" often resorted to their rapiers for close-quarter self-defense.

PAPPENHEIMER
A swept-hilt rapier usually incorporating a perforated guard, named after Marshal Maximilian Pappenheimer, sometimes called a walloon.

PARRY
A defensive move that normally uses the blade's true edge to block or deflect an attacking blade. Standard parries are numbered in sequence of their efficiency once a sword (usually worn on the left hip and held in the right hand) is drawn. When a weapon is held in the left hand, the numbering sequence remains the same, but relative sides of the body are switched. parry 1, or prime, guards the inside low line with the

hand in pronation. Parry 2, or seconde, guards the outside low line with the hand in pronation. Parry 3, or tierce, guards outside high line with the hand in pronation. Parry 4, or quarte, guards the inside high line with the hand in supination. Parry 5, or quinte, guards the head from a vertical cut, hilt held on the outside high line with the hand in pronation. Parry 5A guards the head from a similar attack, but the hilt is held on the inside high line with the hand in supination. Parry 6, or sixte, is similar to parry 3, but made with the blade's false edge, hand in supination. Parry 7, or septime, is an alternative to parry 1, but with the hand in supination. Parry 8, or octave, is similar to parry 2, but made with the blade's false edge, hand in supination.

PARRYING DAGGER
A dagger carried in the left hand while the right hand wields a rapier; used in attack as well as defense.

PAS D'ANE
Literally, "donkey's foot;" a loop of steel between the top of the quillons and the ricasso to protect the forefinger when it is hooked over the quillon to increase control of the blade.

PASS FORWARD
A purposive walking step in which the trailing foot moves forward to become the leading foot. During a pass, the body remains in balance, forward facing, with its center of gravity held relatively low.

PASS TO THE REAR
Pass to the rear, or pass back; a purposive backward step in which the leading foot moves rearward to become the trailing foot while the body is held low, forward facing, and in balance.

PERCUSSION WEAPONS
A class of impact weapons used to bludgeon or batter opponents with the intention of knocking them down, off balance, or of breaking the bones beneath their armor. Examples: mace, war club, morningstar, war hammer, unhoned broadsword.

PHRASE
In a stage fight, an interconnected set of moves that tells a specific part of the story of the fight.

PIKE
A very long spear.

PILLOW SWORD
A sword, usually with a simple hilt, hung at the head of a bed for domestic defense.

PISTOL
A short-barrelled, hand-held firearm.

PLATE ARMOR
Inflexible body armor made of solid sheets of metal molded to fit the arms, legs, and torso.

POLEARM
A cutting or thrusting weapon consisting of a metallic head fitted to a long wooden shaft and wielded by hand (not thrown). Examples: spears, pikes, halberds, pole axes.

POMMEL
The bottom of the hilt; the part of the sword farthest from the tip, usually somewhat heavy and used to counterbalance the blade. The pommel is the last part of the hilt assembled and holds the rest of the furniture in place.

POMMEL ATTACK
An attack made with the pommel of a sword.

PREPARATION
Preparation or "prep," is the second step in the four-step stage combat sequence of eye contact–preparation–reaction–and action. A prep signals the defender that the agreed-upon attack, or action, is about to come.

PRIS-DE-FER
Pris-de-fer: literally, "taking of the blade (iron or steel);" an attack on the opponent's blade made from a parry, intended to control the attacker's weapon, taking it from one line or position to another, while the defender transitions from defense to attack. The term pris-de-fer includes the croisé, bind, envelopment, and glissade.

PRONATION
A sword grip in which the knuckles are up and the palm faces down.

PUNTO REVERSO
A thrust made from the attacker's inside line to the defender's outside line with the hand usually in supination.

QUILLONS
The arms of the crossguard that protect the hand.

RAPIER
A class of swords featuring a long, thin blade, with sharpened point and true edge, used primarily for thrusting, with a secondary threat of a cut. Rapiers often have elaborate knuckle bows and hand guards.

REACTION
The third step in the four-step stage combat sequence of eye contact, preparation, reaction, action in which the defender signals the attacker that the preparation has been seen and understood. A proper reaction typically takes the form of beginning the required defensive move, such as a parry or evasion.

REBATED WEAPON
A cutting or thrusting weapon whose pointed and honed edges have been blunted, usually for use in a tournament.

RECOVERY
To return to the en garde position from a lunge. To "recover forward," the trailing foot is brought forward while the leading foot remains in place. To "recover back" or "recover to the rear," the trailing foot is left in place while the leading foot is brought back.

RETREAT
The opposite of an advance: the trailing foot steps back, followed by the leading foot.

REVERSE LUNGE
A lunge in which the leading foot remains stationary while the trailing foot steps even farther back, allowing the torso to sink behind the deeply bent forward knee.

RICASSO
The lowest part of the forte just before the hilt; in a rapier, the part of the blade between the pas d'anes.

RIPOSTE
To counterattack immediately after a successful parry.

RONDEL
A metal disc fitted to daggers and polearms to protect the hand. It became the generic name for ice pick-like daggers used to stab fallen knights between gaps in their plate armor.

SABER
A one-handed sword with a curved, single-edged blade, used by cavalry in the eighteenth and nineteenth-centuries.

SCABBARD

A protective case for carrying a sword. (The term "sheath" generally describes the protective case for carrying a knife or dagger.)

SCALE ARMOR

Flexible body armor comprised of small, overlapping metal or bone plates sewn or laced onto a padded shirt.

SCIMITAR

A thin-bladed, single-edged sword of Middle Eastern origins featuring small quillons and a curved blade.

SECTION

In a stage fight, a series of phrases that completes one part of the story of the fight.

SEMI-CIRCULAR PARRY

A parry in which the blade must move between high and low lines (or vice versa) to assume the end position.

SHORT FORM

Quarterstaff technique in which the staff is held approximately one third the distance from each end, allowing the opponent to be engaged at very close quarters (see also, Long Form).

SHORT SWORD

A broad-bladed (and often double-edged) weapon longer than a dagger but shorter than a broadsword. Example: the Roman gladius.

SMALLSWORD

Used widely in the late seventeenth, eighteenth, and early nineteenth centuries, a relatively short but deadly sword used only for thrusting; called a "courtsword" in its highly ornamented, decorative or presentation versions, it was the immediate precursor to the modern fencer's foil.

SPEAR

A polearm featuring a wooden shaft fixed with a leaf-shaped metal, bone, or stone point at one end. A spear is used for thrusting and is never thrown. Lightweight "spears" thrown at game or the enemy are called javelins.

STEEL

An alloy of iron and carbon, steel is hardened by repeated heating and cooling (called quenching) in water. To keep the hardened steel from becoming too brittle, it is gently reheated, or tempered. The best sword blades are made from high carbon, highly tempered steel.

SUPINATION

A sword grip in which the knuckles face down while the palm faces up.

SWIPE

An energetic, roundhouse cut in which the blade travels approximately 180 degrees in a horizontal plane aimed at the head, or the stomach, or the feet; or on a diagonal plane passing from high to low (or vice versa). In stage combat, the defender usually reacts to a swipe by beginning an evasion.

SWORD BREAKER

A device mounted on quillons, ricasso, dagger, or buckler to catch and trap, and if possible to break an opponent's blade.

SWORD CANE

A smallsword concealed in a walking stick.

SWORD KNOT
A cord or leather strap, ending in a tassel, looped from the hilt and secured to the wrist to prevent dropping the sword in battle.

SWORDSMITH
A sword maker, or one who assembles and repairs swords. Typically, there are two types of swordmakers: those who make their own blades (true swordsmiths), and those who make and install hilts (also called hiltsmiths or swordcutlers).

TALHOFFER
 A fifteenth century fencing master; See Zweihander.

TANG
The portion of the blade that extends from the ricasso through the inside of the handle, onto which the pommel is fixed to hold the furniture in place.

TAPER
The change in the width of a blade from ricasso to tip.

TARGET
In stage combat, a point related to, but slightly removed from, a specific part of the body.

TEMPER
To bring steel to a degree of hardness and flexibility by repeated heating and cooling in water (annealing).

THRUST
An attack made with the point of the sword, intended to stab or impale.

TOMAHAWK
A lightweight war axe of Native American origin.

TOURNAMENT
A formal convocation of nobility in the Middle Ages for entertainment and mock combat by knights. Tournament weapons were usually rebated to avoid serious injury to combatants.

TRAVERSE
Any footwork that takes one partner off line; also called a "lateral (or diagonal) pass."

TRUE EDGE
The sharpened cutting edge of a rapier or knife; on a double-edged weapon, the edge furthest the web of the thumb.

TUCK
(See Estoc.)

VOLTE
From the normal en garde stance (with right foot forward) a method of reducing the frontal area of the body exposed to attack by swinging the trailing leg back and to the right. This flattens the torso, leaving only the outside line (right shoulder, sword arm, and right leg) facing the opponent. A volte may also be made to the left by swinging the right leg to the rear and behind the left foot. A "full volte" moves the right foot almost 270 degrees to the left, or the left foot approximately 180 degrees to the right; a "demi-" or "half-volte" takes the moved foot only half this distance.

WAR HAMMER
Also called a "martel," a short-hafted hammer used as a percussive weapon in the fifteenth and sixteenth centuries. War hammers with a single, long spike extending from behind the hammer head were often called the "horseman's pick."

YIELD PARRY

A parry in which the defender gives way while keeping the swords engaged. In stage combat, a yield (or "ceding") parry often leads to a corps a corps, or an attack with the free hand.

ZA!

A term coined by Patrick (Paddy) Crean, Dean of fight choreographers, for the irresistible charismatic allure and charm of a gallant swashbuckler.

ZWEIHANDER

Literally, "two hander;" also known as the Bidenhander (sometimes called a Talhoffer, after the German swordmaster by that name): a large (five to six feet long), two-handed crosshilt used almost exclusively for cutting.

BIBLIOGRAPHY

Adcock, FE. *The Roman Art of War Under the Republic*. Martin Classical Lectures, Vol. VIII, Cambridge: W. Heffer & Sons, Ltd., 1970.

Agrippa, Camillo. *Trattato di Scientia d'Arme*. Rome: Bladig, 1553.

Anderson, Bob. *Stretching*. Bolinas, CA: Shelter Publications, 1980.

Angelo, Domenico. *L'Ecole des Armes*. 1765. Reprint. *The School of Fencing*. New York: Land's End Press, 1971.

Anonymous. *Chinese Martial Arts*. Beijing: Morning Glory Press, 1982.

Aylward, JD. *The English Master of Arms*. London: Routledge & Kegan Paul Limited, 1956.

Baldick, Robert. *The Duel*. London: Chapman and Hall Ltd., 1965.

Barbasetti, Luigi. *The Art of the Sabre and the Épée*. New York: E.P. Dutton & Co., 1936.

—————. *The Art of the Foil, with a Short History of Fencing*. New York: E.P. Dutton & Co., 1932.

Barber, Richard. *The Arthurian Legends: An Illustrated Anthology*. Totowa, NJ: Littlefield Adams & Co., 1979.

Bassoff, Lawrence. *Errol Flynn: The Movie Posters*. Beverly Hills, CA: The Lawrence Bassoff Collection, Inc., 1995.

Bazancourt, Baron de. *Les Secrets de l'épée*. Paris: Amyot, 1862.

Berriman, Wm. *The Militiaman's Manual and Sword-play*. New York: D. Van Nostrand, 1861.

Bottomley, I, and AP Hopson. *Arms and Armor of the Samurai*. New York: Crescent Books, 1988.

Bryson, Frederick R. *The Sixteenth Century Italian Duel*. Chicago: University Of Chicago Press, 1938.

Burt, Payson H. *Of Paces*, Norristown, PA: Payson H. Burt, 1993.

Burton, Richard F. *The Book of the Sword*. New York: Dover Publications, Inc., 1987.

Burton, Sir Richard. *The Sentiment of the Sword*. London: Horace Cox, 1911.

Byam, Michele. *Arms & Armor*. New York: Alfred A. Knopf, Inc., 1988.

Caldwell, Lloyd. "Slapstick in the Commedia Dell'Arte," *The Fight Master*, May, 1987.

Callahan, John. "Some Methods of Weaponless Stage Combat," *The Fight Master*, Jan. 1983.

Castle, Egerton. *Schools and Masters of Fence*. York, PA: George Shumway, 1969.

Cernenko, EV. *The Scythians, 700-300 B.C.* London: Osprey Publishing, 1983.

Chow, David, and Richard Spangler. *Kung Fu: History, Philosophy, and Technique*. Burbank, CA: Unique Publications, 1982.

Coe, Michael D, et al. *Swords and Hilt Weapons*. London: Barnes & Noble, Inc./Multimedia Books Limited, 1993.

Colbin, Rod. "The Not So Funny Art or the Quest for Fun," *The Fight Master*, Jan. 1987.

Connolly, Peter. *The Roman Army*. London: Macdonald Educational, 1975.

—————. *The Greek Armies*. London: Macdonald Educational, 1977.

—————. *Hannibal and the Enemies of Rome*. London: Macdonald Educational, 1978.

Conwell, Charles. "Of Fights and Film: A Conversation with William Hobbs," *The Fight Master*, Fall, 1993.

Cook, Eiler Robert. "Theatrical Weaponry," *The Fight Master,* Jan. 1987.

Corbesier, *Theory of Fencing with the Small Sword Exercise*. Annapolis, MD: Government Printing Office, 1873.

Craig, Darrell. *Iai: The Art of Drawing the Sword*. Tokyo: Charles E. Tuttle Company, Inc., 1981.

Craig, Horace S. *Dueling Scenes and Terms in Shakespeare's Plays*. University Of California Publications in English, Vol. 9, No. 1. Berkeley: University of California Press, 1940.

Crean, Patrick. *More Champagne Darling*. Toronto, Canada: McGraw-Hill Ryerson Limited, 1981.

De Loque, Bertrand. *Discourses of Warre and Single Combat*. London: J. Wolfe, 1591.

Dennhardt, Paul. "Serving Time: the Fight Master's Apprentice," *The Fight Master*. Fall 1990.

Di Grassi, Giacomo. *His True Arte of Defence*. London: Appresso Georgio de'Cavalli, 1594.

Dillon, Robert W. "Classical Japanese Martial Art," *The Fight Master*, Spring, 1992.

——————. "Beyond Acting in Fights: Stage Combat as a New Martial Art," *The Fight Master*, Spring/Summer, 1994.

Draeger, Donn F. and Robert W Smith. *Comprehensive Asian Fighting Arts*. Tokyo: Kodansha International Ltd., 1982.

Duchartre, Pierre Louis. *The Italian Comedy*. New York: Dover Publications, Inc., 1966.

Dunn, HA Colmore. *Fencing*. London: George Bell & Sons, 1889.

D'Eon, F. *System of Fencing*. Boston: Frederick D'eon, 1823.

Edge, David and John M Paddock. *Arms & Armor of the Medieval Knight: An Illustrated History of Weaponry in the Middle Ages*. Avenal, NJ: Crescent Books/Random House, 1995.

Evangelista, Nick. *The Encyclopedia of the Sword*. Westport, CT: Greenwood Press, 1995.

Evered, DF. *Sabre Fencing*. London: Gerald Duckworth & Co., Ltd., 1982.

Fabris, Salvator. *De Lo Schermo Overo Scienza d'Arme*. Copenhaven: Henrico Waltkirch, 1606.

Ffoulkes, Charles. *The Armourer and His Craft from the XIth to the XVIth Century*. New York: Dover Publications, Inc., 1988.

Fraser, George MacDonald. *The Hollywood History of the World*. New York: William Morrow and Company, Inc., 1988.

Freeman, John W. *Stories of the Great Operas*. New York: The Metropolitan Opera Guild/W.W. Norton & Company, Inc., 1984.

Girard, Dale Anthony. *Actors on Guard*. New York: Routledge/Theatre Arts Books, 1997.

——————. *The Fight Arranger's Companion*. Long Island City, NY: Dale Anthony Girard, 1994.

Gleich, James R. "Fencing vs. Ballet: to the Point - Modern Dualism," *The Fight Master*, Summer, 1995.

Glenn, TJ. "How To Teach Stage Combat to Martial Artists," *The Fight Master*, Spring, 1989.

Gravett, Christopher, and Angus McBride. *Knights at Tournament*. London: Osprey Publishing, Ltd., 1985.

——————. *German Medieval Armies 1300-1500*. London: Osprey Publishing, Ltd., 1985.

Gummerson, Tony. *Strength Training for the Martial Arts*. London: A&C Black, Ltd., 1990.

Hart, Harold H. *Weapons & Armor*. New York: Dover Publications, Inc., 1982.

Herrigel, Eugene. *Zen in the Art of Archery*. New York: Random House, 1989.

Hill, Michael Wayne. *A Selected and Annotated Bibliography of Stage Combat Resource Materials*. Ann Arbor, MI: UMI Dissertation Services, 1995.

Hobbs, William. *Fight Direction for Stage and Screen*. London: A&C Black, Ltd., 1995.

——————. *Stage Combat: The Action to the Word*. New York: St. Martin's Press, 1980.

Hope, Sir William. *The Compleat Fencing Master*. London: Printed for Dorman Newman. London: The King's Arms in the Poultrey, 1692.

Horgan, Paul. *Conquistadores in North American History*. New York: Farrar & Straus, 1963.

Howell, Maxwell L. *Chairman Mao's 4-Minute Physical Fitness Plan*. Millbrae, CA: Celestial Arts, 1973.

Hutton, Alfred. *The Sword and the Centuries or Old Sword Days and Old Sword Ways*. Rutland, VT: Charles E. Tuttle Company, Inc., 1973.

——————. *Old Sword-Play*. London: H. Grevel & Co., 1892.

Jackson, James L. *Three Elizabethan Fencing Manuals: Giacomo di Grassi, "His True Arte of Defense" (1594); Vincentio Saviolo, "His Practice" (1595); George Silver, "Paradoxes of Defense" and "Bref Instructions Upon My Paradoxes of Defense."* New York: Scholars' Facsimiles & Reprints, Delmar, 1972.

Jenks, Harold J, and Michael H Brown. *Bloody Iron*. Cornville, AZ: Desert Publications, 1978.

Jou, Tsung Hwa. *The Tao of Tai-Chi Chuan*. Rutland, VT: Charles E. Tuttle Co., 1980.

Jwing-Ming, Yang. *How to Defend Yourself*. Hong Kong: Yang's Martial Arts Association, 1992.

Kapit, Wynn, and Lawrence M Elson. *The Anatomy Coloring Book*. New York: Harper and Row, 1977.

Keegan, John. *The Face of Battle*. New York: Viking Press, 1976.

——————. *A History of Warfare*. New York: Alfred A. Knopf, 1994.

Kelton, JC. *A New Manual of the Bayonet*. New York: D. Van Nostrand, 1861.

L'abbat, M. *The Art of Fencing or the Use of the Smallsword*. Andrew Mahon, trans. Dublin: James Hoey, Printer, 1734.

Lee, Bruce. *Tao of Jeet Kune Do*. Santa Clarita, CA: Ohara Publications, Inc., 1975.

Leong, David S. "Teaching Stage Combat: Helpful Hints," *The Fight Master*, January, 1986.

Marozzo, Achille. *Opera Nova*. Venice: M. Sessa, 1517.

Marshall, Henry. *Stage Swordplay, or "So You Want To Be Errol Flynn?": A Manual of Dramatic Armed Combat for Actors*. Tarrytown, NY: Marymount College, 1977.

Martinez, JD. *Combat Mime*. Chicago: Nelson-Hall Publishers, 1982.

——————. "A Tale of Jealousy, Swordplay and a Certain Italian," *The Fight Master*, Fall, 1990.

——————. *The Swords of Shakespeare*. Jefferson, NC: McFarland & Company, 1996.

McClellan, GB. *Manual of Bayonet Exercise*. Philadelphia: Lippincott & Co., 1861.

McCollum, Linda. "Weight Consciousness," *The Fight Master*, April, 1983.

——————. "Special Workshop Report," *The Fight Master*, Spring, 1993.

——————. "Dennis Graves, Premier Swordcutler," *The Fight Master*, Winter, 1990.

Melville, Lewis. and Reginald Hargreaves. *Famous Duels and Assassinations*. New York: JJ. Sears and Co. Date unknown.

Miller, Douglas, and GA Embleton. *The Swiss at War 1300-1500*. London: Osprey Publishing, Ltd., 1979.

Montross, Lynn. *War Through the Ages*. 3rd Edition. New York: Harper, 1960.

Morley, Margaret. *The Films of Laurence Olivier*. Secaucus, NJ: The Citadel Press, 1978.

Musashi, Miyamoto. *A Book of Five Rings*. Woodstock, NY: The Overlook Press, 1982.

Nadi, Aldo. *On Fencing*. Sunrise, FL: Laureate Press, 1994.

Neergaard, Lauran. "Dancers And Actors Raked By Injuries," *San Francisco Examiner, (AP)*, Feb. 4, 1996.

Newark, Timothy. *Medieval Warfare*. London: Bloomsbury Books, 1988.

Nicole, David, and Richard Hook. *The Crusades*. London: Osprey Publishing, Ltd., 1988.

——————, and Angus McBride. *French Medieval Armies 1000-1300*. London: Osprey Publishing, Ltd., 1991.

——————. *Arthur and the Anglo-Saxon Wars*. London: Osprey Publishing, Ltd., 1984.

Norman, Vesey. *Arms and Armour*. London: Octopus Books Limited, 1972.

North, Anthony. *European Swords*. Owings Mills, MD: Stemmer House Publishers Inc., 1982.

Nuland, Sherwin B. *How We Die: Reflections on Life's Final Chapter*. New York: Vintage books, Random House, 1995.

Obata, Toshishiro. *Naked Blade*. Thousand Oaks, CA: Dragon Books, 1985.

Olivier, Laurence. *Henry V by William Shakespeare*. London: Lorrimer Publishing Limited, 1984.

Olsen, Mark. "The Metaphysics of Stage Combat," *The Fight Master*, Jan. 1988.

Pallazoil, Richard. "A Musketeer History Lesson," *The Fight Master*, Fall, 1983.

Richards, Jeffrey. *Swordsmen of the Screen*. London: Routledge & Kegan Paul, Ltd., 1977.

Rolfe, Bari. *Movement for Period Plays*. Berkeley, CA: Personabooks, 1985.

Rothero, Christopher. *The Armies of Crécy and Poitiers*. London: Osprey Publishing, 1981.

Rowse, AL. *The Annotated Shakespeare*. Vol. III. New York: Clarkson N. Potter, Inc., 1978.

San-Feng, Chang. "T'ai Chi Ch'uan Ching:" In *The Essence of T'ai Chi Chuan: The Literary Tradition*. Berkeley, CA: North Atlantic Books, 1979.

Saviolo, Vincentio. *His Practise, in Two Bookes: the first intreating of the use of the Rapier and Dagger, the second, of Honor and honorable Quarrels*. London: John Wolfe, 1595.

Seder, John W. *Shakespeare's Book of Insults, Insights & Infinite Jests*. Springfield, IL: Octavo Press, 1984.

Silver, George. *Paradoxes of Defence*, 1599. Shakespeare Association Facsimiles, No. 6. London: Oxford University Press, 1933.

Simkins, Michael. *The Roman Army from Caesar to Trajan*. London: Osprey Publishing, Ltd., 1984.

Simonian, Charles. *Basic Foil Fencing*. Dubuque, IA: Kendall/Hunt Publishing, 1990.

Smith, Raymond G. *The Art of the Sword in the Late Middle Ages*. Ann Arbor, MI: U.M.I. Dissertation Services, 1993.

Soper, Tony. "Stage Manager's Fight-Call Checklist," *The Fight Master*, May, 1984.

Stevens, John. *Abundant Peace, the Biography of Morihei Ueshiba*. Boston: Shambala Publications, 1987.

Stone, George Cameron. *A Glossary of the Construction, Decoration and Use of Arms and Armor in all Countries and in all Times*. New York: Jack Brussel, Publisher, 1961.

Suddeth, J. Allen. *Fight Directing for the Theatre*. Portsmouth, NH: Heinemann, 1996.

Suino, Nicklaus. *The Art of Japanese Swordsmanship: A Manual of Eishin-Ryu Iaido*. New York: Weatherhill, 1994.

Swetnam, Joseph. *The Schoole of Defence*. London: Nicholas Okes, 1617.

Tarassuk, Leonid. *Parrying Dagger and Poinards*. Blue Diamond, NV: The Society of American Fight Directors, 1987.

Taylor, John. *The Art of Defence on Foot*. London: Egerton, 1804.

Thimm, Carl A. *A Complete Bibliography of Fencing and Duelling*, 1896. New York: Benjamin Blom, Inc., 1968.

Tung, Timothy. *Wushu*. London: Mitchell Beazley Publishers, 1981.

Turnbull, Stephen R. *The Book of the Samurai*. New York: Gallery Books, 1982.

Turner, Craig. "Notes From the Elizabethan Swordplay Masters," *The Fight Master*, Spring, 1989.

Vegetius, Flavius Renatus. *The Military Institutions of the Romans*. Harrisburg, PA: Stackpole, 1960.

Viggiani, Angelo. *Lo Schermo*. Vinitia: Appresso Giorgio Angelieri, 1575.

Von Volbroth, Carl Alexander. *Heraldry of the World*. New York: Macmillian Publishing Co., 1972.

Wagner, Eduard. *Cut and Thrust Weapons*. London: Spring Books, 1967.

Warner, Gordon, and Donn F. Draeger. *Japanese Swordsmanship*. Tokyo: Weatherhill, 1987.

Westbrook, A, and O Ratti. *Aikido and the Dynamic Sphere*. Tokyo: Charles A. Tuttle Co., 1970.

Wise, Arthur. *The Art and History of Personal Combat*, Greenwich, CN: New York Graphic Society, 1971.

Wise, Terence. *Medieval European Armies*. London: Osprey Publishing, Ltd., 1975.

—————. *Armies of the Carthaginian Wars, 265-146 BC*. London: Osprey Publishing, 1982.

Witchel, Alex. "Co-star Exits During Broadway Play," *New York Times*. May 4, 1991.

Wolkomir, Richard. "En Garde! We Seem To Be Getting the Point of Fencing," *Smithsonian*, June, 1996.

Young, Jack. "What Happened To the Actor in Actor/Combatant?" *The Fight Master*, Spring, 1995.

Zi, Sun. *The Art of War*. Leong Weng Kam, trans. Singapore: Asiapac Books, 1991.

| FURTHER READING

Alaux, Michel. *Modern Fencing: Foil, Épée, and Sabre.* New York: Charles Scribner's Sons, 1975.

Allanson-Winn, RG, and C Phillips-Wooley. *Broad-Sword and Single-Stick.* London: George Bell and Sons, 1898.

Allcock, Hubert. *Heraldic Design: Its Origins, Ancient Forms and Modern Usage.* New York: Tudor Publishing Company, 1962.

Annis, PGW. *Naval Swords: British and American Edged Weapons 1660-1815.* Harrisburg, PA: Stackpole Books, 1970.

Anonymous. *The British Code of Duel: A Reference to the Laws of Honour, and the Character of a Gentleman.* London: Knight and Lacey, 1824. Reprint: The Richmond Publishing Co., Ltd., 1971.

Ashby-Beach, Genette. *The Song of Roland: A generative study of the formulaic language in the single combat.* Amsterdam: Rodopi, 1985.

Ashdown, Charles Henry. *Armour & Weapons in the Middle Ages.* London: New Holland Publishers, 1988.

Ashdown, Charles Henry. *An Illustrated History of Arms & Armour.* Hertfordshire: Wordsworth Editions, Ltd, 1988.

——————. *European Arms and Armor.* New York: Barnes & Noble, 1995.

Asquith, Stuart, and Chris Warner. *New Model Army 1645-60.* London: Osprey Publishing, 1981.

Aylward, JD. *The House of Angelo.* London: Batchworth Press, 1945.

——————. *The Small Sword in England.* London: Hutchinson, 1945.

Bacon, Francis. *The Charge of Sir F. Bacon. . . His Majesties Attourney Generall, touching duells, upon an information in the star-chamber against Priest and Wright. With the decree of the Star-Chamber in the same cause.* London: Great Britian Attourney Generall, 1614. Reprinted as: *The Charge of Sir F. Bacon Touching Duells.* New York: DaCapo Press, 1968.

Baker, Michael K. *The Sword.* Oklahoma City: M.B. Publishing, 1985.

Bacon, John Lord. *Elementary Forge Practice.* Lindsay Publications, Inc., 1986.

Barber, Richard, and Juliet Barker. *Tournaments, Jousts, Chivalry and Pageants in the Middle Ages.* New York: Weildenfeld & Nicolson, 1989.

Barber, Richard. *The Knight and Chivalry.* London: Cox and Wyman, Ltd., 1970.

Barney, Richard W, and Robert Loveless. *How To Make Knives.* North Hollywood, CA: Beinfeld Publishing, 1977.

Barthop, Michael, and GA Embleton. *The Jacobite Rebellions 1689-1745.* London: Osprey Publishing, 1982.

——————, and Angus McBride. *Marlborough's Army 1702-1711.* London: Osprey Publishing, 1980.

Bealer, Alex. *The Art of Blacksmithing.* New York: Funk & Wagnalls, 1976.

Belous, Russell E. *Arms and Armor.* Los Angeles: The Ward Ritchie Press, 1968.

Bennetton, Norman Adrian. *Social Significance of the Duel in Seventeenth Century French Drama.* Baltimore: The Johns Hopkins Press, 1938.

Berry, Herbert. *The Noble Science: A Study and Transcription of Sloane Ms. 2530, Papers of the Masters of Defence of London. Henry VIII to 1590.* Delaware: University of Delaware Press, 1991.

Billacois, Francois. *The Duel: Its Rise & Fall in Early Modern France.* New Haven, CT: Yale University Press, 1990.

Blackmore, Howard L. *Arms and Armour.* New York: E.P. Dutton and Co., 1965.

Blair, Claude. *European Armour.* London: B.T. Batsford, Ltd., 1958.

——————. *European and American Arms circa 1100-1850.* New York: Crown Publishers, 1962.

Blakeslee, F. *Sword Play for Actors: A Manual of Stage Fencing.* New York: M.N. Hazen Co., 1905.

Bosenquet, Henry TA. *The Naval Officer's Sword.* London: Her Majesty's Stationery Office, 1955.

Boutell, Charles. *Armes and Armour.* Gibbings & Co., Ltd., 1902.

——————. *Arms and Armour in Antiquity and the Middle Ages.* Conshohchken, PA: Combined Books, 1906.

Bowers, Fredson. *Elizabethan Revenge Tragedy 1587-1642.* Princeton, NJ: Princeton University Press, 1966.

Bryson, Fredrick Robertson. *The Point of Honor in Sixteenth-Century Italy: an Aspect of the Life of the Gentleman,* Chicago: University of Chicago Press, 1935.

Brzezinski, Richard, and Angus McBride. *Polish Armies 1569-1696*. London: Osprey Publishing, 1987.

—————————, and Richard Hook. *The Army of Gustavus Adolphus: Infantry*. London: Osprey Publishing, 1991.

Buehr, Walter. *Chivalry and the Mailed Knight*. New York: G.P. Putnam's Sons, 1963.

Bull, Stephen. *An Historic Guide to Arms and Armor*. New York: Facts on File, 1991.

—————————. *European Swords*. Princes Risborough, UK: Shire Publications Ltd., 1994.

Carlyle, Thomas. "Two-Hundred and Fifty Years Ago—Dueling," in: *English and Other Critical Essays*. London: J.M. Dent and Sons, 1915. Reprint: 1967.

Cass, Eleanor Baldwin. *The Book of Fencing*. Boston: Lothrop, Lee and Shepard, Co., 1930.

Cassidy, William. *The Complete Book of Knife Fighting*. Boulder, CO: Paladin Press, 1975.

Cassin-Scott, Jack. *The Greek and Persian Wars 500-323 B.C.* London: Osprey Publishing, 1977.

Castello, Julio. The *Theory and Practice of Fencing*. New York: Charles Scribner's Sons, 1933.

Castello, Hugo and James. *Fencing*. New York: The Ronald Press Company, 1962.

Chartrand, Rene, and Francis Back. *Louis XIV's Army*. London: Osprey Publishing, 1988.

—————————. *The French Army in the American War of Independence*. London: Osprey Publishing, 1991.

Chevalier, Guillaume de. *The ghosts of the deceased Sieurs De Villemor and de Fountains. A most necessarie discorse of duells: wherein is shewed the means to roote them out quite. With a discourse of valour*. Trans: Thomas Heigham, Esq. Cambridge: C. Legge, Printer to the University of Cambridge, 1624.

Clephan, R Coltman. *The Tournament: Its Periods and Phases*. New York: Frederick Ungar Publishing Co., 1967.

Colby, CB. *Revolutionary War Weapons*. New York: Coward, McCann and Geoghegan, 1963.

Comber, Thomas. *A discourse of duels, shewing the sinful nature and mischievous effects of them and answering the usual excuses made for them by challengers, accepters, and seconds*. London: Samuel Roycroft, 1687.

Constable, George, ed. *The Age of Calamity: Time Frame A.D. 1300-1400*. Alexandria, VA: Time-Life Books, 1989.

Cornish, Paul, and Angus McBride. *Henry VIII's Army*. London: Osprey Publishing, Ltd., 1987.

Council, Norman. *When Honour's at the Stake*. New York: Barnes and Noble, 1973.

Cowper, Henry S. *The Art of Attack. Being a Study in the Development of Weapons and Appliances of Offence from the Earliest Times to the Age of Gunpowder*. Ulverston, Westmorland, UK: W. Holmes Ltd., 1906.

Craven, Kurt. *101 Sucker Punches*. Boulder CO: Paladin Press, 1989.

Crosnier, Roger. *Fencing with the Foil*. A.S. Barnes and Company. Date unknown.

Curtis, Howard M. *2,500 Years of European Helmets*. North Hollywood, CA: Beinfeld Publishing Inc., 1978.

De Saillans, Francois. *Discourses of warre and single combat*. Trans. I. Eliot. London: John Wolfe, Printer, 1591.

D'Espagne, Jean. *Anti-duello. The anatomie of duells, with the symptomes thereof*. London: Published by His Majesties command, 1632.

Darling, Anthony D. *Swords for the Highland Regiments 1757-1784*. Andrew Mowbray Inc., 1988.

Dean, Bashford. *Catalogue: Loan Exhibition of Arms and Armor*. New York: The Metropolitan Museum of Art, 1911.

Demmin, Auguste. *An Illustrated History of Arms and Armour: From the Earliest Period to the Present Time*. Trans. C.C. Black. London: George Bell and Sons, 1901.

DeVries, Kelly. *Medieval Military Technology*. Ontario: Broadview Press Ltd., 1992.

Dillon, Robert W Jr. *Towards a Theatrical Hoplology: An Approach to Staging, Performance, and Critical Theory for Weapons-Play in the Theatre*. Columbia, MO: University of Missouri, 1989.

Donovan, Frank R. *The Vikings*. New York: Harper and Row, 1964.

Dufty, Arthur Richard. *European Armour in the Tower of London*. London: Her Majesty's Stationery Office, 1968.

Dupuy, TN. *The Evolution of Weapons and Warfare*. New York: The Bobbs-Merrill Company, 1980.

Fawcett, William. *Rules and Regulations for the Sword Exercise of the Cavalry*. Military Library, Whitehall, London, 1796. Ottawa, ON: Reprint, Museum Restoration Service, 1970.

Figiel, Leo. *On Damascus Steel*. Atlantis Arts Press, 1991.

Fosten, Bryan. *Wellington's Infantry*. London: Osprey Publishing Ltd., 1981.

Franco, Sammy. *Street Lethal: Unarmed Urban Combat*. Boulder, CO: Paladin Press, 1989.

Fraser, John. *Violence in the Arts*. London: Cambridge University Press, 1974.

Frey, Edward. *The Kris. Mystic Weapon of the Malay World*. Singapore: Oxford University Press, 1986.

Gambordella, Ted. *Fight for Your Life: Secrets of Street Fighting*. Boulder, CO: Paladin Press, 1982.

Garder, Robert E. *Five Centuries of Gunsmiths, Swordsmiths and Armourers, 1400-1900*. Columbus, OH: W.F. Heer, 1948.

Gardner, Robert E. *Small Arms Makers*. Bonanza Books, 1963.

Gordon, Gilbert. *Stage Combat: A Simple Handbook of Techniques*. New York: Routledge, Chapman & Hall, 1974.

Grancsay, Stephen. *Arms and Armor*. New York: The Metropolitan Musuem of Art, 1986.

——————. *Catalogue of Armor: The John Woodman Higgins Armory*. New York: Davis Press Inc., 1961.

Grant, Michael. *Gladiators*. New York: Delacorte Press, 1967.

Gravett, Christopher. *Hastings 1066: The Fall of Saxon England*. London: Osprey Publishing, 1992.

——————, and Richard and Christine Hook. *Medieval Siege Warfare*. London: Osprey Publishing, 1990.

Great Briton Sovereigns, etc., James I, 1603-1625. *By the King. A proclamation against private challenges and combats: vvith articles annexed for the better directions to be used therein, and for the most judiciall proceeding against offenders*. London: r. Baker, 1613. In: Early English Books, 1475-1640, University Microfilms: Ann Arbor, MI.

——————. *By the King. A proclamation prohibiting the publishing of any reports or writings of duels*. London: R. Barker, 1613. In: Early English Books, 1475-1640, University Microfilms: Ann Arbor, MI.

Hakusui, Inami. *Nippon-To, the Japanese Sword*. Kyoei Printing Co. Ltd., 1948.

Hale, John R. *The Art of War & Renaissance England*. Folger Books, 1979.

——————. *Artists & Warfare in the Renaissance*. New Haven, CT: Yale University Press, 1991.

Hale, JR. *War and Society in Renaissance Europe, 1450-1620*. New York: St. Martin's Press, 1985.

Hammond, Peter. *Royal Armouries Official Guide*. Philip Wilson Publishers Ltd., 1986.

Harding, David, ed. *Weapons: An International Encyclopedia from 5,000 B.C. to 2,000 A.D.* London: Galley Press, 1984.

Hardy, Robert. *Longbow: A Social and Military History*. New York: Arco Publishing Co., 1976.

Harrington, Peter. *Culloden 1746*. London: Osprey Publishing, 1991.

Haythornwaite, Philip, and Bryan Fosten. *Frederick the Great's Army: Cavalry*. London: Osprey Publishing, 1991.

Hayward, JF. *Swords and Daggers*. London: Her Majesty's Stationery Office, 1963.

Heath, Ian, and Angus McBride. *Byzantine Armies 886-1118*. London: Osprey Publishing, 1979.

Held. Robert. *Art, Arms and Armour: an International Anthology*. Acquafresca Editrice, SA., 1979.

Herndon, Myrtis. *Selected Fencing Articles*. Washington, DC: American Association for Health, Physical Education and Recreation, 1971.

Hindley, Geoffrey. *Medieval Warfare*. New York: G.P. Putnam's Sons, 1971.

Hobbs, William. *Techniques of the Stage Fight*. London: Studio Vista, 1967.

Hogg, Ian V, and John H Batchelor. *Armies of the American Revolution*. Englewood Cliffs, NJ: Prentice-Hall, Inc., 1975.

Holden, Matthew. *The Legions of Rome*. East Sussex, England: Wayland Publishers, 1973.

Holmes, Martin R. *Arms and Armour in Tudor and Stuart London*. London: Her Majesty's Stationery Office, 1970.

Hrisoulas, Jim. *The Complete Bladesmith: Forging Your Way to Perfection*. Boulder, CO: Paladin Press, 1987.

——————. *The Master Bladesmith: Advanced Studies in Steel*. Boulder, CO: Paladin Press, 1991.

Humble, Richard. *Warfare in the Ancient World*. London: Cassell, 1980.

Hunt, M. Briggs, and Norman Miller. *Beginning Wrestling*. Belmont, CA: Wadsworth Publishing Co., 1970.

Hutton, Alfred. *Cold Steel*. London: Clowes, 1889.

Jeffreys, Steven. *A Medieval Siege*. London: Wayland Publishers, 1973.

Jorgensen, Paul Alfred. *Shakespeare's Military World*. Berkeley: University of California Press, 1974.

Kane, Harnett T. *Gentlemen, Swords and Pistols*. New York: Morrow, 1951.

Kapp, Leon and Hiroko, and Yoshindo Yoshihara. *The Craft of the Japanese Sword*. Tokyo: Kodansha International Ltd., 1988.

Katz, Albert M. *The Theatre Student: Stage Violence, Techniques of Offense, Defense and Safety*. New York: Richard Rosen Press, Inc., 1976.

Keegan, John, and Richard Holmes. *Soldiers: A History of Men in Battle*. New York: Viking Penguin, 1986.

Kelso, Ruth. *The Doctrine of the English Gentleman in the Sixteenth Century*. Gloucester, MA: Peter Smith, 1964.

Kezer, Claude D. *Principals of Stage Combat*. Schulenburg, TX: I.E. Clark, Inc., 1983.

Kiernan, VG. *The Duel in European History: Honour & the Reign of Aristocracy*. New York: Oxford University Press, Inc., 1989.

Kist, JB. *Jacob de Gheyn: The Exercise of Arms; a Commentary*. New York: McGraw-Hill Book Company, 1971.

—————, JP Puype, W Van Der Mark, and RBF Van Der Sloot. *Dutch Muskets and Pistols*. York, PA: George Shumway Publisher, 1974.

Koch, HW. *History of Warfare*. New York: Gallery Books, 1981.

Koson, Honami. *Teiryo Yoji*. NewYork: David Scott, 1984.

Kottenkamp, F. *The History of Chivalry and Armor*. New York: Portland Press, 1988.

Kowalski, Bruce W, and James McElhinney. *Art and the Sword: The Bulletin of the Japanese Sword Society of the United States*. Volume 1. The Japanese Sword Society of the United States, Inc., 1988.

—————. *Art and the Sword: The Bulletin of the Japanese Sword Society of the United States*. Volume 2. The Japanese Sword Society of the United States, Inc., 1989.

Lacombe, MP. *Arms and Armour in Antiquity and the Middle Ages*. Trans. Charles Boutell, London: Reeves and Turner, 1905.

Laking, Guy F. *A Record of European Armor and Arms Through Seven Centuries*. London: G. Bell and Sons, Ltd., 1922.

Latham, Sid. *Knifecraft*. Harrisburg PA: Stackpole Books, 1978.

Lost Technology Series: *Blacksmith Shop & Iron Forging*. Lindsay Publications, 1983.

MacYoung, Marc "Animal." *Fists, Wits, and a Wicked Right: Surviving on the Wild Side of the Street*. Boulder, CO: Paladin Press, 1991.

—————. *Knives, Knife Fighting, and Related Hassles: How To Survive a Real Knift Fight*. Boulder, CO: Paladin Press, 1991.

Maertz, Richard C. *Wrestling Techniques: Takedowns*. New York: A.S. Barnes and Company, 1970.

Manley, Albert. *Complete Fencing*. Garden City, NY: Doubleday and Company, 1979.

Mann, Sir James. *Wallace Collection Catalogues: European Arms and Armour*. Lindon: Spottiswoode Ballantyne Ltd., 1962.

Manus, Willard. *The Fighting Men*. Los Angeles: Panjandrum Books, 1982.

Martone, John. *Handbook of Self-Defense*. New York: Arco Publishing Co., 1955.

May, Robin, and GA Embleton. *The British Army in North America*. London: Osprey Publishing, 1974.

May, WE, and PGW Annis. *Swords for Sea Service*. Vols. I and II. London: Her Majesty's Stationery Office, 1970.

Mayes, Jim. *How To Make Your Own Knives*. New York: Everest House Publishers, 1978.

McCallum, Paul. *A Practical Self-Defense Guide for Women*. Whitehall, VA: Betterway Publications, Inc., 1991.

McCreight, Tim. *The Complete Metalsmith*. Davis Publications Inc., 1991.

McIan, RR, and James Logan. *The Clans of the Scottish Highlands*. New York: Alfred A. Knopf, 1980.

Meilach, Dona. *Decorative and Sculptural Ironwork*. New York: Crown Publishers Inc., 1977.

Miller, Douglas, and GA Embleton, *The Landsknechts*. London: Osprey Publishing, 1976.

Moore, Warren. *Weapons of the American Revolution*. New York: Funk and Wagnalls, 1967.

Morsberger, Robert E. "Swordplay and the Elizabethan and Jacobean Stage," *Salzburg Studies in Elizabethan Literature*. James Hogg, ed. Salzburg, Austria: Universitaet Salzburg, 1974.

Morton, ED. *Martini A-Z of Fencing*. London: Queen Anne Press. Date unknown.

Mowbray, Andrew E. *Arms-Armor, from the Atelier of Ernst Schmidt, Munich*. Providence, RI: Mowbray Company, 1967.

Murtha, Gary. *The Samurai Sword: An American Perspective*. Independence, MO: H.S.M. Publications, 1984.

—————. *The Samurai Sword: An American Perspective*. Volume 2. Independence, MO: H.S.M. Publications, 1984.

Neumann, George C. *Swords and Blades of the American Revolution*. Texarkana, TX: Rebel Publishing Company, 1991.

Newark, Timothy. *The Barbarians: Warriors & Wars of the Dark Ages*. New York: Blandford Press, 1985.

—————. *Celtic Warriors 400 BC to AD 1600*. New York: Blandford Press, 1986.

—————. *Medieval Warlords*, London: Blandford Press, 1994.

—————. *Women Warlords*, London: Blandford Press, 1989.

Nicolle, David, and GA Embleton. *Italian Medieval Armies*. London: Osprey Publishing, 1983.

—————, and Angus McBride. *Rome's Enemies: The Desert Frontier*. London: Osprey Publishing, 1984.

—————. *Hattin 1187*. London: Osprey Publishing, 1993.

Nicolle, David, and Angus McBride. *The Age of Charlemagne*. London: Osprey Publishing, 1984.

Norman, AVB. *A History of War and Weapons 499-1660*. New York: Thomas Y. Crowell, 1966.

—————. The *Rapier and Small Sword, 1460-1820*. New York: Arco Press, 1980.

—————, and Don Pottinger. *English Weapons and Warfare 499-1660*. Englewood Cliffs, NJ: Prentice-Hall, 1979.

—————, and GM Wilson. *Treasures from the Tower of London*. London: Sainsbury Center for Visual Arts by Lund Humphries Publishers Ltd., 1982.

Norman, Vesey. *Waffen und Rüstungen*. Harrisburg, PA: George Weidenfeld and Nicolson Ltd., 1964.

Oakeshott, R Ewart. *The Archeology of Weapons*. Woodbridge, UK: Boydell Press, 1994.

—————. *European Weapons and Armor*. North Hollywood, CA: Beinfeld Pub. Inc., 1980.

—————. *A Knight and his Armour*. London: Lutterworth, 1961.

—————. *Records of the Medieval Sword*. Rochester, NY: Boydell & Brewer, 1991.

—————. *The Sword in the Age of Chivalry*. London: Lutterworth, 1964.

Ogasawara, Nobuo. *Sword Guards & Fittings*. Tokyo: Kodansha, 1984.

—————. *Japanese Swords*. Osaka: Hoikusha Publishing Co. Ltd., 1980.

Oman, Charles W. *A History of the Art of War in the Sixteenth Century*. New York: Dutton, 1937; New York: AMS Press, Reprint 1979.

—————. *The Art of War in the Middle Ages: A.D. 378-1515*. London: Methuen & Co., 1924; Ithaca, NY: Cornell University Press, Reprint 1986.

Onions, CT. *A Shakespeare Glossary*. Oxford: Clarendon Press, 1988.

Oxenstierna, Eric, Count. *The Norseman*. Trans. Catherine Hutter, ed. Greenwich, CN: New York Graphic Society Publishers, 1959.

Palffy-Alpar, Julius. *Sword and Masque*. Philadelphia: F.A. David Company, 1967.

Payne-Gallway, Sir Ralph. *The Crossbow*. New York: Bramhall House, 1958.

Perry, Edward. *Rapiers*. Stackpole Books, 1968.

Peterson, Harold, L. *History of Body Armor*. New York: Scribner, 1968.

—————. *Daggers & Fighting Knives of the Western World: from the Stone Age Till 1900*. New York: Bonanza Books, 1968.

Peterson, Susan L. *Self-Defense for Women*. New York: Leisure Press, 1984.

Pitman, Brian. *Fencing:Techniques of Foil, Épée and Sabre*. Ramsbury, Marlborough, Wiltshire: The Crowood Press, 1988.

Pollock, Frederick. *The Forms and History of the Sword*. London: Macmillan, 1890.

Quinn, Peyton. *Bouncer's Guide to Barroom Brawling: Dealing with the Sucker Puncher, Streetfighter and Ambusher.* Boulder, CO: Paladin Press, 1990.

Ratti, O, & A Westbrook. *Secrets of the Samurai.* Tokyo: Charles E. Tuttle Co., Inc., 1992.

Reid, Stuart, and Bryan Fosten. *Wellington's Highlanders.* London: Osprey Publishing, 1992.

Reid, William. *Weapons Through the Ages.* New York: Crescent Books, 1976.

————. *Arms Through the Ages.* New York: Harper & Row Publishers, 1976.

Roberts, Keith, and Angus McBride. *Soldiers of the English Civil War: Infantry.* London: Osprey Publishing, 1989.

Robinson, H Russell. *The Armour of Imperial Rome.* London: Arms and Armour Press, 1975.

Sabine, Lorenzo. *Notes on Duels & Duelling: Alphabetically Arranged with a Preliminary Historical Essay.* Boston: Crosby, Nichols & Co., 1855.

Sanchez, John. *Blade Master: Advanced Survival Skills for the Knife Fighter.* Boulder, CO: Paladin Press, 1983.

Sato, Kanzan. *The Japanese Sword.* Tokyo: Kodansha America Inc., 1983.

Saxon, K. *Weaponeer: an Encyclopedia of Weapons.* Gordon Press, 1986.

Schmidt, Alexander. *Shakespeare Lexicon and Quotation Dictionary.* New York: Dover Publications, 1971.

Schroen, Karl. *The Hand Forged Knife.* Knife World Publications, 1984.

Segar, William. *The Book of Honor and Arms (1590)* and *Honor Military and Civil (1602).* Diane Bornstein, ed. Delmar, New York: Scholars' Facsimiles and Reprints, 1975.

Segar, Sir William. *The Book of Honor and Arms.* Printed for Richard Ihones. London: T. Orwin, Printer, 1590.

Sekunda, Nicholas, and Angus McBride. *The Ancient Greeks.* London: Osprey Publishing, 1986.

Selden, John. *The duello or single combat: from antiquite derived into this kingdome of England, with severall kindes, and ceremonious formes there of from good authority described.* Printed for J. Helme. London: G. E[ld] Printer, 1610.

Sietsema, Robert. *Weapons and Armor.* New York: Hart Publishing Company, 1978.

Silver, George. *The Works of George Silver.* contains *Paradoxes of Defence* 1599, and *Brief Instructions on My Paradoxes of Defence* c. 1600, Capt. Cyril GR Matthey, ed. London: G. Bell, 1898.

Simkins, Michael. *Warriors of Rome.* London: Blandford Press, 1988.

Smith, Cyril Stanley. *A History of Metalography.* Cambridge, MA: MIT Press, 1988.

Snodgrass, AM. *Arms and Armour of the Greeks.* Ithaca, New York: Cornell University Press, 1967.

Sprague, Arthur Colby. *Shakespeare and the Actors: The Stage Business in His Plays.* Cambridge, MA: Harvard University Press, 1948. Steiner, Bradley J. *No Second Chance: Disarming the Armed Assailant.* Boulder, CO: Paladin Press, 1986.

Styers, John. *Cold Steel: Techniques of Close Combat.* Boulder, CO: Paladin Press, 1974.

Szabo, Laszlo, and Corvina Kiado. *Fencing and the Master.* Trans. Gyula Gulyas, Budapest, Hungary: Franklin Printing House, 1982.

Tarassuk, Leonid and Claude Blair. *The Complete Encyclopedia of Arms and Weapons.* New York: Simon and Schuster, 1982.

Tarassuk, Leonid. *Antique European and American Firearms at the Hermitage Museum.* Arco Publishing Company Inc., 1972.

Tegner, Bruce. *Bruce Tegner's Complete Book of Self-Defense.* Ventura, CA: Thor Publishing Company, 1977.

Thomas, Bruno, Ortwin Gamber, and Hans Schedelmann. *Die Schönsten Waffen und Rustungen.* Wiesbaden: R. Lowit.

Thornbury, GW. *Shakespeare's England; or Sketches of Our Social History in the Reign of Elizabeth.* Two Volumes. London: Longman, Brown, Green and Longmans, 1856.

Tincey, John and Richard Hook. *The Armada Campaign: 1588.* London: Osprey Publishing, 1988.

————, and Angus McBride. *Soldiers of the English Civil War: Cavalry.* London: Osprey Publishing, 1990.

Treece, Henry, and Ewart Oakeshott. *Fighting Men.* New York: G.P. Putnam's Sons, 1963.

Trevino, Rafael, and Angus McBride. *Rome's Enemies: Spanish Armies.* London: Osprey Publishing, 1986.

Truman, Ben C. *The Field of Honor.* New York: Fords, Howard & Hulbert, 1884.

————. *Dueling in America, 1884.* Reprint, Steven R. Wood, ed. San Diego, CA: Joseph Tablor Books, 1992.

Tunis, Edwin. *Weapons: A Pictorial History*. New York: Thomas Y. Crowell Company, 1954.

Turnbull, Stephen. *The Book of the Medieval Knight*. New York: Crown Publishers, 1985.

Turner, Craig, and Tony Soper. *Methods & Practice of Elizabethan Swordplay*. Carbondale, IL: Southern Illinois Press, 1990.

Turner, Sir James. *Pallas Armata: Military Essayes of the Ancient Grecian, Roman and Modern Art of War Written in the Years 1670 and 1671*. London: Richard Chiswell, 1683. Reprint. New York: Greenwood Press, 1968.

Umbach, Arnold, and Warren R Johnson. *Wrestling*. Dubuque, IA: Wm. C. Brown Company, 1966.

Valentine, Eric. *Rapiers: An Illustrated Reference Guide to the Rapiers of the 16th and 17th Centuries with Their Companions*. Harrisburg, PA: Stackpole Books, 1968.

Von Volbroth, Carl Alexander. *Heraldry: Customs, Rules and Styles*. Dorset, England: Blandford Press, Poole, 1981.

Vuksic V, and Z Grbasic. *Cavalry: The History of a Fighting Elite*. Srdjan Vujica, trans. London: Cassell Books, 1993.

Wagner, Eduard. *Medieval Costume, Armour and Weapons*. Jean Layton, trans. London: Paul Hamlyn, 1958.

—————. *European Weapons and Warfare 1618-1648*. London: Octopus Books Ltd., 1979.

Walker, Donald. *Defensive Exercises; Comprising Wrestling, Boxing, Defence Against Brute Force, by Various Methods: Fencing and Broad Sword, with Simpler Methods: the Gun, and its Exercise: the Rifle, and its Exercise*. London: Thomas Hurst, 1840.

Wallace, John. *Scottish Swords and Dirks*. London: Arms and Armour Press, 1970.

Warry, John. *Alexander 334-323 B.C.: Conquest of the Persian Empire*. London: Osprey Publishing, 1991.

Weiland, Gerald. *A Collector's Guide to Swords, Daggers & Cutlasses*. Quintet Publishing Ltd., 1991.

Weygers, Alexander. *The Modern Blacksmith*. New York: Van Nostrand Reinhold Company Inc., 1974.

Wilcox, Peter and GA. Embleton. *Rome's Enemies: Germanics and Dacians*. London: Osprey Publishing, 1982.

Wilkinson, Frederick. *Swords and Daggers*. Bungay, Suffolk, UK: Ward Lock Limited, 1972.

—————. *Arms and Armour*. New York: The Hamlyn Publishing Group Limited, 1978.

Wilkinson-Latham, R. *Sword in Color: including Other Edged Weapons*. New York: Arco Publishing Company, Inc., 1978.

Wilkinson-Latham, John. *British Cut and Thrust Weapons*. Rutland, VT: Charles E. Tuttle Co., Publishers, 1971.

Wilkinson-Latham, Frederick. *Phaidon Guide to Antique Weapons and Armour*. Englewood, NJ: Prentice-Hall, Inc., 1981.

Wilson, Jim, and Paul Evans. *Commando Fighting Techniques*. Boulder, CO: Paladin Press, 1983.

Wilson, John Lyde. *The Code of Honor: of Rules for the Government of Principals and Seconds in Duelling*. Charleston, SC: James Phinney, 1858. Reprint. Kennesaw, GA: Continental Book Company, 1959.

Wise, Terence. *European Edged Weapons*. London: Almark Publishing Co., 1974.

Wise, Arthur. *Weapons in the Theatre*. New York: Barnes & Noble, Inc., 1968.

Wright, LB. "Stage Duelling in the Elizabethan Theatre," *The Seventeenth Century Stage: A Collection of Critical Essays*. Gerald Eades Bentley, ed. Chicago: University of Chicago Press, 1968.

Yumoto, John. *The Samurai Sword*. Charles E. Tuttle Company, 1958.

INSTRUCTIONAL AND EDUCATIONAL VIDEOS

Ancient Warriors: A Soldier's-Eye View of History's Legendary Armies. Bethesda, MD: Seventh Art Productions, The Learning Channel, 1994.

Barroom Brawling: The Art of Staying Alive in Beer Joints, Biker Bars, and Other Fun Places. Peyton Quinn, Marc "Animal" MacYoung and Mike Haynack. Boulder, CO: Paladin Press, 1991.

Blitzkrieg Attacks: Knock Out Blows from the Bouncer Trade. Peyton Quinn. Boulder, CO: Paladin Press, 1993.

The Blow by Blow Guide to Swordfighting in the Renaissance Style. Mike Loades. London: Running Wolf Productions, 1992.

Broadsword for the Stage and Screen: The De Longis Method. Anthony De Longis. Hollywood, CA: Palpable Hit Productions, 2001.

Combat for the Stage. Raoul Johnson. Indianapolis, IN: D.V.C. Inc., 1989.

Combat for the Stage: Medieval Weaponry (Segment #1), *Elizabethan Weaponry* (Segment #2), *Unarmed Combat* (Segment #3). David L. Boushey. Seattle, WA: Instructional Media Services Television, University of Washington, 1985.

The Complete Unarmed Stage Combat Video Library (Unarmed Stage Combat I: Learning the Basics; Unarmed Stage Combat II: Perfecting the Fundamentals; Unarmed Stage Combat III: Mastering the Techniques). David Leong and J. Allen Suddeth. Roslyn Heights, NY: Combat Masters International, 1993.

The Crusades. Four Videos. New York: BBC/A&E Home Video, 1995.

Deadly Duels. Non-fiction Films, A. Michael Hoff and A La Carte Communications Production, Discovery Channel, 1995.

How a Man Schall Be Armyed. Anthony Wilkinson. London: Royal Armouries, HM Tower of London, 1990.

Knights and Armor. New York: A&E Television Networks, 1994.

A Legacy of Knights. Los Angeles, CA: Terra Entertainment, 2000.

Masters of Defence: Civilian Swords and Swordsmanship in Europe 1500–1800. London: Royal Armouries, HM Tower Of London, 1990.

The Myth of the Sword. Hank Reinhardt. Boulder, Co: Paladin Press, 2001.

Rapier for the Stage and Screen: The De Longis Method. Anthony De Longis. Hollywood, CA: Palpable Hit Productions, 2001.

The Stage Fight Director: A Look Behind the Scenes with David Boushey. Leucadia, CA: Theatre Arts Video Library, 1990.

Staged Fencing Techniques. Charles H. Morris. Weslaco, TX: Summit Productions, 1990.

Surviving a Street Knife Fight: Realistic Defensive Techniques. Marc "Animal" MacYoung and Richard Dobson. Boulder, CO: Paladin Press, 1992.

"Swordplay to Fencing" from *The David Frost Show.* From the United States Fencing Association, when available.

SAFD CERTIFIED TEACHERS, COLLEGES, AND OTHERS OFFERING STAGE COMBAT TRAINING

ALABAMA

UNIVERSITY OF ALABAMA

Department of Theatre and Dance
Box 870239
Tuscaloosa, AL 35487
Phone: 205.348.3127
e-mail: tgarland@bama.ua.edu
Teacher of Stage Combat: Tiza Garland

Ms. Garland teaches acting movement and stage combat in the University's BA and MFA programs. She is the resident movement coach and fight director for university productions and travels out of state as a guest artist teaching workshops, classes, and directing staged violence and fights at theatres and universities in the southern, midwestern, and eastern US.

CALIFORNIA

THE ACADEMY OF THE SWORD

587 Lisbon Street
San Francisco, CA 94112
Phone: 415.957.3622
Fax: 415.239.6650
e-mail: Richard@academyofthesword.org
http://www.academyofthesword.org
Executive Director: Richard Lane, Fight Director/Certified Teacher, Pacific Western Regional Representative, SAFD
Fight direction, stage combat classes and workshops

The Academy of the Sword and its performance company offer armed and unarmed stage fighting and historical swordplay choreography, training, and demonstrations to schools, colleges, universities, theatres, opera and ballet companies, community groups, and individuals. SAFD Certified Teacher and Fight Director, Lane and his associates have won numerous awards and nominations for their choreography, including the Drama Critics' Circle Award. Lane is the author of *Swashbuckling: A Step-By-Step Guide to the Art of Stage Combat and Theatrical Swordplay*, published by Limelight Editions.

ACADEMY OF THEATRICAL COMBAT

Los Angeles, CA 90035
Studio: 6560 Hollywood Blvd.
Hollywood, CA 90035
Phone: 818.364.8420
http://www.theatricalcombat.com
Artistic Director: Dan Speaker, Master of Theatrical Combat

Teachers of Stage Combat (Provosts): Jan Bryant, Dave Speaker, Darrin Jaques
Offering teaching and qualifications (certificate) in Basic Combat; Intermediate & Advanced
Historical Weapons
Performances in Stage and Film

The Academy of Theatrical Combat is intensely dedicated to quality in the Art of Combat and
to keeping alive elements of swordplay and its history that are in danger of being lost. To that
end they run a year-round, ongoing training program in Los Angeles, teach workshops for
regional theatre and schools, and train performers and choreographers to work in all facets of
the theatrical industry including stage, screen, TV and CD-ROM.

THE ALBION SCHOOLE OF DEFENSE

1222 S. 56th Street
Richmond, CA 94804
Phone: 510.215.5735
e-mail: captglbr@pacbell.net
Director/Instructor: Michael Cawelti

Stage Combat training is open enrollment; classes meet weekly
Performances at Renaissance Pleasure Faire in northern California in the fall.

Historical swordplay taught through stage combat performance and safety techniques. Swordplay is a recreation of period practice as taught in the English Renaissance. Beginning through
advanced techniques of stage combat are taught, with a focus on reenactment-style performances including: historical realism, exciting/spontaneous-looking choreography, period training techniques, and the ambiance of a 16th century schoole. Previous fencing/stage combat
experience is helpful but not required.

ANTHONY DE LONGIS

Answering Service: 818.980.2123
e-mail: anthony@delongis.com
http://www.delongis.com

Anthony De Longis is an experienced fight choreographer for stage, film and television. He has
occupied the staff position of fight director for the Los Angeles Music Center Opera since
1986, and has directed fights for the Old Globe Theater in San Diego, the Hollywood Bowl, the
Mark Taper Forum and Ahmanson Theatres in Los Angeles. He was Sword Master and Stunt
Co-coordinator for episodes 1-6 of the Fireworks/Paramount action series *The Queen of
Swords*. In 1991, Anthony was honored with a Dramalogue Award for his work at the Mark
Taper Forum.

Anthony is also an experienced and accomplished instructor. He has taught Acting Action class-
es at the world-famous Inosanto Academy in Los Angeles, and Fencing, Stage Combat and
Character Movement at UCLA's Theater Arts Department (1974 to 1993) and at the UCLA
extension when his schedule permits. He has taught master classes at Los Angeles City College
(Calif.), York University (Toronto, Canada), and the Atlanta School of Stage Combat (Ga.). De
Longis carries U.S. citizenship and Canadian permanent resident status. He is a member of the
Academy of Motion Picture Arts and Sciences, Screen Actors Guild, Actors Equity Association,
American Federation of Television and Radio Actors, Academy of Canadian Television and
Radio Actors, Union of British Columbia Performers, Fight Directors, Canada, and an hon-
orary member of the Society of American Fight Directors.

In 1999, Anthony, along with director/fight choreographer Ed Douglas, created Palpable Hit
Productions, to produce quality instructional videos on combat for stage and screen and historical swordplay. *Rapier for the Stage and Screen: The De Longis Method* and *Broadsword for
the Stage & Screen: The De Longis Method*, featuring theatrical combat techniques, are currently available. These videos reflect skills honed during thirty years of study as a swordsman,
martial artist and professional teacher. Visit his web site (www.delongis.com) to read video
reviews from Fight Master Bob Anderson (*Star Wars*, *Princess Bride*, *Mask of Zorro*, *Lord of*

the Rings), martial arts great Dan Inosanto and Fencing Master and author, Nick Evangelista (*Encyclopedia of the Sword*, *The Art and Science of Fencing*).

La Verdadera Destreza, also available from Palpable Hit, features instruction in the combative form of this Spanish martial art, presented by the premier expert in the field, Maestro Ramon Martinez. This is the first time that his instruction has been made available outside of his salle or workshops; the system is presented in two volumes, with assistance from Maestro Jeannette Acosta-Martinez and Anthony De Longis. Delivered in short, sequential lessons, the videos are designed to allow the modern swordsperson the opportunity to study this historical form of swordplay as documented in the original Spanish treatises of its developer Don Jeronimo Sanchez de Carranza and his protégé Don Luis Pacheco de Narvaez. Note: This is not a theatrical combat video, and Palpable Hit Productions strongly recommend the use of appropriate safety gear for practicing this contact sport.

LOS ANGELES FIGHT ACADEMY (LAFA)

4335 Van Nuys Blvd., #140
Sherman Oaks, CA 91403
Phone: 818.446.0246
http://www.4lafa.org

President: Payson Burt, Fight Director, SAFD
Direction, Fight Direction and stage combat classes and workshops
Meets weekly and monthly at various San Fernando Valley area locations.

LAFA is a school of theatrical movement dedicated to developing and teaching skills that celebrate the expressive body in motion, and how to apply these skills in relationship to comedy, conflict and performance. LAFA is a member of the Los Angeles Artists Coalition, an organization dedicated to exploring the human body in motion as communicative art. In recognizing the diverse training in the movement arts, LAAC acts as a cooperative with other artists throughout the performing community.

ROBERT CHAPIN

Los Angeles, CA
e-mail: bob@robertchapin.com
http://www.robertchapin.com

With twenty years of experience in stage combat, Robert Chapin has worked with some of Hollywood's finest directors, combat choreographers, and performers, including Steven Spielberg (*Hook*), Sam Raimi (*Army of Darkness*), Mel Brooks (*Robin Hood: Men in Tights*), and Penny Marshall (*Renaissance Man*). His credits include starring roles in *Ring of Steel* (MCA/Universal), *Dragon Fury I & II*, and leading roles in *Night of the Hyena, Lancelot: Guardian of Time*, and *Sinbad: The Battle of the Dark Knights*. Mr. Chapin also appears in a series of instructional videotapes on stage combat produced by Anthony De Longis.

He has benefited from a variety of formal stage combat training programs, including the Academy of Theatrical Combat in Los Angeles, The Ring of Steel and Royal Chessmen in Miami, and studies with martial arts masters Hee Il Cho, Dan Inosanto, and Eric Chen. Certified with the Societies of American, British, and Canadian Fight Directors, Robert is also a trained gymnast, stuntman, and horseman. He continues to develop his many skills, working behind the camera as a fight choreographer, second unit director, and writer.

SKIRMISHERS

1751 Ellis Street, Suite #301
Concord, CA 94520
Phone: 510.687.2634
e-mail: Skirmishers@ix.netcom.com

Artistic Director: Cecily M. McMahan

Focused on stage combat performance and training, Skirmishers specializes in European fight choreography styles spanning the 14th through early 20th centuries—History with an Edge.

SWORDS OF GLORY

2219 West Olive Avenue, #255
Burbank, CA 91506-2648
Phone: 818.892.1264
Fax: 818.892.0665
Director: Melodee M. Spevack

S.O.G. provides actor coaching/training, technical advisors and personnel to the entertainment industry and is affiliated with SAG, AFTRA, Equity and the SAFD. Credits include TV, film and CD-ROM.

TODD LOWETH

Certified Teacher, SAFD
11030 Aqua Vista Street, Suite #10
Studio City, CA 91602
Phone: 818.760.4712
e-mail: toddloweth@mac.com

Offers: Skills Proficiency Testing, SAFD.

Todd Loweth teaches private classes in unarmed, broadsword, rapier & dagger, quarterstaff, smallsword and conducts SAFD group workshops and SAFD Proficiency testing in the Hollywood area. As a free-lance Fight Director and Teacher, he is available for travel.

COLORADO

GEOFFREY KENT

Fight Director/Certified Teacher, SAFD
3047 West 47th Avenue, Unit #512
Denver, CO 80211
Phone: 303.877.2670
e-mail: fightdirector@attbi.com

Geoffrey offers stage combat classes/workshops, private instruction as well as fight direction in the Colorado area and beyond. He has choreographed countless professional productions in regional LORT theatres as well as AGMA opera and ballet houses.

DISTRICT OF COLUMBIA

MICHAEL JEROME JOHNSON

Fight Director/Certified Teacher, SAFD
e-mail: Foundart@hotmail.com

Michael is the teacher and director of stage combat training at the National Conservatory of Dramatic Arts and stage combat teacher for the Maryland Opera Studio, University of Maryland, College Park. He has been the fight director for various professional theatres, and universities and has garnered much critical praise. He has taught at several regional workshops, universities, and community groups, taught many seminars, and was privileged to share how he created knife fighting for the SAFD with the teachers of the British Academy of Stage and Screen Combat.

FLORIDA

JOHN CASHMAN

Certified Teacher, South Eastern Regional Representative, SAFD
10353 Alameda Alma Road

Clermont, FL 34711
Phone: 352.394.8522
e-mail: cashman@gdi.net

John Cashman is a free-lance fight director and stage combat instructor teaching private classes, SAFD group workshops, and SAFD proficiency testing primarily in Central Florida. As a free-lance fight director and teacher, he is available for travel.

GEORGIA

THE ATLANTA STAGE COMBAT STUDIO

Phone: 404.423.8504
http://www.stagecombat.com

Executive Director: Scot J. Mann, Fight Director, SAFD/BASSC
Assistant Director: Jason Armit, Actor Combatant, SAFD

The Atlanta Stage Combat Studio offers choreography, training and weapons rental services for theatres, universities, conservatories, and motion capture projects. Training is offered leading to Actor Combatant Recognition testing with the SAFD and the British Academy of Stage and Screen Combat. Previous clients include the Alliance Theatre Company, The Alabama Shakespeare Festival, the North Carolina School of the Arts, the Asolo Conservatory and various CD-ROM and DVD motion capture productions.

HAWAII

UNIVERSITY OF HAWAII AT MANOA

Kennedy Theatre
115 East-West Road
Honolulu, HI 96822
Phone: 808.956.7677
e-mail: Gregory Hoffman: gehoffman@att.net

Tony Pisculi: tonyp@lava.net
Aaron Anderson: adanderson@vcu.edu

Offers: Training in stage and film at fully funded state university with 600-seat mainstage theatre.

The University Of Hawaii at Manoa offers specialized training in many Asian theatre forms, many of which include unique stylized martial components (such as Japanese Tachimawari, the acrobatic stylization of Chinese Beijing Opera, Indian Kathakali, Balinese Kecak, and others). Practicing masters from Asia are routinely brought in to teach these specialized forms. Other related courses offered at the university included QiQong and advanced Wu style Tai Chi Quan training with weapons taught by Lao Shih Patricia Leong, senior disciple of Wu Yan Hsia. Additionally, every summer, UH hosts the three-week-long Swords and Surf Stage Combat Workshop (in Western stage-combat techniques) taught by Gregory Hoffman (SAFD Fight Director and Founder of Dueling Arts International), Aaron Anderson (Certified Teacher, SAFD, BASSC, and Dueling Arts International), and Tony Pisculi (Certified Teacher, Dueling Arts International).

ILLINOIS

ART OF COMBAT, INC. (See Michigan)

Chicago, IL
e-mail: artofcombat@myne.com
http://www.artofcombat.org

Chapter Head: J.J. Pido, Certified Actor/Combatant, SAFD
Fight direction, classes and workshops, combatant services

BABES WITH BLADES

Chicago, Illinois
e-mail: babeswithblades@juno.com
http://www.babeswithblades.org

Founder, Producer, Director, Instructor: Dawn "Sam" Alden, SAFD Actor/Combatant, MFA in Acting
Offers: Training and Performance in stage combat; an original show of combat scenes produced whenever possible.

Babes With Blades, an all-female stage combat troupe, was originally conceived to give women in Chicago an opportunity to showcase their training and talent in stage combat. Although, across the United States, women are in the majority in stage combat classes, their opportunities for work in the field once they receive the training are practically nonexistent. The preconception, in both the theatre world and the minds of the public at large, is that women have never truly wielded weapons, and therefore the dearth of representations of female warriors on stage is excusable and justified. But merely scratching the surface of history reveals a very different picture. Women have been bearing arms, for either personal or patriotic aims, in every culture and every time period on record. In dueling societies, on pirate ships, in jousting competitions, in standing armies, and on every revolution's roster, women have had an historic martial presence that is repeatedly denied or ignored!

Babes With Blades is an attempt to revive and revitalize the archetype of the Woman Warrior, the Amazon, and to show the theatrical world the wonderful resource of combat-trained women available to fill that archetype.

DAVID WOOLLEY

Fight Master, SAFD
72 E. 11th Street
Chicago, IL 60605
Phone: 312.344.6123
e-mail: guido@theswordsmen.com

Artist-in-Residence at Columbia College of Chicago, SAFD certification offered
Offers: Training and performance for both stage and film.

Theatrical Fight Director David Woolley is also known as Guido Crescendo of Dirk & Guido: The Swordsmen!, a comedy swashbuckling duo. At Columbia College Mr. Woolley teaches four levels of stage combat in the undergraduate program and oversees the fight direction on all productions. Proficiency testing in all the weapons offered by the SAFD is available under instruction at the college.

NEW AMERICAN THEATER

118 N. Main Street
Rockford, IL 61101
Phone: 815.963.9454

Artistic Director: Richard Raether, Fight Master, SAFD

Richard Raether is the Artistic Director at this regional theater in Rockford, Ill. that operates on an Equity S.P.T. Contract. The Theater Center houses 2 theatres: The 282-seat David W. Knapp Theater and the 90-seat Amcore Cellar Theater. There is currently no training program in stage combat.

SWORD & CLOAK PRODUCTIONS

Chicago, IL
e-mail: webmaster@swordandcloak.com
http://www.swordandcloak.com

Artistic Director: David Schmidt
Teachers of Stage Combat: Andrew Dannhorn/David Schmidt, SAFD Actor/Combatants
Offers basic classes in stage combat as an introduction to forms and safety.

"Renaissance Theatre, Comedic Improvisations and Stage Combat for all occasions"-Sword & Cloak is dedicated to pursuing the best in historical drama and action-oriented entertainment. This includes accessible Shakespeare and other classical authors, original productions, Renaissance Faires and other environmental theatre, comedic stage acts, historical weapons and stage combat demonstrations, and public access television. They place special interest in developing more active roles for women through original scripts and gender-blind casting.

THE THEATRE SCHOOL

DePaul University
2135 N. Kenmore Avenue
Chicago, IL 60614-4111
Phone: 773.325.7917 (DePaul)
         773.398.3034 (Sandys)

Teacher Of Combat: Nick Sandys, MA, Fight Director, SAFD

The Theatre School at DePaul University is a 4-year undergraduate and 3-year graduate, highly competitive training program with a strong emphasis on performance. Sandys teaches BFA2 and MFA2 and DePaul offers the SAFD Skills Proficiency Test in an "advanced" class for graduating seniors, combined undergraduate and graduate.

In addition, Mr. Sandys is the Resident Fight Director at Lyric Opera of Chicago and an Artistic Associate with Remy Bumppo Theatre Company.

UNIVERSITY OF ILLINOIS, URBANA-CHAMPAIGN

Department of Theatre
4-122 The Krannert Center for Performing Arts
500 South Goodwin Avenue
Urbana, IL 68101
Phone: 217.333.1659

Teacher of Stage Combat: Robin H. McFarquhar, PHD, Fight Director/Certified Teacher, SAFD
Degrees offered: BFA and MFA with a year of Stage Combat
Actor/Combatant Skills Proficiency Test, SAFD

Dr. McFarquhar teaches all the movement classes in the Professional Actor Training Program. The program also includes work in Circus Techniques, Mask, Physical Character, Relaxation techniques, Alignment, some Tai Chi, Yoga, and more. All of this work basically leads up to and informs the stage combat and culminates in the SAFD Skills Proficiency Test.

WESTERN ILLINOIS UNIVERSITY

Theatre Department
1 University Circle
Macomb, IL 61455
Phone: 309.298.1926
e-mail: DC-Wright@wiu.edu

Chair: Gene Kozlowski
Teacher of Stage Combat: D.C. Wright, MFA, Assistant Professor, Certified Teacher, SAFD
Degrees Offered: BA, MFA, SAFD Skills Proficiency Test

Western Illinois University offers a three semester sequence of courses designed to prepare students to take the Actor/Combatant Skills Proficiency Test, SAFD (THEA 470: Unarmed Combat, THEA 474a: Medieval Weaponry, THEA 474b: Elizabethan Weaponry). Facilities include three theaters, a well-stocked armory and spacious classrooms.

D.C. Wright, Certified Teacher, SAFD, teaches stage combat at WIU. He also works extensively with Dueling Arts International, and has written, directed and/or performed in several live action stunt shows, as well as teaching at numerous workshops across the country. D.C. has been on staff at the SAFD's National Stage Combat Workshop, and at the United Stuntmen's Association's International Stunt School.

INDIANA

DEPAUW UNIVERSITY

Communication Arts Department
Greencastle, IN 46135
Phone: 765.658.4596
e-mail: amhayes@depauw.edu

Andrew M. Hayes, Certified Teacher, SAFD

Offers: Courses in stage combat.

KENTUCKY

DREW FRACHER

Fight Master, SAFD
61 Bon Jan Lane
Highland Heights, KY 41076
Phone: 859.441.9433
e-mail: vern10th@worldnet.att.net

Drew conducts university guest artist residencies and is a Master Teacher at the SAFD National Stage Combat Workshop.

LOUISIANA

LOUISIANA TECH UNIVERSITY

School of Performing Arts
PO Box 8608 TS
Ruston, LA 71272
Phone: 318.257.2930
Fax: 318.257.4571

Chair: Dr. Kenneth Robbins
Teacher of Combat: Mark D. Guinn, MFA, Certified Teacher, SAFD
Offers: Skills Proficiency Testing, SAFD.

Louisiana Tech is an educational institution with one dedicated performance space and one shared concert hall. Movement for the Stage and Dance for the Theatre are offered in Fall, winter and spring semesters. Tech's 5 Theatre and 15 Music faculty teach 50 majors in both stage and film.

The University Theatre within Louisiana Tech's School of the Performing Arts holds a seventy year tradition of excellence. Since its inception, the Theatre has provided quality education for the Tech student. In addition to the academic mission of the organization, the Theatre has provided the campus and North Louisiana with entertaining and enriching productions. Since 1920, a regular season of plays has been produced without interruption. The theatre curriculum provides the student with a strong liberal arts education and a rich foundation in the practice, theory, and history of the art form. Hands-on courses in the craft of acting, directing, set construction, design, etc., are offered in tandem with history, criticism, and development. The student graduates with a thorough knowledge in his or her area of concentration (performance, design, management, etc.) and a basic working knowledge of the entire field of theatre.

MAINE

NATIONAL FIGHT DIRECTORS TRAINING PROGRAM
FIGHT DIRECTORS & ACTORS ENSEMBLE WORKSHOPS

Celebration Barn Theatre
190 Stock Farm Road
South Paris, ME 04281
Phone: 207.743.8452
Fax: 207.743.3889
e-mail: info@celebrationbarn.com—Carol Brett, Barn producer
    nyfgtdirctr@aol.com—J. Allen Suddeth, Barn coordinator
http://www.celebrationbarn.com (click on Fight Workshops)

Faculty have included: J. Allen Suddeth, Rick Sordelet, David Woolley, Dale Girard, David Leong, Richard Ryan, Mark Olsen, k. Jenny Jones, Colleen Kelly, Steve Vaughan, and A. C. Weary.

Program: two weeks in late June, yearly

Offers: Re-certification with SAFD

THE ACTORS ENSEMBLE WORKSHOP is composed of 12 people from diverse backgrounds, from working Equity members, to professors at various universities throughout the country, to young performers at the beginning of their careers. The two-week Workshop stretches your emotional muscles, line learning, character building, and performance skills. It provides the opportunity to work on the classics, the "big" roles, as well as the best of new and modern work. Participants are cast in a non-gender-specific ways, and learn more about collaboration with a director and a fight director. They kick the rust off of fight techniques, and learn to apply them to character and situation.

THE FIGHT DIRECTORS WORKSHOP is provided for talented young Fight Directors who wish to expand their skills working with actors in the pressured atmosphere of professional theatre, film and television. The six Fight Directors work on several pieces, both classical and modern. They work on comedy, improvisation, battle scenes, and contemporary violence, including polishing up their gun safety. As well as researching, they read plays, analyze scripts and ground plans, choose music, and work on a short video movie. Liability and the ins and outs of contracts are discussed. The Fight Directors rehearse and prepare the actors, help them create character and movement, and discover the acting beats within a scene. Finally, they create a show of scenes which is presented publicly on the workshop's last night.

RICHARD HEDDERMAN

Actor/Combatant, SAFD
PO Box 378
York Harbor, ME 03911
Phone: 207.363.0595
e-mail: rhedderman@mos.org

Richard Hedderman is available for fight direction, workshops, classes and performances throughout New England. Based in Boston, Richard teaches with Certified Teacher Robert Walsh at both Boston and Brandeis University (see below).

MASSACHUSETTS

ROBERT WALSH

Certified Teacher, SAFD
60 Tolman Street
W. Newton, MA 02465
Phone: 617.244.9656
e-mail: robertwalsh@rcn.com

Robert Walsh teaches MFA students at Brandeis University and BFA students at Boston University as well as teaching privately. A free-lance fight director, Mr. Walsh is affiliated with SAG, Equity, AFTRA and SSDC (Society of Stage Directors and Choreographers). Bob is on the faculty of American Repertory Theatre/Moscow Art Theatre School/Institute for Advanced Theatre Training at Harvard University. Bob usually offers the SAFD Skills Proficiency Test once a year and also has stage combat weapons available for rental.

MICHIGAN

ART OF COMBAT, INC. (see Illinois)

605 W. High Street
Jackson, MI 49203
Phone: 517.783.2823
Fax: 253.399.5033
e-mail: artofcombat@myne.com
http://www.artofcombat.org

Co-Chairmen & Founders, John Lennox, Member, Association for Historical Fencing, Dawn Duellists Society, British Federation for Historical Swordplay; Ian Griffin
Offers: Fight direction, classes and workshops, acting and combatant services.

Art of Combat, Inc., currently combines the talents of five fight directors with a total of over 30 years of stage combat experience. Based in Lansing, MI, Art of Combat, Inc., also has chapters in Chicago, Ill., New York, N.Y., and Edinburgh, Scotland. The company works predominantly locally in these areas, but is willing to travel. Company members are trained in historical as well as "industry standard" combat styles, and since 1999 have been actively transferring historical techniques to stage and film.

UNIVERSITY OF MICHIGAN-ANN ARBOR

Department of Theatre and Drama
2550 Frieze Building
Ann Arbor, MI 48109
Phone: 313.764.5350
e-mail: theatre.info@umich.edu
http://www.theatre.music.umich.edu

Instructor: Erik Fredriksen, Full Professor, Fight Master, SAFD
Offers: BFA and Actor Combatant Skills Proficiency Test, SAFD.

Two levels of stage combat are taught-Combat I and Combat II-which culminate with a skills test conducted by an SAFD fight master. The University presents 5 "straight" plays, 2 musical theatre, 2 opera, and 1 dance per season. Fight Master Fredricksen is also an instructor with United States Fencing Coaches Association and is an active member of United States Aikido Federation.

NEVADA

THE SOCIETY OF AMERICAN FIGHT DIRECTORS (SAFD)

Department Of Theatre Arts
University of Nevada, Las Vegas
4505 S. Maryland Parkway
Las Vegas, NV 89154-5044
Phone: 702.895.3662
Fax: 800.659.6579
http://www.safd.org

On-site coordinator: Linda McCollum
Offerings: Actor/Combatant Workshop, Advanced Actor/Combatant Workshop, Teacher Training Workshop and Actor/Combatant Skills Proficiency Test.

Schedule: Last three weeks of July on the campus of UNLV

The Society of American Fight Directors in association with the Department of Theatre Arts of the University of Nevada, Las Vegas conducts annual National Stage Combat Workshops. The SAFD offers two workshops that operate concurrently. The first is a basic skills or Actor/Combatant Workshop, in which the students are given up to eight hours of instruction per day, offered by four Fight Masters, in rapier & dagger, smallsword, broadsword, quarterstaff, and unarmed combat techniques.

The second workshop rotates between an Advanced Actor/Combatant Workshop and a Certified Teacher Workshop. The Advanced Actor/Combatant Workshop participants are taught advance techniques in rapier & dagger, smallsword, broadsword, sword & shield, sword & buckler, quarterstaff, and unarmed stage combat by six Fight Masters. Every third year ther is a Certified Teacher Workshop conducted in which students receive intense instruction on the art of teaching stage combat. Enrollment in both workshops is limited and is determined through an application process.

The Actor/Combatant Workshop participants are given the opportunity to take the SAFD Skills Proficiency Test in rapier & dagger, unarmed combat and broadsword. Those participating in the Advanced Actor/Combatant workshop are given the opportunity to take the SAFD Skills Proficiency Test in up to six weapons.

NEW MEXICO

NEW MEXICO STATE UNIVERSITY

Department of Theatre Art
Box 30001/Dept. 3072
Las Cruces, NM 88003-0001
Phone: 505.646.4517
Instructor: Tim Pinnow, Certified Teacher, SAFD

New Mexico State offers the SAFD Skills Proficiency Test which is available to all majors. The American Southwest Theatre Company is on NMS campus.

NEW YORK

ART OF COMBAT, INC. (See Michigan)

New York, NY
e-mail: artofcombat@myne.com
http://www.artofcombat.org

Chapter Head: Jared Kirby; Certified Intermediate, British Academy of Dramatic Combat, Member, Dawn Duellists Society, Certified Actor/Combatant, SAFD

Offers: Fight direction, classes and workshops, combatant services.

IFV, INC.

100 Judd Falls Road., #135
Ithaca, NY 14850
Phone: 607.277.3262
http://www.classicalfencing.com

Master of Defense: Adam Adrian Crown, FM, AFA; Maître d'Armes d'Escrime, USFCA; Maître de l'Academie d'Armes, IAA, Paris

In Ferro Veritas ("In the Sword is Truth")

Mr. Crown offers instruction in classical and historical swordplay in his own studio and at clubs and schools in the Ithaca area, teaching men and women of all skill levels and all ages. As well as teaching the "modern weapons"—the foil, the dueling sword and the sabre—he is one of a very few masters who also teaches the "ancient weapons"—the smallsword of the 17th and 18th centuries and the rapier & dagger of the Elizabethan period. He uses Classical Fencing to mean practice based on and intended to simulate as closely as possible a "frank encounter," i.e., an actual fight with sharps. By Historical Fencing he means authentic sword-fighting of the late 15th through 18th centuries. He also teaches practical unarmed self-defense.

In addition to his regular teaching schedule, Mr. Crown presents interactive fencing exhibitions at historical-theme events. His "in character" appearances combine improvisational acting with swordplay to teach visitors the fencing techniques of a particular period.

Over the years Mr. Crown has created and developed a new and unique approach to fencing as a martial art the purpose of which is to cultivate a strong, healthy body, an acute and agile mind, a gallant and gracious manner, and a dauntless and joyful spirit rather than as merely a sport. His "I.F.V. Method" incorporates learning/teaching strategies from diverse disciplines. In 1995, he founded I.F.V., Inc., a not-for-profit 501c (3) tax-exempt educational corporation dedicated to Classical and Historical Fencing.

Mtr. Crown accepts a small number of apprentices for instructor training and certification in the IFV method.

MICHAEL G. CHIN

Fight Director/Certified Teacher, SAFD
New York, NY
e-mail: Nscwboss@aol.com
http://www.Fights4.com

Michael is the co-founder of an actor/combatant training school in New York City called Fights4. and teaches full time at the American Musical and Dramatic Academy.

He also serves as coordinator for the National Stage Combat Workshop and New York Regional Workshop for the SAFD.

RON PIRETTI

Certified Teacher, SAFD, BA, BFA, MFA
15 Leroy Street., #12
New York, NY 10014
Phone: 212.675.4688

Offers: Training for Stage and Screen.

Mr. Piretti teaches privately and at various institutions in the New York City area and on the East Coast. Ron offers classes for actors and also choreographs the fights for productions in New York.

STATE UNIVERSITY OF NEW YORK-FREDONIA

Department of Theatre and Dance
Rockefeller Arts Center
Fredonia, NY 14063
Phone: 716.673.3597
e-mail: tlsharon@hotmail.com

Ted Sharon, Certified Teacher, SAFD, Voice and Movement Specialist

Offers: Stage combat classes, workshops, private training and fight direction.

NORTH CAROLINA

DALE ANTHONY GIRARD

Fight Master, SAFD
North Carolina School of the Arts
School of Drama
969 LaPlata Drive
Kernersville, NC 27284

Phone: 336. 993.3255
Cell: 336.403.6434
Fax: 336.993.5955
Director of Stage Combat Studies

Mr. Girard coordinates and teaches a three-year stage combat training program for the North Carolina School of the Arts (NCSA), School of Drama. In this position he oversees all course work, student development, and technical and artistic integrity specific to stage combat within the undergraduate actor training program. His duties include stocking and maintaining a theatrical armory, overseeing artist safety and the staging of all physical violence in school scene and production work, working closely with members of the faculty to assure proper integration of technique and to function as chief spokesman for NCSA School of Drama in all matters dealing with stage combat and theatrical violence.

Students at NCSA receive training in unarmed/hand-to-hand, single sword, rapier and dagger as well as knife techniques. Course work culminates in performance scene work, and the opportunity to test for recognition with the SAFD.

JEFF A.R. JONES

Fight Director/Certified Teacher, SAFD
2917 Isabella Drive
Raleigh, NC 27603
Phone: 919.835.3557
e-mail1: jarjones@nc.rr.com
e-mail2: jarjones@aol.com

Jeff teaches SAFD Skills Proficiency Test classes in all areas in addition to many more specialized weapons styles. A fight director who has had rave reviews in *The New York Times* and *The Washington Post*.

OHIO

REGINA CERIMELE-MECHLEY

Certified Teacher, SAFD
2325 Park Avenue, #4
Cincinnati, OH 45206
Phone: 513.200.5866
e-mail: swordlady@sprintmail.com

Ms. Cerimele-Mechley offers Actor/Combatant Skills Proficiency Testing and workshops year-round privately, at Northern Kentucky University, Highland Heights, and at Miami University, Oxford, Ohio. Affiliated with American Guild of Musical Artists (AGMA) and trained as a dancer, Gina is available to ballet companies, theatres, and universities looking for a free-lance fight director and teacher. Her workshops and training are offered year-round to high school programs and students in stage combat, Shakespeare, and movement for the actor. She has weapons available for rental.

OKLAHOMA

PAUL STEGER

Certified Teacher, Southwest Regional Representative, SAFD
1614 E. Boyd
Norman, OK 73071
e-mail1: Bucy1999@aol.com
e-mail2: steger@ou.edu

Offers: Stage combat classes, workshops, private training and fight direction.

PENNSYLVANIA

INDIANA UNIVERSITY OF PENNSYLVANIA

Department of Theater and Dance
Waller Hall 104
Indiana, PA 15705-1087
Phone 724.357.2965
Email: bblackle@iup.edu

Teachers of Stage Combat: Ed Simpson, Associate Professor Acting and Movement
            Michael Hood, Dean of Fine Arts and Certified Teacher, SAFD

Offers: BA in theater, minor in dance, Actor/Combatant Skills Proficiency Test.

IUP's Department of Theater and Dance hosts a full-time faculty of nine with approximately 115 majors. The department is dedicated to theater and dance as collaborative and highly disciplined fine arts, which demand a broad-based education. Courses are offered in acting, history, all areas of design, and playwriting. The program is production based and is accredited by the National Association of Schools of Theatre.

PENNSYLVANIA SHAKESPEARE FESTIVAL AT DESALES UNIVERSITY

2755 Station Avenue.
Center Valley, PA 18034
http://www.pashakespeare.org

Artistic Director: Jack Young, Fight Director/Certified Teacher, SAFD

"Sharp minds...brave hearts...fast wits."
The Official Shakespeare Festival of the Commonwealth of Pennsylvania.

PENNSYLVANIA STATE UNIVERSITY

School of Theatre
103 Arts Building
University Park, PA 16802-1919
Phone: 814.865.7586
Fax: 814.865.5754

Director: Dan Carter, Fight Director, SAFD
Teachers of Stage Combat: Professor Mark Olsen, Certified Teacher, SAFD, Professor Jane Ridley & Richard Nichols, Actor/Combatants, SAFD
Performances on fully operating mainstage and blackbox
Offers: BA, BFA, MFA, Actor/Combatant Skills Proficiency Testing, SAFD

This highly respected training program in both stage and film, supported by the Commonwealth of Pennsylvania, offers BA, BFA, and MFA programs in all aspects of theatrical craft. Because only eight graduate acting students are accepted they receive superb training in movement, voice, and all aspects of acting. All degree programs are top-flight and fully supported. Excellent stipends and extensive international experiences.

TEMPLE THEATERS

Temple University
1301 W. Norris Street
Philadelphia, PA 19122
Phone: 215.204.8414
Fax: 215.204.8566
e-mail: theater@temple.edu

Teacher of Stage Combat: John Bellomo, Certified Teacher, SAFD
Offers: BA, MFA.

The Department of Theater offers the BA at the undergraduate level and MFA at the graduate level with an emphasis in Acting, Design and Directing.

The production program is an extension of the department's studio work and is an opportunity for all the theatre artists to take what they have learned to the next level of realization. All students have the opportunity to participate in fully-mounted production experiences which greatly enhance the practical classroom education.

UNIVERSITY OF THE ARTS

School of Theatre Arts
320 South Broad Street
Philadelphia, PA 19102
Phone: 215.717.6454

Teacher of Stage Combat: Charles Conwell, Professor of Theatre, Fight Director, SAFD
Offers: BFA with 8 semesters of stage combat, Actor/Combatant Proficiency Sills Test, SAFD.

The successful integration of aggressive intent and safe technique is stressed throughout the theatre school's program. Courses include training in Unarmed Combat & Knife, Introduction to the Sword, Saber, or Singe Rapier, Rapier & Dagger, Bastard Broadsword. Advanced Combat, Fight Direction & Performance includes Smallsword, Broadsword & Shield, Broadsword & Buckler, Axe, Mace, Rapier & Cloak, Japanese Sword, Cavalry Saber, Competitive Saber, Competitive Foil, Épée, Cratehook, Wrestling, Asian Sticks, Quarterstaff, Group Fights, Comic Fights.

SOUTH CAROLINA

TRUSTUS THEATRE

520 Lady Street
PO Box 11721
Columbia, SC 29211-1721
Phone: 803.254.9732
Fax: 803.771.9153
http://www.trustus.org

Artistic Director: Jim Thigpen
Offers: Monthly workshops to their Apprentice Company.

TRUSTUS employs five actors full-time to maintain the quality of their productions along with a Technical Director, Box Office Manager and Producing and Artistic Directors. TRUSTUS boasts a company of 25 additional actors and technicians, as well as an Apprentice company of 20 of the best and brightest high school students in the midlands. The Apprentice company is a free program that presents monthly workshops for the students and allows them to work in a professional setting. Internships are offered to interested high school and college students.

TRUSTUS, the only professional theatre in the midlands, and the only theatre in the state of South Carolina to receive funding from the National Endowment for the Arts, serves as a resource of information and guidance to other groups throughout the state, helping to raise the cultural environment of South Carolina.

TENNESSEE

AMERICAN ACADEMY OF STAGE & SCREEN COMBAT CHOREOGRAPHERS (AASSCC)

1998 Pleasant Grove Road
Westmoreland, TN 37186
Phone: 615.644.2722
http://www.faire.net/freelancers/training.html

Artistic Director: Roy William Cox, MFA, Black Belt Karate, Black Sash Gung Fu
Teaching Staff: The Coxes, Dubro, Dudley, Patterson, Robin, Stout, The Westfields

Combat oriented entertainers banded together in 1987 to form the AASSCC. Their goal is to promote the training of individuals in the styles of classical period fighting, using realistic techniques. They have established a training facility at a 66-acre farm in the hills of Westmoreland, TN. Each year in February and in November at a location near Dallas, Texas, the AASSCC sponsors a seminar in Stage Combat techniques. Students have the opportunity to receive certification at different levels in a wide range of weapons and empty hand styles. For seven consecutive days, students train for 12 hours per day which assures the participants of an abundance of knowledge.

Course are taught in heavy weapons (sword, staff, axe, mace, polearms and shields), medium weapons (rapier, dagger, cloak, buckler and case), light weapons (smallsword, lantern and sabre), hand to hand (including falls, flips and rolls), full contact jousting, and firearms (black powder through automatics).

TEXAS

PIERROT PRODUCTIONS

PO Box 1032
Seabrook, TX 77586
Phone: 281.474.2253
e-mail: pierrot@flash.net
http://www.flash.net/~lalvarez

Artistic Director/Teacher of Combat: Richard Alvarez, Fencing Instructor, IAA; Recommended Actor/Combatant, SFAD

Offers: Certification in Mounted Combat.

Theatrical and media production company, Pierrot Productions, specializes in action theatre for theme productions, such as Houston's Tower Theatre, Astroworld's Showcase Theatre, and the Excalibur Hotel/Casino. Pierrot maintains a troupe of trained horses for jousting/equestrian combat. Pierrot offers master classes in all periods of stage combat by request. Pierrot Productions also provides consultation, costumes and props to stage and film productions, such as *Ivanhoe*, *The Babe* and *Exploding Angel*.

UNIVERSITY OF HOUSTON

School of Theatre & Division of Dance
133 Wortham Theatre
University of Houston
Houston, TX 77204-4016
Phone: 713.743.1788
Fax: 713.749.1420
e-mail: BByrnes@UH.edu

School of Theatre Director: Dr. Sidney Berger

Teacher of Stage Combat: Brian Byrnes, Professor of Movement & Stage Combat, Fight Master, SAFD

The theatre program offers training in acting, movement, stage combat, voice, directing, costume design, scenic design, lighting design, directing, stage management, theatre history, as well as dance. Each year, productions include four mainstage shows, two dance concerts, and several student productions.

Stage Combat training includes two semesters of training and scene work, leading toward an SAFD Skills Proficiency Test, adjudicated by an SAFD Fight Master. Students may continue stage combat training beyond the initial two semesters, working intermediate and advanced skills, with testing in additional stage weapon skills.

Fight Master Brian Byrnes' credits include New York theatres, regional theatres, and Shakespeare companies. He works regularly in Houston with The Alley Theatre, Stages Repertory Theatre, Houston Grand Opera, Houston Ballet, Houston Shakespeare Festival, and many other companies. He continues to work professionally as a fight director, actor (AEA), and director.

VIRGINIA

J. D. MARTINEZ

Fight Master Emeritus, SAFD
Maple Spring Farm
3786 Collierstown Road
Lexington, VA 24450
Phone: 540.458.8005
Fax: 540.458.8041
e-mail: martinezjd@wlu.edu

Mr. Martinez is a free-lance director and teacher of Stage Combat. He regularly teaches classes on the university level and accepts selected advanced private students. J.D. directs stage fights at all levels of professional and semi-professional theatre. His facilities include a 40 x 40 foot dance studio with sprung floors, mirrors and an armory.

NOBLE BLADES

c/o Reston Community Players
2310 Colts Neck Road
Reston, VA 20191
e-mail: noble@nobleblades.org
http://www.nobleblades.org

Liaison: Al Myska
Teacher of Stage Combat: Michael Johnson, Fight Director, SAFD
Offers: Training in winter and spring includes Actor Combatant Proficiency Renewal, SAFD.

Fight choreography for area theater groups.
Workshops and demonstrations throughout the year.
Touring performances in summer and fall.

Noble Blades, founded in 1991, is the resident stage combat troupe of the Reston Community Players. It provides the area's only professionally-trained, community-based fight group. The Noble Blades are committed to the performance of Stage Combat in an entertaining, educational, historically accurate, and safe manner. All its members receive training; many qualify as SAFD actor/combatants. Beginner and advanced classes are offered. Performance venues include plays, festivals, schools, and civic groups.

VIRGINIA COMMONWEALTH UNIVERSITY

Department of Theatre
922 Park Avenue
Richmond, VA 23284
Phone: 804.828.1514
e-mail: dsleong@vcu.edu or adanderson@vcu.edu

Professional training for stage and film at a fully funded state university

Offers: SAFD and BASSC Skills Proficiency Tests.

Teachers: David Leong, Fight Master, SAFD
          Aaron Anderson, Certified Teacher, SAFD/BASSC

Virginia Commonwealth University's theatre department offers both a BFA in Performance and an MFA in Theatre Pedagogy with an emphasis in Stage Combat and Movement. The BFA program trains students for a career in performance by offering both armed and unarmed techniques with special emphasis given to performance skills and professional development. The MFA program is customized according to the specific needs of each group of students in order to develop strong directing aesthetics and maximize future career opportunities.

Specific classes include Graduate Seminar in Choreographic Technique, Business of Theatre, Physical Acting, Movement Analysis, Mime and Mask, Physical Comedy, Contemporary Violence and Weapons Technique. Both the BFA and MFA programs strongly emphasize performance aesthetics, pedagogical principals, choreographic techniques, and marketing skills. Both programs offer the opportunity for SAFD and BASSC Skills Proficiency Tests with award winning SAFD Fight Master David Leong and SAFD and BASSC Certified Teacher Aaron Anderson.

WASHINGTON

GEOFFREY ALM

Fight Director/Certified Teacher, SAFD
6418 NE 184th Street
Kenmore, WA 98028
Phone: 206.871.8526 or 425.483.2857
e-mail: gbald@juno.com
Offers: Stage combat classes, workshops, private training and fight direction.

TONY SOPER

1127 S. Dawson
Seattle, WA 98108
Phone: 206.762.3985
e-mail: tonyso@msn.com
Offers: Training for Stage and Screen.

Mr. Soper is the co-author of *Methods and Practice of Elizabethan Swordplay*. He has taught in professional actor training programs from the University of Washington to the Juilliard School. He teaches privately and choreographs for regional theaters on a free-lance basis. He has trained with the SAFD.

UNITED STUNTMEN'S ASSOCIATION

2723 Saratoga Lane
Everett, WA. 98203
Phone: 206.290.9957
http://www.stuntschool.com
Director: David Boushey, Stunt Coordinator, Fight Master, SAFD
Offers: Stunt and Stage Combat Training every June at National Stunt Workshop for "Certificate of Completion."
Performances for Stage and Screen

The foremost stunt training facility in North America with a direct conduit to several stunt shows in Asia and Europe. United Stuntmen's is also the premier stunt organization in the Pacific Northwest with more than 100 film credits.

WYOMING

UNIVERSITY OF WYOMING

PO Box 3951
Laramie, WY 82071-3951
Phone: 307.766.3287
Fax: 307.766.2197
e-mail: selting@uwyo.edu

Instructor: Leigh Selting, Professor of Theatre, Recommended Actor/Combatant, SAFD

The University of Wyoming offers 2 levels of stage combat within a BFA Performance degree program and is available to anyone who enrolls for 2 semester hours of credit at the university. Stage Combat instruction includes: (I) Unarmed, and (II) Rapier & dagger, small sword, broadsword, and quarterstaff.

INTERNATIONAL

BEARDSLEY ENTERTAINMENT INC.

e-mail: Intljr@aol.com

http://www.showcreators.com

John Robert Beardsley, writer and director, has worked in the entertainment industry for over 25 years and has a strong theatrical, action and fight choreography background. He has worked and lived in Europe, Scandinavia, Australia, New Zealand, and Japan and has choreographed for theatre, television, video, theme park action attractions, corporate shows and commercials including Universal Studios Hollywood/Florida, MGM, Burbank Studios, NHK Japan, Channel 2 Oslo, Target, and Channel 2 Reno. His repertoire includes classical to contemporary, slapstick comedy to drama. See resume and detailed information on website.

AUSTRALIA

THE SOCIETY OF AUSTRALIAN FIGHT DIRECTORS INC. (SAFDI)

Suite 1/Level 3
Metro Arts Building
109 Edwards Street
Brisbane
Qld 4000.
e-mail: rapieroz@hotmail.com (Scott Witt)
e-mail: kaboom@powerup.com.au (Nigel Poulton)
http://www.rahcreations.com.au/SAuFD/

President: Scott Witt
Vice President: Nigel Poulton
Treasurer: Niki-J Witt
Secretary: Denez Nassif
Management Member: Jason King

"Setting the standard in stage combat and fight direction on the boards and in film."

The Society of Australia Fight Directors Inc. (SAFDi) is a representative body and training organization set up to enhance and further the education of performing artists and the entertainment industry with respect to the art and skills of stage combat and fight direction throughout Australia. Society members express their common interest in the field of stage combat studies, stage combat practices and fight direction (i.e. choreography) in the Australian entertainment marketplace.

CANADA

FIGHT DIRECTORS, CANADA

c/o Steve Wilsher
547 Parliament Street
Toronto, ON M4X 1P7
Phone: 416.462.3551
e-mail: info@fdc.ca
http://www.fdc.ca

President: Paul Gelianeu.
Vice-President of Training: Dr. Kara Wooten
Vice-President of Membership: Simon Fon
Workshop Co-ordinator: Steve Wilsher

Safety, education, training and certification in the "Illusion of Physical Conflict" for stage, screen and television.

Fight Directors, Canada was founded in 1993 and is recognized internationally as the sole regulatory and governing body for Fight Direction in Canada. It is a federally incorporated, not-for-profit, professional association. Its mandate is to promote and maintain a national standard of safety and esthetics in the art of fight choreography as an integral part of the entertainment industry; to educate, train, examine, and confer grades of proficiency on its members; to safeguard the diversity, interests and concerns of those members, and to inform the general public of the safety and esthetics of well choreographed fight sequences for television, film and theater.

The levels that Fight Directors, Canada members can achieve are Actor/Combatant, Advanced Actor/Combatant, Teacher, Fight Director, Fight Master and, eventually, Maître D'Armes. Additional membership categories include, Associate, for individuals interested in physical stage techniques, and who want to keep abreast of the field, and Honorary, for individuals designated worthy by a quorum of Fight Masters and Maîtres d'Armes. Members are welcome and have a voice in the associations, no matter how they choose to apply their knowledge.

Every May/June, FDC conducts a 2-week National Workshop with training in unarmed combat, single sword, rapier & dagger, broadsword, smallsword, Eastern martial arts and quarterstaff, with close attention paid to the acting component. The Canadian Nationals are the only time that professionals (or any other individuals interested in stage, screen and television) will have the opportunity to cover all aspects of the certification process to a recognized international professional standard. The process includes Red Cross/CPR certification and firearms training.

DENMARK

NORDIC STAGE FIGHT SOCIETY

c/o Tina Robinson-Hansen, President
Phone: +45 40 79 26 79
e-mail: fight_for_it@mail.danbbs.dk
http://www.nordicstagefight.com

Established officially in 1995, the Nordic Stage Fight Society (NSFS) encompasses Scandinavia and the Baltic States. The Society, which is based on the system established by the SAFD, emphasizes safety, quality and acting the fight for stage, film, and television. The NSFS stresses the necessity for a solid foundation in basic weapons and acting techniques. Students are encouraged to begin their training with various workshops/courses offered throughout the year before trying to be certified.

The certification process includes: First Level: rapier & dagger, unarmed combat, broadsword. Second Level: smallsword, quarterstaff, sword & shield. Third Level: teacher. Fourth Level: choreographer.

Specialty classes such as Viking and medieval combat weapons, women and fighting, stunts, and physical theatre, are also available.

ENGLAND

THE BRITISH ACADEMY OF DRAMATIC COMBAT

3 Castle View
Helmsley
North Yorkshire YO62 5AU

Phone: 1439 770546
e-mail: info@badc.co.uk
http://www.badc.co.uk
Chairman: Jonathan Howell
Secretary: Dr Ian Stapleton
Stage combat and fight direction tuition and workshops

The BADC supplies stage combat teachers to the major UK drama schools, and administers the "industry standard" test of fight proficiency among UK actors. The Academy also trains fight teachers and fight directors for stage, film and TV. Offers irregular weekend workshops on a wide variety of stage combat subjects throughout the UK, and an annual summer school leading to the various examinations in this field.

BRITISH ACADEMY OF STAGE AND SCREEN COMBAT (BASSC)

Suite 280
37 Store Street
London WC1E 7BS
Phone: 208 352 0605
e-mail: info@bassc.org
http://www.bassc.org

Training in stage combat for stage, film and TV

BASSC was founded in 1993 to promote a unified code of practice for the training, teaching and assessing of stage combat within the UK with the aims of improving the standards of safety, quality and training of stage combat for all visual media.

BASSC is an educational organization dedicated to developing and promoting the art of staged violence. Its philosophy focuses on safety and the belief that stage combat is a dramatic, rather than a martial, art; an acting skill as well as a physical one.

Because stage combat is a constantly evolving art, the Academy encourages members to keep abreast of new developments. For all classifications of membership, the Academy offers a comprehensive structured testing that includes a three-year renewal process, which allows members to maintain their high standards.

British Equity recognizes the BASSC's Advanced Actor/Combatant status as a valid qualification for entry onto the Equity Fight Directors' training scheme and also sanctions the BASSC Fight Director training and Assessment. To avoid confusion with the British Equity's Register of Fight Directors, the BASSC does not have a Fight Director classification.

Member classifications advance from Actor/Combatant, to Advanced Actor/Combatant, Certified Teacher and Master Teacher.

The Academy is dedicated to promoting full and open communication with other Stage Combat Academies, Schools, Societies and individuals within both the UK and the International stage combat community.

The BASSC hosts the British National Stage Combat Workshops, incorporating the Actor/Combatant Workshop, the Advanced Actor/Combatant Workshop and the Teacher Training Programme and the Teacher Certification Workshop.

BRITISH ACTOR'S EQUITY FIGHT DIRECTORS' REGISTER

The Secretary of the Fight Directors' Register
Guild House
Upper St. Martin's Lane
London WC2H 9EG

A specialist body within Equity, The Register is recognized by the various Theatre Managements. Under the agreements that Equity has with the SOLT (Society of London Theatre), TMA (Theatre Managements Association), and the ITC (Independent Theatre Council), in productions involving a fight (defined as a specialized performance involving two or more people using fists, implements or weapons, which require choreography or supervision for safety) the Management is obliged to engage a suitably qualified Fight Director. Membership in the Fight Directors' Register shall be regarded as proof.

Requirements for entry to the Register are obtainable from Equity Head Office. (use the above address.)

RICHARD RYAN

Phone: 7973 195887
E-mail: Richard@stagefight.com
http://www.stagefight.com

Mr. Ryan is an internationally respected Fight Director with over 300 professional credits including theatre, opera, film and TV.

He is Master-at-Arms to the Royal Academy of Dramatic Art (RADA) and has been recognized as a Master Teacher by the British Academy of Stage and Screen Combat, as a Fight Master by the former Society of British Fight Directors, and a Fight Director by the SAFD.

YOUNGBLOOD LTD

20 Aintree Street
Fulham
London SW6 7QU
Phone: 207 385 4783
e-mail: info@youngblood.org.uk
http://www.youngblood.org.uk

Directors: Tim Klotz Fight Director, FDC, Certified Instructor, BADC
          Toby Gaffney, Certified Instructor, BADC

Offers: Ongoing Classes in London. Intensives in UK and Europe. Mounted Combat training. Fight direction and performance combat instruction courses offered with resident UK and visiting masters.

Dramatic action specialists providing dramatic action personnel for theatre, film and TV.

YoungBlood Ltd is a collective of young Fight Directors and Instructors who work in film, TV and theatre. The company exists to provide personnel in all roles—from casting performers to training actors to arranging fights. YoungBlood also provides consultation, workshops and training.

FRANCE

LA DAME DU LAC

17, Avenue de la Bartavello
13470 Carnoux en Provence
France
Phone: +33 4 42 73 70 18
e-mail: guettier_c@yahoo.fr

Artistic Director/Teacher of Combat: Christophe Guettier

The La Dame du Lac group specializes in medieval reenactment, crusades history, and theatrical combat to promote both old style and historical fencing. La Dame provides fight reconstructions and old weapon demonstrations in historical milieus that offer a natural or authentic period stage. La Dame also promotes historic fencing by teaching theater groups styles of swordplay from the eleventh to the twentieth centuries.

To reach these objectives (and to attract people) La Dame investigates: 1) the study of the epics, chronicles and legends of the medieval time relevant to where they are performing; 2) reconstruction of medieval fencing based on the study of monuments, figurines, illustrations, and post-medieval treatises; 3) methods of adapting the fight to the stage, which can be risky due to the age of construction (eleventh to the seventeenth centuries in general), and; 4) the design of stage weapons that are also realistic.

Other show-producers and sword fighters in France include:

1. Maître Promard, La Sorbonne, Cité Universitaire, Paris. Specializes in theatrical fencing.
2. Maître Rostaing, Escrime Club La Tour d'Auvergne, 26, Rue Buffault, 75009 Paris.
3. Les Compagnons de Gabriel, Association Loi 1901, 63790 Murol. Specializes in medieval shows.
4. Office du Tourisme, 77160 Provins. Provins is a large medieval city, which has a medieval association that organizes shows in the town.
5. Maître J-L Bougle, Cercle d'Escrime Adamois, L'Isle-Adam. This is a new company working in all periods.
6. Les Cavaliers Voltigeurs de France. Working in all periods of combat, excellent with horses.

NEW ZEALAND

THE NEW ZEALAND STAGE COMBAT SOCIETY

PO Box 38 046
Wellington Mail Center
New Zealand
Phone: +64 4 587 0045
e-mail: lone_wolf_9@hotmail.com

Founding Members: Fight Directors Tony Wolf, Giovanni Tomillo, Peter Hassall, and SAFD Fight Master J.R. Beardsley

The New Zealand Stage Combat Society is a nonprofit educational organization that offers training and national certification in the Re:Action system of performance combat movement training. This system, devised by founder Tony Wolf, incorporates six essential principles: Synergy (moving in cooperation with another performer), Extension (efficient use of momentum control), Articulation (clarity of movement), Deception (concealment and misdirection), Alignment (efficient use of posture and body weight), and Sequential Flow (falling and rolling). Once these principles are mastered they can be applied to teaching, staging and performing any of a wide variety of combat styles.

PETER HASSALL

PO Box 27432
Marion Square,
Wellington 1
New Zealand
e-mail: stunts@paradise.net.nz
http://homepages.paradise.net.nz/rowlf/index.html

Mr. Hassall is a fight choreographer, stunt coordinator, and stuntman based in New Zealand. Occasionally he holds film fighting and stage combat workshops—mostly in Wellington, sometimes at other places around New Zealand but individual tuition is also available. Peter has 22 year's experience performing live shows and 11 year's experience working for film and television. He has choreographed and performed fights for Peter Jackson's film *Braindead*, TV series *The Tribe*, *Atlantis High*, etc. For stage productions such as *Hamlet*, *I Hate Hamlet*, *Macbeth*, *Romeo and Juliet*, etc. Peter instructs in the use of safe and spectacular techniques for unarmed fights (both street fighting and martial arts style), long sword or broadsword, rapier, and staff fights; and in breakfalls, pratfalls, basic wrestling and gymnastics moves.

SCOTLAND

ART OF COMBAT, INC. (See Michigan, USA)

e-mail: artofcombat@myne.com

http://www.artofcombat.org

Chapter Head: Maestro Paul MacDonald, Founding Member-Dawn Duellists Society, British Federation for Historical Swordplay, International Masters-at-Arms Federation, MacDonald Academy of Arms, Owner/Proprietor-MacDonald Armouries.

Fight direction, classes and workshops, combatant and armory services

Art of Combat, Inc., currently combines the talents of five fight directors with a total of over 30 years of stage combat experience. Company members are trained in historical as well as "industry standard" combat styles, and since 1999 have been actively transferring historical techniques to stage and film.

WEAPONS, PROPS, AND COSTUME SUPPLIERS

ALCONE CO., INC.

5-49 49th Avenue
Long Island City, NY 11101
Phone: 718.361.8373
Fax: 718.729.8296
http://www.alconeco.com

Separate catalogs for theatrical makeup and technical supplies. Handles wide range of products, from scenic to lighting and stage hardware. Some swords, knives, and props.

ARMORSTUFF

PO Box 26165
Fresno, CA 93729-6165
Phone: 559.222.4568
e-mail: armorstuff@earthlink.net

Rick Shupe, an armorer for 30 years, provides "knightstuff for the 21st century": decoration- to presentation-style armor, hand formed and finished, custom-built to individual measurements. Pieces are designed for practical function, safety, and wearability as well as appearance. Products include custom leatherwork and accessories. Catalog available.

THE ARMOURY AMERICAN FENCERS SUPPLY

1180 Folsom Street
San Francisco, CA 94103
Phone: 415.863.7911
Fax: 415.431.4931

Extensive catalog of stage combat-worthy weapons from all historical eras: broadswords, arming swords, shortswords, rapiers, transitional rapiers, smallswords, daggers, sabers, pole arms, and leather gauntlets. Weapons may be customized with regard to furniture and blade type. Also some Spanish replica armory of Oscar Kolombatovich still available. Catalog available.

ARMS & ARMOR, INC.

1101 Stinson Blvd., NE
Minneapolis, MN 55413
Phone: 800.745.7345
e-mail: aa@armor.com
http://www.armor.com

Created in 1981, Arms & Armor provides high-quality weapons and armor handcrafted in the U.S. Periods range from antiquity to the late 17th century, with most work done in the Medieval and Renaissance styles. Replicas, modeled from originals found in museums and private collections, are produced using historical construction methods. A special line of stage combat weapons is available. Operates in association with the Oakeshott Institute (www.oakeshott.org). Custom work and catalog available.

COLLECTOR'S ARMOURY, LTD.

Mail: PO Box 59, Alexandria, VA 22313-0059
Retail Store and Showroom: 1101 North Union Street, Alexandria, VA
Phone Orders: 800.336.4572
Phone Inquiries: 703.684.6111
Fax: 703.683.5486
e-mail: jwh@collectorsarmoury.com
http://www.collectorsarmoury.com

In business over 30 years, Collector's Armoury deals mainly in historic replicas for decoration, theatrical performers, hobbyists, and resale by specialty stores. Products range from "wall hanger" medieval weaponry to nonfunctional (but quite realistic looking) firearms from all eras, including American Revolution, Civil War, the Wild West, WWII, and modern times. Some costume accessories and novelty items. Catalog available.

COSTUME ARMOUR, INC.

2 Mill Street
PO Box 85
Cornwall, NY 12518
Phone: 845.534.9120
e-mail: info@costumearmour.com

Billing itself as a "custom armour studio producing authentic, highly durable, medium-priced theatrical armor," its products are vacuum-formed using the same material found in molded airplane luggage and have been featured on Broadway and in TV, opera, and films. Custom designs and rentals possible. Catalog available.

THE EDGE COMPANY

17 Kit Street
Keene, NH 03431
Phone: 800.732.9976
e-mail: edgecompany@yahoo.com

Tools, gifts, knives and action gear of all kinds, including European and Asian swords—although mostly for decorative, costume or solo uses. Catalog available.

EDGES2, INC.

Bob Burgee
6805 Furman Parkway
Riverdale, MD 20737
Phone: 301.306.0194
Fax: 301.306.5382
e-mail: bob@trainingblades.com
http://www.trainingblades.com

EDGES2 has been hand-building high-quality, reasonably priced aluminum training knives and swords since 1992. Founder/craftsman Bob Burgee wanted to provide trainers and performers with more realistic alternatives to plastic props and safer alternatives than live steel. Custom work available.

FIOCCHI SWORD CUTLERY

305 E. State Street
Athens, OH 45701
Phone: 740.593.5645
Fax: 740.593.4817
e-mail: fiocchi@ohiou.edu

Provides custom stage combat weapons.

FORTE STAGE COMBAT

Tim Frawley, Master at Arms
859 Chancel Circle
Glen Ellyn, IL 60048
Phone: 630.942.9102
e-mail: fortestage@aol.com
http://www.fortestage.tripod.com

Forte Stage Combat is a weapons rental source located in the Chicago area. They have an extensive stock of combat-worthy broadswords, shortswords, rapiers, daggers, axes, staffs, bucklers, and scabbards, as well as a generous supply of dress "wall hangers" for costume use—all from nationally recognized manufacturers. Custom leatherwork is available for hangers, frogs, and scabbards. Stage combat choreography is also available.

MARK HANEY

Theatre Arts Department
6000 J Street
Sacramento, CA 95819-6069
Phone: 916.278.6287
Pager: 916.328.3738

Builds general purpose stage combat-worthy, European-style swords (no foils) upon request, generally to a standard, inexpensive design, with further savings possible based on quantity ordered. Also supplies curved swords, scabbards and hangers, knives, axes, pikes, halberds, shields, and some armor—including large-scale set pieces like cannons and wagons. No catalog.

I.T.S. CUTLERY

PO Box 200
Dayton, TN 37321
Phone: 423.332.7400

I.T.S. is a retail supplier of C.A.S. Iberia, Inc., products. Swords in the "Iberia" line are advertised as suitable for theatrical use; others are clearly costume or decorative quality. Their "classic rapiers" use France-Lames blades but are available with either the schlagered double-wide épée blade or the Mansur theatre blade. Catalog available.

KNIGHTS EDGE, LTD.

5696 N. Northwest Highway
Chicago, IL 60646
Phone: 800.516.EDGE
Fax: 733.775.3339
http://www.KnightsEdge.com

Designs functional, hand forged "battle ready" weaponry for collectors, hobbyists, and performers. Styles span all historical eras, including fantasy weapons. Exclusive designs include Ritter Steel, Stage Steel, and Valiant Arms series. Some jewelry and decorative items. Catalog available. Chicago showroom open by appointment.

KRIS CUTLERY

2314 Monte Verde Drive
Pinole, CA 94564
Phone: 510.758.9912
Fax: 510.223.8968

http://www.kriscutlery.com

Features a growing list of medieval swords and daggers, fantasy swords, Asian weapons, and scabbards. Catalog available.

LEGENDARY ARMS, INC.

PO Box 197
Califon, NJ 07830
Phone: 800.528.2767
Fax: 908.832.0812

Replicas and decorative weapons from all historical periods: broadswords, rapiers, smallswords, daggers, sabers, fantasy swords, Asian swords and scabbards. Also offers helmets, chain mail, leather and steel gauntlets, war axes, shields, bayonets and knives, Civil War uniforms, black-powder firearms, and other militaria. Catalog available.

LUNDEGAARD ARMOURY

PO Box 155
High Bridge, NJ 08829
Phone: 908.638.4107
e-mail: thelunde@lundegaard.com
http://www.lundegaard.com

Imaginative and whimsical hiltsmith Lars Lunde offers a variety of unique, fantasy-oriented sword and dagger furniture (as standard ensembles or for customer mix-and-match) mounted on imported, stage combat-worthy blades, along with period accessories. Catalog available.

MUSEUM REPLICAS, LTD.

2143 Gees Mill Road
Box 840
Conyers, GA 30207
Phone: 800.883.8838
Fax: 770.388.0246

"Battle ready" replica swords (broadswords, rapiers, two-handed greatswords, fantasy swords, Asian swords, most with scabbards available), daggers, axes (including war hammers, maces, and pole arms), shields (and bucklers), and helmets. Replicas from all historical periods, including leather gauntlets, chain mail, Renaissance and Medieval costumes and period accessories. Catalog available.

THE NOBLE COLLECTION

PO Box 1476
Sterling, VA 20167
Phone: 800.866.2538
Fax: 800.866.0025

http://www.noblecollection.com

Decorative arms and armor, both fantasy and historical, most not intended for stage combat. Various tabletop and wall displays. Catalog available.

NO QUARTER ARMS

Dennis L. Graves, Swordcutler
255 S. 41st Street
Boulder, CO 80303
Phone: 303.494.4685

Elegantly simple and practical arming swords, shortswords, rapiers, smallswords, and daggers of all historical periods. Rapier carriers and broadsword baldrics also available. Rental service and catalog available.

NORCOSTCO, INC.

Please call for mailing address pertinent to your region.
Phone: 800.220.6920

Technical equipment (lighting, effects, fabrics, etc.) and costume/makeup supplies for theatrical, concert, dance, film, opera, and television productions. Offers a variety of props, including weapons, but not for stage combat use. Catalog showing equipment and local/regional outlets available.

PIERRE'S COSTUMES

211 N. Third Street
Philadelphia, PA 19106
Phone: 856.486.1188

During the last five decades, Pierre has maintained a complete full-service professional costume house, designing and manufacturing on the premises. Also offers movie-quality makeup ranging from sci-fi and blacklight to horror and special effects, including mascot design and fabrication. Information sheet available.

ROGUE STEEL

Neil Massey
3738 Blanchan Avenue
Brookfield, IL 60513
Phone: 708.485.2089
http://www.roguesteel.com

Rogue Steel weapons are built especially for stage combat use in theater, film, and classes. All weapons are constructed for safety and durability and are primarily of European design with a choice of standard items. Custom work and rentals are available.

SANTELLI

465 South Dean Street
Englewood, NJ 07631
Phone: 201.871.3105
Fax: 201.871.8718

A wide variety of foils, épées, sabers, and related equipment for competitive fencers, including sword-length carrying bags. Catalog available.

STARFIRE SWORDS, LTD.

74 Railroad Avenue
Spencer, NY 14883
Phone: 607.589.7244
Fax: 607.589.6630
http://www.starfireswords.com

Swords and daggers for costume, decoration, and stage combat. Includes: broadswords, rapiers, shortswords, axes, polearms, and scabbards. Catalog available.

SYKE'S SUTLERING

Raffaella Marr
7 Devonshire Drive
Egg Harbor Township, NJ 08234-7111
Phone: 609.926.1297
e-mail: sykesutler@worldnet.att.net
http://www.sykesutler.com

"Purveyors of fine seventeenth century goods," Syke's caters to Elizabethan, Stuart, and Restoration re-enactors, and is expanding to include earlier periods. Products include period reprint and reference books, ready-to-wear costumes, iron cookware, rapiers, and related equipment (mostly from Santelli and Black Rose Creations), and black-powder firearms. Catalog available.

TRIPLETTE COMPETITION ARMS

101 E. Main Street
Elkin, NC 28621
Phone: 336.835.7774
http://www.triplette.com

Fencing equipment, theatrical blades, and Society for Creative Anachronism (SCA) equipment including a variety of leather gauntlets. Offers some decorative swords. Catalog available.

VULCAN'S FORGE

Lewis Shaw, Proprietor
330 West 23rd Street
Baltimore, MD 21211
Phone: 410.231.6519
e-mail: LonnieSC@aol.com

Fine "duelling supplies" specifically designed for stage combat. No catalog as such, but photo samples, with prices, are available.

WEAPONS OF CHOICE/SWORDCRAFTERS

Richard Pallazoil
4075 Browns Valley Road
Napa, CA 94558-4144
Phone: 707.226.2845

Weapons of Choice has provided fight worthy and costume weapons—rapiers, daggers, broadswords, shortswords, sabres, smallswords and courtswords, and exotics like cutlasses, baskethilts, knives, hooks, flails, axes, and polearms, plus prop and working prop firearms from all historical eras—for rent to the theatrical community since 1990. Exclusive representative for Swordcrafters of San Diego. Catalog available.

ARMS & ARCHERY

The Coach House
London Road
Ware, Hertfordshire SG12 9QU
United Kingdom
Phone: 1920 460335
Fax: 1920 461044
e-mail: terry@armsandarchery.co.uk
http://www.armsandarchery.co.uk

A long-established armorer and costumer for stage, TV, and film. Terry Gouldon and Ray Monery have worked on such noted swashbucklers as *Gladiator, Braveheart, First Knight, Robin Hood: Prince of Thieves,* and the first two Highlander films, among many made-for-TV epics. Extensive inventory of weapons, armor and costumes for all periods, including equestrian caparisons. Titanium swords for film use.

ALAN M. MEEK

180 Frog Grove Lane
Wood Street Village
Guildford, Surrey GU3 3HD
United Kingdom
Phone: 1483 234084
Fax: 1482 236684

Supplies theatrical swords, rapiers, daggers, polearms, shields, helmets, mail and plate armor for sale or rental. Clients have included: the Metropolitan Opera, Cleveland Opera, New York Public Theatre, Folger Theatre (Washington) among many others. No catalog.